AngularJS Web Application Development Cookbook

Over 90 hands-on recipes to architect performant
applications and implement best practices in AngularJS

Matt Frisbie

[PACKT] open source
PUBLISHING   community experience distilled

BIRMINGHAM - MUMBAI

AngularJS Web Application Development Cookbook

First published: December 2014

Production reference: 1191214

Published by Packt Publishing Ltd.
Livery Place
35 Livery Street
Birmingham B3 2PB, UK.

ISBN 978-1-78328-335-4

www.packtpub.com

Cover image by Suyog Gharat (yogiee@me.com)

Credits

Author
Matt Frisbie

Reviewers
Pawel Czekaj

Patrick Gillespie

Aakash Patel

Adam Štipák

Commissioning Editor
Akram Hussain

Acquisition Editor
Sam Wood

Content Development Editor
Govindan K

Technical Editors
Taabish Khan

Parag Topre

Copy Editors
Deepa Nambiar

Neha Vyas

Project Coordinator
Shipra Chawhan

Proofreaders
Simran Bhogal

Maria Gould

Ameesha Green

Paul Hindle

Indexer
Mariammal Chettiyar

Graphics
Abhinash Sahu

Production Coordinator
Arvindkumar Gupta

Cover Work
Arvindkumar Gupta

About the Author

Matt Frisbie is currently a full stack developer at DoorDash (YC S13), where he joined as the first engineer. He led their adoption of AngularJS, and he also focuses on the infrastructural, predictive, and data projects within the company.

Matt has a degree in Computer Engineering from the University of Illinois at Urbana-Champaign. He is the author of the video series *Learning AngularJS*, available through O'Reilly Media. Previously, he worked as an engineer at several educational technology start-ups.

About the Reviewers

Pawel Czekaj has a Bachelor's degree in Computer Science. He is a web developer with strong backend (PHP, MySQL, and Unix systems) and frontend (AngularJS, Backbone. js, jQuery, and PhoneGap) experience. He loves JavaScript and AngularJS. Previously, he has worked as a senior full stack web developer. Currently, he is working as a frontend developer for Cognifide and as a web developer for SMS Air Inc. In his free time, he likes to develop mobile games. You can contact him at `http://yadue.eu`.

Patrick Gillespie is a senior software engineer at PROTEUS Technologies. He has been working in the field of web development for over 15 years and has both a Master's and Bachelor's degree in Computer Science. In his spare time, he enjoys working on web projects for his personal site (`http://patorjk.com`), spending time with his family, and listening to music.

Aakash Patel is the cofounder and CTO of Flytenow, a ride sharing platform for small planes. He has industry experience of client-side development using AngularJS, and he is a student at Carnegie Mellon University (CMU).

Adam Štipák is currently a full stack developer. He has more than 8 years of professional experience with web development. He specializes in AMP technologies (where A stands for Apache, M for MySQL, and P for PHP). He also likes other technologies such as JavaScript, AngularJS, and Grunt. He is also interested in functional programming in Scala. He likes open source software in general.

www.PacktPub.com

Support files, eBooks, discount offers, and more

For support files and downloads related to your book, please visit www.PacktPub.com.

Did you know that Packt offers eBook versions of every book published, with PDF and ePub files available? You can upgrade to the eBook version at www.PacktPub.com and as a print book customer, you are entitled to a discount on the eBook copy. Get in touch with us at service@packtpub.com for more details.

At www.PacktPub.com, you can also read a collection of free technical articles, sign up for a range of free newsletters and receive exclusive discounts and offers on Packt books and eBooks.

https://www2.packtpub.com/books/subscription/packtlib

Do you need instant solutions to your IT questions? PacktLib is Packt's online digital book library. Here, you can search, access, and read Packt's entire library of books.

Why subscribe?

- ▶ Fully searchable across every book published by Packt
- ▶ Copy and paste, print, and bookmark content
- ▶ On demand and accessible via a web browser

Free access for Packt account holders

If you have an account with Packt at www.PacktPub.com, you can use this to access PacktLib today and view 9 entirely free books. Simply use your login credentials for immediate access.

Writing about a subject as tumultuous as JavaScript frameworks is a bit like bull riding.

To Jordan, my family, and my friends—you helped me hang on.

Table of Contents

Preface

"Make it work. Make it right. Make it fast."

Back when the world was young, Kent Beck forged this prophetic sentiment. Even today, in the ultra-modern realm of performant single-page application JavaScript frameworks, his idea still holds sway. This nine-word expression describes the general progression through which a pragmatic developer creates high-quality software.

In the process of discovering how to optimally wield a technology, a developer will execute this progression many times, and each time will be a learning experience regarding some new understanding of the technology.

This cookbook is intended to act as a companion guide through this process. The recipes in this book will intimately examine every major aspect of the framework in order to maximize your comprehension. Every time you open this book, you should gain an expanded understanding of the brilliance of the AngularJS framework.

What this book covers

Chapter 1, Maximizing AngularJS Directives, dissects the various components of directives and demonstrates how to wield them in your applications. Directives are the bread and butter of AngularJS, and the tools presented in this chapter will maximize your ability to take advantage of their extensibility.

Chapter 2, Expanding Your Toolkit with Filters and Service Types, covers two major tools for code abstraction in your application. Filters are an important pipeline between the model and its appearance in the view, and are essential tools for managing data presentation. Services act as broadly applicable houses for dependency-injectable modules and resource access.

Chapter 3, AngularJS Animations, offers a collection of recipes that demonstrate various ways to effectively incorporate animations into your application. Additionally, it will dive deep down into the internals of animations in order to give you a complete perspective on how everything really works under the hood.

Chapter 4, Sculpting and Organizing Your Application, gives you strategies for controlling the application initialization, organizing your files and modules, and managing your template delivery.

Chapter 5, Working with the Scope and Model, breaks open the various components involving ngModel and provides details of the ways in which they can integrate into your application flow.

Chapter 6, Testing in AngularJS, gives you all the pieces you need to jump into writing test-driven applications. It demonstrates how to configure a fully operational testing environment, how to organize your test files and modules, and everything involved in creating a suite of unit and E2E tests.

Chapter 7, Screaming Fast AngularJS, is a response to anyone who has ever complained about AngularJS being slow. The recipes in this chapter give you all the tools you need to tune all aspects of your application's performance and take it from a steam engine to a bullet train.

Chapter 8, Promises, breaks apart the asynchronous program flow construct, exposes its internals, then builds it all the way back up to discuss strategies for your application's integration. This chapter also demonstrates how promises can and should integrate into your application's routing and resource access utilities.

Chapter 9, What's New in AngularJS 1.3, goes through how your application can integrate the slew of new features and changes that were introduced in the AngularJS 1.3 and the later AngularJS 1.2.x releases.

Chapter 10, AngularJS Hacks, is a collection of clever and interesting strategies that you can use to stretch the boundaries of AngularJS's organization and performance.

What you need for this book

Almost every example in this book has been added to JSFiddle, with the links provided in the text. This allows you to merely visit a URL in order to test and modify the code with no setup of any kind, on any major browser and on any major operating system. If you want to replicate an example outside of JSFiddle, all the external content (AngularJS, AngularJS modules, third-party libraries and modules) is served from `https://code.angularjs.org/` and `https://cdnjs.com/`.

Chapter 6, Testing in AngularJS, involves setting up a testing framework, which should be able to be accomplished on any major Unix-based operating system (OS X and, Linux). The test suite is built on top of Grunt, Karma, Selenium, and Protractor; all of these and their dependencies can be installed through npm.

Who this book is for

There are already plenty of introductory resources to guide a green developer into the thick of AngularJS. This cookbook is for developers with at least basic knowledge of JavaScript and AngularJS, and who are looking to expand their perspective on the framework.

The goal of this text is to have you walk away from reading about an AngularJS concept armed with a solid understanding of how it works, insight into the best ways to wield it in real-world applications, and annotated code examples to get you started.

Sections

In this book, you will find several headings that appear frequently (Getting ready, How to do it, How it works, There's more, and See also).

To give clear instructions on how to complete a recipe, we use these sections as follows:

Getting ready

This section tells you what to expect in the recipe, and describes how to set up any software or any preliminary settings required for the recipe.

How to do it...

This section contains the steps required to follow the recipe.

How it works...

This section usually consists of a detailed explanation of what happened in the previous section.

There's more...

This section consists of additional information about the recipe in order to make the reader more knowledgeable about the recipe.

See also

This section provides helpful links to other useful information for the recipe.

Conventions

In this book, you will find a number of styles of text that distinguish between different kinds of information. Here are some examples of these styles, and an explanation of their meaning.

Code words in text, database table names, folder names, filenames, file extensions, pathnames, dummy URLs, user input, and Twitter handles are shown as follows: "By cleverly using directives and the $compile service, this exact directive functionality is possible."

A block of code is set as follows:

```
(index.html)

<!-- specify root element of application -->
<div ng-app="myApp">
  <!-- register 'my-template.html' with $templateCache -->
  <script type="text/ng-template" id="my-template.html">
    <div ng-repeat="num in [1,2,3,4,5]">{{ num }}</div>
  </script>

  <!-- your custom element -->
  <my-directive></my-directive>
</div>
```

When we wish to draw your attention to a particular part of a code block, the relevant lines or items are set in bold:

```
(app.js)

.directive('iso', function () {
  return {
    scope: {}
  };
});
```

Any command-line input or output is written as follows:

```
npm install protractor grunt-protractor-runner --save-dev
```

New terms and **important words** are shown in bold. Words that you see on the screen, in menus or dialog boxes for example, appear in the text like this: "The following directive will display **NW**, **NE**, **SW**, or **SE** depending on where the cursor is relative to it."

> Warnings or important notes appear in a box like this.

> Tips and tricks appear like this.

Reader feedback

Feedback from our readers is always welcome. Let us know what you think about this book—what you liked or may have disliked. Reader feedback is important for us to develop titles that you really get the most out of.

To send us general feedback, simply send an e-mail to feedback@packtpub.com, and mention the book title via the subject of your message.

If there is a topic that you have expertise in and you are interested in either writing or contributing to a book, see our author guide on www.packtpub.com/authors.

Customer support

Now that you are the proud owner of a Packt book, we have a number of things to help you to get the most from your purchase.

Downloading the example code

You can download the example code files for all Packt books you have purchased from your account at http://www.packtpub.com. If you purchased this book elsewhere, you can visit http://www.packtpub.com/support and register to have the files e-mailed directly to you.

Errata

Although we have taken every care to ensure the accuracy of our content, mistakes do happen. If you find a mistake in one of our books—maybe a mistake in the text or the code—we would be grateful if you would report this to us. By doing so, you can save other readers from frustration and help us improve subsequent versions of this book. If you find any errata, please report them by visiting http://www.packtpub.com/submit-errata, selecting your book, clicking on the **errata submission form** link, and entering the details of your errata. Once your errata are verified, your submission will be accepted and the errata will be uploaded on our website, or added to any list of existing errata, under the Errata section of that title. Any existing errata can be viewed by selecting your title from http://www.packtpub.com/support.

Piracy

Piracy of copyright material on the Internet is an ongoing problem across all media. At Packt, we take the protection of our copyright and licenses very seriously. If you come across any illegal copies of our works, in any form, on the Internet, please provide us with the location address or website name immediately so that we can pursue a remedy.

Please contact us at copyright@packtpub.com with a link to the suspected pirated material.

We appreciate your help in protecting our authors, and our ability to bring you valuable content.

Questions

You can contact us at questions@packtpub.com if you are having a problem with any aspect of the book, and we will do our best to address it.

1
Maximizing AngularJS Directives

In this chapter, we will cover the following recipes:

- ▶ Building a simple element directive
- ▶ Working through the directive spectrum
- ▶ Manipulating the DOM
- ▶ Linking directives
- ▶ Interfacing with a directive using isolate scope
- ▶ Interaction between nested directives
- ▶ Optional nested directive controllers
- ▶ Directive scope inheritance
- ▶ Directive templating
- ▶ Isolate scope
- ▶ Directive transclusion
- ▶ Recursive directives

Introduction

In this chapter, you will learn how to shape AngularJS directives in order to perform meaningful work in your applications. Directives are perhaps the most flexible and powerful tool available to you in this framework and utilizing them effectively is integral to architecting clean and scalable applications. By the same token, it is very easy to fall prey to directive antipatterns, and in this chapter, you will learn how to use the features of directives appropriately.

Building a simple element directive

One of the most common use cases of directives is to create custom HTML elements that are able to encapsulate their own template and behavior. Directive complexity increases very quickly, so ensuring your understanding of its foundation is essential. This recipe will demonstrate some of the most basic features of directives.

How to do it...

Creating directives in AngularJS is accomplished with a directive definition object. This object, which is returned from the definition function, contains various properties that serve to shape how a directive will act in your application.

You can build a simple custom element directive easily with the following code:

```
(app.js)

// application module definition
angular.module('myApp', [])
.directive('myDirective', function() {
  // return the directive definition object
  return {
    // only match this directive to element tags
    restrict: 'E',
    // insert the template matching 'my-template.html'
    templateUrl: 'my-template.html'
  };
});
```

As you might have guessed, it's bad practice to define your directive template with the `template` property unless it is very small, so this example will skip right to what you will be using in production: `templateUrl` and `$templateCache`. For this recipe, you'll use a relatively simple template, which can be added to `$templateCache` using `ng-template`. An example application will appear as follows:

```
(index.html)

<!-- specify root element of application -->
<div ng-app="myApp">
  <!-- register 'my-template.html' with $templateCache -->
  <script type="text/ng-template" id="my-template.html">
    <div ng-repeat="num in [1,2,3,4,5]">{{ num }}</div>
  </script>

  <!-- your custom element -->
  <my-directive></my-directive>
</div>
```

When AngularJS encounters an instance of a custom directive in the `index.html` template, it will *compile* the directive into HTML that makes sense to the browser, which will look as follows:

```
<div>1</div>
<div>2</div>
<div>3</div>
<div>4</div>
<div>5</div>
```

 JSFiddle: `http://jsfiddle.net/msfrisbie/uwpdptLn/`

How it works...

The `restrict: 'E'` statement indicates that your directive will appear as an element. It simply instructs AngularJS to search for an element in the DOM that has the `my-directive` tag.

Especially in the context of directives, you should always think of AngularJS as an HTML compiler. AngularJS traverses the DOM tree of the page to look for directives (among many other things) that it needs to perform an action for. Here, AngularJS looks at the `<my-directive>` element, locates the relevant template in `$templateCache`, and inserts it into the page for the browser to handle. The provided template will be compiled in the same way, so the use of `ng-repeat` and other AngularJS directives is fair game, as demonstrated here.

There's more...

A directive in this fashion, though useful, isn't really what directives are for. It provides a nice jumping-off point and gives you a feel of how it can be used. However, the purpose that your custom directive is serving can be better implemented with the built-in `ng-include` directive, which inserts a template into the designated part of HTML. This is not to say that directives shouldn't ever be used this way, but it's always good practice to not reinvent the wheel. Directives can do much more than template insertion (which you will soon see), and it's best to leave the simple tasks to the tools that AngularJS already provides to you.

Working through the directive spectrum

Directives can be incorporated into HTML in several different ways. Depending on how this incorporation is done, the way the directive will interact with the DOM will change.

How to do it...

All directives are able to define a `link` function, which defines how that particular directive instance will interact with the part of the DOM it is attached to. The `link` functions have three parameters by default: the directive scope (which you will learn more about later), the relevant DOM element, and the element's attributes as key-value pairs.

A directive can exist in a template in four different ways: as an HTML pseudo-element, as an HTML element attribute, as a class, and as a comment.

The element directive

The element directive takes the form of an HTML tag. As with any HTML tag, it can wrap content, have attributes, and live inside other HTML elements.

The directive can be used in a template in the following fashion:

```
(index.html)

<div ng-app="myApp">
  <element-directive some-attr="myvalue">
    <!-- directive's HTML contents -->
  </element-directive>
</div>
```

This will result in the directive template replacing the wrapped contents of the `<element-directive>` tag with the template. This element directive can be defined as follows:

```
(app.js)

angular.module('myApp', [])
.directive('elementDirective', function ($log) {
  return {
    restrict: 'E',
    template: '<p>Ze template!</p>',
    link: function(scope, el, attrs) {
      $log.log(el.html());
      // <p>Ze template!</p>
      $log.log(attrs.someAttr);
      // myvalue
    }
  };
});
```

JSFiddle: http://jsfiddle.net/msfrisbie/sajhgjat/

Note that for both the tag string and the attribute string, AngularJS will match the CamelCase for elementDirective and someAttr to their hyphenated element-directive and some-attr counterparts in the markup.

If you want to replace the directive tag entirely with the content instead, the directive will be defined as follows:

```
(index.html)

angular.module('myApp', [])
.directive('elementDirective', function ($log) {
  return {
    restrict: 'E',
    replace: true,
    template: '<p>Ze template!</p>',
    link: function(scope, el, attrs) {
      $log.log(el.html());
      // Ze template!
      $log.log(attrs.someAttr);
      // myvalue
    }
  };
});
```

 JSFiddle: http://jsfiddle.net/msfrisbie/oLhrm194/

This approach will operate in an identical fashion, but the directive's inner HTML will not be wrapped with <element-directive> tags in the compiled HTML. Also, note that the logged template is missing its <p></p> tags that have become the root directive element as they are the top-level tags inside the template.

The attribute directive

Attribute directives are the most commonly used form of directives, and for good reason. They have the following advantages:

- They can be added to existing HTML as standalone attributes, which is especially convenient if the directive's purpose doesn't require you to break up an existing template into fragments

- ▶ It is possible to add an unlimited amount of attribute directives to an HTML element, which is obviously not possible with an element directive

- ▶ Attribute directives attached to the same HTML element are able to communicate with each other (refer to the *Interaction between nested directives* recipe)

This directive can be used in a template in the following fashion:

```
(index.html)
```

```html
<div ng-app="myApp">
  <div attribute-directive="aval"
      some-attr="myvalue">
  </div>
</div>
```

 A nonstandard element's attributes need the `data-` prefix to be compliant with the HTML5 specification. That being said, pretty much every modern browser will have no problem if you leave it out.

The attribute directive can be defined as follows:

```
(app.js)
```

```javascript
angular.module('myApp', [])
.directive('attributeDirective', function ($log) {
  return {
    // restrict defaults to A
    restrict: 'A',
    template: '<p>An attribute directive</p>',
    link: function(scope, el, attrs) {
      $log.log(el.html());
      // <p>An attribute directive</p>
      $log.log(attrs.attributeDirective);
      // aval
      $log.log(attrs.someAttr);
      // myvalue
    }
  };
});
```

 JSFiddle: http://jsfiddle.net/msfrisbie/y2tsgxjt/

Other than its form in the HTML template, the attribute directive functions in pretty much the same way as an element directive. It assumes its attribute values from the container element's attributes, including the attribute directive and other directives (whether or not they are assigned a value).

The class directive

Class directives are not altogether that different from attribute directives. They provide the ability to have multiple directive assignments, unrestricted local attribute value access, and local directive communication.

This directive can be used in a template in the following fashion:

```
(index.html)

<div ng-app="myApp">
  <div class="class-directive: cval; normal-class"
       some-attr="myvalue">
  </div>
</div>
```

This attribute directive can be defined as follows:

```
(app.js)

angular.module('myApp', [])
.directive('classDirective', function ($log) {
  return {
    restrict: 'C',
    template: '<p>A class directive</p>',
    link: function(scope, el, attrs) {
      $log.log(el.html());
      // <p>A class directive</p>
      $log.log(el.hasClass('normal-class'));
      // true
      $log.log(attrs.classDirective);
      // cval
      $log.log(attrs.someAttr);
      // myvalue
    }
  };
});
```

 JSFiddle: http://jsfiddle.net/msfrisbie/rt1f4qxx/

It's possible to reuse class directives and assign CSS styling to them, as AngularJS leaves them alone when compiling the directive. Additionally, a value can be directly applied to the directive class name attribute by passing it in the CSS string.

The comment directive

Comment directives are the runt of the group. You will very infrequently find their use necessary, but it's useful to know that they are available in your application.

This directive can be used in a template in the following fashion:

```
(index.html)

<div ng-app="myApp">
  <!-- directive: comment-directive val1 val2 val3 -->
</div>
```

The comment directive can be defined as follows:

```
(app.js)

angular.module('myApp', [])
.directive('commentDirective', function ($log) {
  return {
    restrict: 'M',
    // without replace: true, the template cannot
    // be inserted into the DOM
    replace: true,
    template: '<p>A comment directive</p>',
    link: function(scope, el, attrs) {
      $log.log(el.html())
      // <p>A comment directive</p>
      $log.log(attrs.commentDirective)
      // 'val1 val2 val3'
    }
  };
});
```

 JSFiddle: `http://jsfiddle.net/msfrisbie/thfvx275/`

Formerly, the primary use of comment directives was to handle scenarios where the DOM API made it difficult to create directives with multiple siblings. Since the release of AngularJS 1.2 and the inclusion of `ng-repeat-start` and `ng-repeat-end`, comment directives are considered an inferior solution to this problem, and therefore, they have largely been relegated to obscurity. Nevertheless, they can still be employed effectively.

How it works...

AngularJS actively compiles the template, searching for matches to defined directives. It's possible to chain directive forms together within the same definition. The `mydir` directive with `restrict: 'EACM'` can appear as follows:

```
<mydir></mydir>

<div mydir></div>

<div class="mydir"></dir>

<!-- directive: mydir -->
```

There's more...

The `$log.log()` statements in this recipe should have given you some insight into the extraordinary use that directives can have in your application.

See also

▸   The *Interaction between nested directives* recipe demonstrates how to allow directives attached to the same element to communicate with each other

Manipulating the DOM

In the previous recipe, you built a directive that didn't care what it was attached to, what it was in, or what was around it. Directives exist for you to program the DOM, and the equivalent of the last recipe is to instantiate a variable. In this recipe, you will actually implement some logic.

How to do it...

The far more common use case of directives is to create them as an HTML element attribute (this is the default behavior for `restrict`). As you can imagine, this allows us to decorate existing material in the DOM, as follows:

```
(app.js)

angular.module('myApp', [])
.directive('counter', function () {
  return {
    restrict: 'A',
    link: function (scope, el, attrs) {
      // read element attribute if it exists
      var incr = parseInt(attrs.incr || 1)
        , val = 0;
      // define callback for vanilla DOM click event
      el.bind('click', function () {
        el.html(val += incr);
      });
    }
  };
});
```

This directive can then be used on a `<button>` element as follows:

```
(index.html)

<div ng-app="myApp">
  <button counter></button>
  <button counter incr="5"></button>
</div>
```

 JSFiddle: http://jsfiddle.net/msfrisbie/knk5znke/

How it works...

AngularJS includes a subset of jQuery (dubbed jqLite) that lets you use a core toolset to modify the DOM. Here, your directive is attached to a singular element that the directive sees in its linking function as the element parameter. You are able to define your DOM modification logic here, which includes initial element modification and the setup of events.

In this recipe, you are consuming a static attribute value `incr` inside the `link` function as well as invoking several jqLite methods on the element. The element parameter provided to you is already packaged as a jqLite object, so you are free to inspect and modify it at your will. In this example, you are manually increasing the integer value of a counter, the result of which is inserted as text inside the button.

There's more...

Here, it's important to note that you will never need to modify the DOM in your controller, whether it is a directive controller or a general application controller. Because AngularJS and JavaScript are very flexible languages, it's possible to contort them to perform DOM manipulation. However, managing the DOM transformation out of place causes an undesirable dependency between the controller and the DOM (they should be totally decoupled) as well as makes testing more difficult. Thus, a well-formed AngularJS application will never modify the DOM in controllers. Directives are tailor-made to layer and group DOM modification tasks, and you should have no trouble using them as such.

Additionally, it's worth mentioning that the `attrs` object is read-only, and you cannot set attributes through this channel. It's still possible to modify attributes using the element attribute, but state variables for elements can be much more elegantly implemented, which will be discussed in a later recipe.

See also

▶ In this recipe, you saw the `link` function used for the first time in a fairly rudimentary fashion. The next recipe, *Linking directives*, goes into further detail.

▶ The *Isolate scope* recipe goes over the writable DOM element attributes that can be used as state variables.

Linking directives

For a large subset of the directives you will eventually build, the bulk of the heavy lifting will be done inside the directive's `link` function. This function is returned from the preceding compile function, and as seen in the previous recipe, it has the ability to manipulate the DOM in and around it.

How to do it...

The following directive will display **NW**, **NE**, **SW**, or **SE** depending on where the cursor is relative to it:

```
angular.module('myApp', [])
.directive('vectorText', function ($document) {
```

```
    return {
      template: '<span>{{ heading }}</span>',
      link: function (scope, el, attrs) {

        // initialize the css
        el.css({
          'float': 'left',
          'padding': attrs.buffer+"px"
        });

        // initialize the scope variable
        scope.heading = '';

        // set event listener and handler
        $document.on('mousemove', function (event) {
          // mousemove event does not start $digest,
          // scope.$apply does this manually
          scope.$apply(function () {
            if (event.pageY < 300) {
              scope.heading = 'N';
            } else {
              scope.heading = 'S';
            }
            if (event.pageX < 300) {
              scope.heading += 'W';
            } else {
              scope.heading += 'E';
            }
          });
        });
      }
    };
  });
```

This directive will appear in the template as follows:

```
(index.html)

<div ng-app="myApp">
  <div buffer="300"
       vector-text>
  </div>
</div>
```

JSFiddle: `http://jsfiddle.net/msfrisbie/a0ywomq1/`

How it works...

This directive has a lot more to wrap your head around. You can see that it has $document injected into it, as you need to define event listeners relevant to this directive all across $document. Here, a very simple template is defined, which would preferably be in its own file, but for the sake of simplicity, it is merely incorporated as a string.

This directive first initializes the element with some basic CSS in order to have the relevant anchor point somewhere you can move the cursor around fully. This value is taken from an element attribute in the same fashion it was used in the previous recipe.

Here, our directive is listening to a $document mousemove event, with a handler inside wrapped in the scope.$apply() wrapper. If you remove this scope.$apply() wrapper and test the directive, you will notice that while the handler code does execute, the DOM does not get updated. This is because the event that the application is listening for *does not occur* in the AngularJS context—it is merely a browser DOM event, which AngularJS does not listen for. In order to inform AngularJS that models might have been altered, you must utilize the scope.$apply() wrapper to trigger the update of the DOM.

With all of this, your cursor movement should constantly be invoking the event handler, and you should see a real-time description of your cursor's relative cardinal locality.

There's more...

In this directive, we have used the scope parameter for the first time. You might be wondering, "Which scope am I using? I haven't declared any specific scope anywhere else in the application." Recall that a directive will inherit a scope unless otherwise specified, and this recipe is no different. If you were to inject $rootScope to the directive and log to the $rootScope.heading console inside the event handler, you would see that this directive is writing to the heading attribute of the $rootScope of the entire application!

See also

▸ The *Isolate scope* recipe goes into further details on directive scope management

Interfacing with a directive using isolate scope

Scopes and their inheritance is something you will frequently be dealing with in AngularJS applications. This is especially true in the context of directives, as they are subject to the scopes they are inserted into and, therefore, require careful management in order to prevent unexpected functionalities. Fortunately, AngularJS directives afford several robust tools that help manage visibility of and interaction with the surrounding scopes.

If a directive is not instructed to provide a new scope for itself, it will inherit the parent scope. In the case that this is not desirable behavior, you will need to create an isolate scope for that directive, and inside that isolate scope, you can define a whitelist of parent scope elements that the directive will need.

Getting ready

For this recipe, assume your directive exists inside the following setup:

```
(index.html)

<div ng-app="myApp">
  <div ng-controller="MainCtrl">
    <div iso></div>
  </div>
</div>

(app.js)

angular.module('myApp', [])
.controller('MainCtrl', function ($log, $scope) {
  $scope.outerval = 'mydata';
  $scope.func = function () {
    $log.log('invoked!');
  };
})
.directive('iso', function () {
  return {};
});
```

How to do it...

To declare a directive with an isolate scope, simply pass an empty object literal as the `scope` property:

```
(app.js)

.directive('iso', function () {
  return {
    scope: {}
  };
});
```

With this, there will be no inheritance from the parent scope in `MainCtrl`, and the directive will be unable to use methods or variables in the parent scope.

If you want to pass a read-only value to the directive, you will use @ inside the isolate scope declaration to indicate that a named attribute of the relevant HTML element contains a value that should be incorporated into the directive's isolate scope. This can be done as follows:

```
(index.html)

<div ng-app="myApp">
  <div ng-controller="MainCtrl">
    <div>Outer: {{ outerval }}</div>
    <div iso myattr="{{ outerval }}"></div>
  </div>
</div>

(app.js)

.directive('iso', function () {
  return {
    template: 'Inner: {{ innerval }}',
    scope: {
      innerval: '@myattr'
    }
  };
});
```

With this, the scope inside the directive now contains an `innerval` attribute with the value of `outerval` in the parent scope. AngularJS evaluates the expression string, and the result is provided to the directive's scope. Setting the value of the variable does nothing to the parent scope or the attribute in the HTML; it is merely copied into the scope of the directive.

[JSFiddle: http://jsfiddle.net/msfrisbie/cjkq6n1n/]

While this approach is useful, it doesn't involve data binding, which you have come to love in AngularJS, and it isn't all that more convenient than passing in a static string value. What is far more likely to be useful to you is a true whitelist of the data binding from the parent scope. This can be accomplished with the = definition, as follows:

```
(index.html)

<div ng-app="myApp">
  <div ng-controller="MainCtrl">
    <div>Outer: {{ outerval }}</div>
    <div iso myattr="outerval"></div>
  </div>
</div>

(app.js)

.directive('iso', function () {
  return {
    template: 'Inner: {{ innerval }}',
    scope: {
      innerval: '=myattr'
    }
  };
});
```

[JSFiddle: http://jsfiddle.net/msfrisbie/b0g9o3xq/]

Here, you are instructing the child directive scope to examine the parent controller scope, and bind the parent `outerval` attribute inside the child scope, aliased as the `innerval` attribute. Full data binding between scopes is supported, and all unnamed attributes and methods in the parent scope are ignored.

Taking a step further, methods can also be pulled down from the parent scope for use in the directive. In the same way that a model variable can be bound to the child scope, you can alias methods that are defined in the parent scope to be invoked from the child scope but are still in the parent scope context. This is accomplished with the & definition, as follows:

```
(index.html)

<div ng-app="myApp">
  <div ng-controller="MainCtrl">
    <div iso myattr="func()"></div>
  </div>
</div>

(app.js)

.directive('iso', function () {
  return {
    scope: {
      innerval: '&myattr'
    },
    link: function(scope) {
      scope.innerval();
      // invoked!
    }
  };
});
```

 JSFiddle: `http://jsfiddle.net/msfrisbie/1u24c4o8/`

Here, you are instructing the child directive to evaluate the expression passed to the `myattr` attribute within the context of the parent controller. In this case, the expression will invoke the `func()` method, but any valid AngularJS expression will also work. You can invoke it as you would invoke any other scope method, including parameters as required.

How it works...

Isolate scope is entirely managed within the `scope` attribute in the directive's returned definition object. Using `@`, `=`, and `&`, you are instructing the directive to ignore the scopes it would normally inherit, and only utilize data, variables, and methods that you have provided interfaces for instead.

There's more...

If the directive is designed as a specific modifier for an aspect of your application, you might find that using isolate scope isn't necessary. On the other hand, if you're building a reusable, monolithic component that can be reused across multiple applications, it is unlikely that the directive will be using the parent scope in which it is used. Hence, isolate scope will be significantly more useful.

See also

> ▶ The *Recursive directives* recipe utilizes the isolate scope to maintain inheritance and separation in a recursive DOM tree

Interaction between nested directives

AngularJS provides a useful structure that allows you to build channels of communication between directive siblings (within the same HTML element) or parents in the same DOM ancestry without having to rely on AngularJS events.

Getting ready

For this recipe, suppose that your application template includes the following:

```
(index.html)

<div ng-app="myApp">
  <div parent-directive>
    <div child-directive
         sibling-directive>
    </div>
  </div>
</div>
```

How to do it...

Inter-directive communication is accomplished with the `require` attribute, as follows:

```
return {
  require: ['^parentDirective', '^siblingDirective'],
  link: function (scope, el, attrs, ctrls) {
    $log.log(ctrls);
    // logs array of in-order required controller objects
  }
};
```

Using the stringified directive names passed through `require`, AngularJS will examine the current and parent HTML elements that match the directive names. The controller objects of these directives will be returned in an array as the `ctrls` parameter in the original directive's `link` function.

These directives can expose methods as follows:

```
(app.js)
angular.module('myApp', [])
.directive('parentDirective', function ($log) {
  return {
    controller: function () {
      this.identify = function () {
        $log.log('Parent!');
      };
    }
  };
})
.directive('siblingDirective', function ($log) {
  return {
    controller: function () {
      this.identify = function () {
        $log.log('Sibling!');
      };
    }
  };
})
.directive('childDirective', function ($log) {
  return {
    require: ['^parentDirective', '^siblingDirective'],
    link: function (scope, el, attrs, ctrls) {
      ctrls[0].identify();
      // Parent!
```

```
        ctrls[1].identify();
        // Sibling!
    }
  };
});
```

 JSFiddle: http://jsfiddle.net/msfrisbie/Lnxeyj60/

How it works...

The `childDirective` fetches the requested controllers and passes them to the `link` function, which can use them as regular JavaScript objects. The order in which directives are defined is not important, but the controller objects will be returned in the order in which they are requested.

See also

▸ The *Optional nested directive controllers* recipe demonstrates how to handle a scenario where parent or sibling controllers might not be present

Optional nested directive controllers

The AngularJS construct that allows you to build channels of communication between directive siblings or parents in the same DOM ancestry also allows you to optionally require a directive controller of a sibling or parent.

Getting ready

Suppose that your application includes the following:

```
(index.html)

<div ng-app="myApp">
  <div parent-directive>
    <div child-directive
        sibling-directive>
    </div>
  </div>
```

```
    </div>

    (app.js)

    angular.module('myApp', [])
    .directive('parentDirective', function ($log) {
      return {
        controller: function () {
          this.identify = function () {
            $log.log('Parent!');
          };
        }
      };
    })
    .directive('siblingDirective', function ($log) {
      return {
        controller: function () {
          this.identify = function () {
            $log.log('Sibling!');
          };
        }
      };
    });
```

How to do it...

Note that in `index.html`, the `missingDirective` is not present. A `?` prefixed to the `require` array element denotes an optional controller directive. This is shown in the following code:

```
    (app.js)

    .directive('childDirective', function ($log) {
      return {
        require: [
          '^parentDirective',
          '^siblingDirective',
          '^?missingDirective'
        ],
        link: function (scope, el, attrs, ctrls) {
          ctrls[0].identify();
          // Parent!
          ctrls[1].identify();
```

```
        // Sibling!
        $log.log(ctrls[2]);
        // null
    }
  };
});
```

 JSFiddle: `http://jsfiddle.net/msfrisbie/kr6w2hvb/`

If the controller exists, it will be served in the same fashion as the others. If not, the returned array will be a null value at the corresponding index.

How it works...

An AngularJS controller is merely a JavaScript constructor function, and when `parentDirective` and `siblingDirective` are required, each directive returns their controller object. As you are using the controller object and not the controller scope, you must define your public controller methods on `this` instead of `$scope`. The `$scope` doesn't make sense in the context of a foreign directive—recall that the directive is in the process of being linked when all of this happens.

Directive scope inheritance

When a directive is not instructed to create its own isolate scope, it will inherit the scope of whatever scope it exists inside.

Getting ready

Suppose that you begin with the following skeleton application:

```
(index.html - uncompiled)

<div ng-app="myApp">
  <div ng-controller="MainCtrl">
    <my-directive>
      <p>HTML template</p>
      <p>Scope from {{origin}}</p>
      <p>Overwritten? {{overwrite}}</p>
    </my-directive>
  </div>
```

```
    </div>

    (app.js)

angular.module('myApp', [])
.controller('MainCtrl', function ($scope) {
    $scope.overwrite = false;
    $scope.origin = 'parent controller';
});
```

How to do it...

The most basic setup is to have the directive scope inherit from the parent scope that will be used by the directive within the `link` function. This allows the directive to manipulate the parent scope. This can be done as follows:

```
    (app.js)

.directive('myDirective', function () {
    return {
        restrict: 'E',
        link: function (scope) {
            scope.overwrite = !!scope.origin;
            scope.origin = 'link function';
        }
    };
});
```

This will compile into the following:

```
    (index.html – compiled)

<my-directive>
    <p>HTML template</p>
    <p>Scope from link function</p>
    <p>Overwritten? true</p>
</my-directive>
```

 JSFiddle: http://jsfiddle.net/msfrisbie/c3b3a38t/

How it works...

There's nothing tricky going on here. The directive has no template, and the HTML inside it is subject to the modifications that the `link` function makes to the scope. As this does not use isolate scope and there is no transclusion, the parent scope is provided as the `scope` parameter, and the `link` function writes to the parent scope's models. The HTML output tells us that the template was rendered from our `index.html` markup, the `link` function was the last to modify the scope, and the `link` function overwrote the original values set up in the parent controller.

See also

▶ The *Directive templating* recipe examines how a directive can apply an external scope to a transplated template

▶ The *Isolate scope* recipe gives details on how a directive can be decoupled from its parent scope

▶ The *Directive transclusion* recipe demonstrates how a directive handles the application of a scope to the interpolated existing nested content

Directive templating

Directives will frequently load HTML templates from outside their definition. When using them in an application, you will need to understand how to properly manage them, how they interact (if at all) with the directive's parent scope, and how they interact with the content nested inside them.

Getting ready

Suppose that you begin with the following skeleton application:

```
(index.html - uncompiled)

<div ng-app="myApp">
  <div ng-controller="MainCtrl">
    <my-directive>
      Stuff inside
    </my-directive>
  </div>
```

```
</div>

(app.js)

angular.module('myApp', [])
.controller('MainCtrl', function ($scope) {
  $scope.overwrite = false;
  $scope.origin = 'parent controller';
});
```

How to do it...

Introduce a template to the directive as follows:

```
(index.html - uncompiled)

<div ng-app="myApp">
  <div ng-controller="MainCtrl">
    <my-directive>
      Stuff inside
    </my-directive>
  </div>

  <script type="text/ng-template" id="my-directive.html">
    <div>
      <p>Directive template</p>
      <p>Scope from {{origin}}</p>
      <p>Overwritten? {{overwrite}}</p>
    </div>
  </script>
</div>

(app.js)

angular.module('myApp', [])
.controller('MainCtrl', function ($scope) {
  $scope.overwrite = false;
  $scope.origin = 'parent controller';
})
.directive('myDirective', function() {
```

```
  return {
    restrict: 'E',
    replace: true,
    templateUrl: 'my-directive.html',
    link: function (scope) {
      scope.overwrite = !!scope.origin;
      scope.origin = 'link function';
    }
  };
});
```

This snippet will compile the directive element into the following:

```
(index.html - compiled)

<div>
  <p>Directive template</p>
  <p>Scope from link function</p>
  <p>Overwritten? true</p>
</div>
```

 JSFiddle: `http://jsfiddle.net/msfrisbie/cojb59b1/`

How it works...

The parent scope from `MainCtrl` is inherited by the directive and is provided as the `scope` parameter inside the directive's `link` function. The directive template is inserted to replace the `<my-directive>` tag and its contents, but the supplanting template HTML is still subject to the inherited scope. The `link` function is able to modify the parent scope as though it were the directive's own. In other words, the link scope and the controller scope are the same object in this example.

See also

▶ The *Directive scope inheritance* recipe goes over the basics that involve carrying the parent scope through a directive

▶ The *Isolate scope* recipe gives details on how a directive can be decoupled from its parent scope

▶ The *Directive transclusion* recipe demonstrates how a directive handles the application of a scope to the interpolated existing nested content

Isolate scope

Often, you will find that the inheritance of a directive's parent scope is undesirable somewhere in your application. To prevent inheritance and to create a blank slate scope for the directive, isolate scope is utilized.

Getting ready

Suppose that you begin with the following skeleton application:

```
(index.html - uncompiled)

<div ng-app="myApp">
  <div ng-controller="MainCtrl">
    <my-directive>
      Stuff inside
    </my-directive>
  </div>

  <script type="text/ng-template" id="my-directive.html">
    <div>
      <p>Directive template</p>
      <p>Scope from {{origin}}</p>
      <p>Overwritten? {{overwrite}}</p>
    </div>
  </script>
</div>

(app.js)

angular.module('myApp', [])
.controller('MainCtrl', function ($scope) {
  $scope.overwrite = false;
  $scope.origin = 'parent controller';
});
```

How to do it...

Assign an isolate scope to the directive with an empty object literal, as follows:

```
(app.js)

.directive('myDirective', function() {
  return {
```

```
        templateUrl: 'my-directive.html',
        replace: true,
        scope: {},
        link: function (scope) {
          scope.overwrite = !!scope.origin;
          scope.origin = 'link function';
        }
    };
});
```

This will compile into the following:

```
(index.html - compiled)

<div>
  <p>Directive template</p>
  <p>Scope from link function</p>
  <p>Overwritten? false</p>
</div>
```

 JSFiddle: http://jsfiddle.net/msfrisbie/a2vmuhd3/

How it works...

The directive creates its own scope and performs the modifications on the scope instead of performing them inside the `link` function. The parent scope is unchanged and obscured from inside the directive's `link` function.

See also

▶ The *Directive scope inheritance* recipe goes over the basics that involve carrying the parent scope through a directive

▶ The *Directive templating* recipe examines how a directive can apply an external scope to an interpolated template

▶ The *Directive transclusion* recipe demonstrates how a directive handles the application of a scope to the interpolated existing nested content

Directive transclusion

Transclusion on its own is a relatively simple construct in AngularJS. This simplicity becomes muddied when mixed with the complexity of directives and scope inheritance. Directive transclusion is frequently used when the directive either needs to inherit from the parent scope, manage nested HTML, or both.

How to do it...

Assemble all the pieces required to use transclusion. This is shown here:

```
(index.html - uncompiled)

<div ng-app="myApp">
  <div ng-controller="MainCtrl">
    <my-directive>
      <p>HTML template</p>
      <p>Scope from {{origin}}</p>
      <p>Overwritten? {{overwrite}}</p>
    </my-directive>
  </div>

  <script type="text/ng-template" id="my-directive.html">
    <ng-transclude></ng-transclude>
  </script>
</div>

(app.js)

angular.module('myApp', [])
.controller('MainCtrl', function ($scope) {
  $scope.overwrite = false;
  $scope.origin = 'parent controller';
})
.directive('myDirective', function() {
  return {
    restrict: 'E',
    templateUrl: 'my-directive.html',
    scope: {},
    transclude: true,
    link: function (scope) {
      scope.overwrite = !!scope.origin;
```

```
        scope.origin = 'link function';
      }
    };
});
```

This will compile into the following:

```
(index.html - compiled)

<p>HTML template</p>
<p>Scope from parent controller</p>
<p>Overwritten? false</p>
```

In the directive's template, the location of `ng-transclude` informs `$compile` that the directive's original HTML contents are to replace the contents of the specified element. Furthermore, using transclusion means that the parent scope will continue to be in the directive to be used for the interpolated HTML.

To see the main reason to use transclusion more clearly, modify the `my-directive.html` directive template slightly in order to see the results side by side. This can be done as follows:

```
(index.html - uncompiled)

<script type="text/ng-template" id="my-directive.html">
  <ng-transclude></ng-transclude>
  <hr />
  <p>Directive template</p>
  <p>Scope from {{origin}}</p>
  <p>Overwritten? {{overwrite}}</p>
</script>
```

This will compile into the following:

```
(index.html - compiled)

<p>HTML template</p>
<p>Scope from parent controller</p>
<p>Overwritten? false</p>
<hr />
<p>Directive template</p>
<p>Scope from link function</p>
<p>Overwritten? false</p>
```

 JSFiddle: http://jsfiddle.net/msfrisbie/1a11d3mk/

How it works...

It should now be apparent exactly what is going on inside the directive that uses transclusion. The directive's template is subject to the `link` function (which necessarily uses the isolate scope), and the original wrapped HTML template maintains its relationship with the parent scope without the directive interfering.

See also

▸ The *Directive scope inheritance* recipe goes over the basics that involve carrying the parent scope through a directive

▸ The *Directive templating* recipe examines how a directive can apply external scope to an interpolated template

▸ The *Isolate scope* recipe details how a directive can be decoupled from its parent scope

Recursive directives

The power of directives can also be effectively applied when consuming data in a more unwieldy format. Consider the case in which you have a JavaScript object that exists in some sort of recursive tree structure. The view that you will generate for this object will also reflect its recursive nature and will have nested HTML elements that match the underlying data structure.

Getting ready

Suppose you had a recursive data object in your controller as follows:

```
(app.js)

angular.module('myApp', [])
.controller('MainCtrl', function($scope) {
  $scope.data = {
    text: 'Primates',
    items: [
      {
        text: 'Anthropoidea',
        items: [
          {
            text: 'New World Anthropoids'
          },
          {
            text: 'Old World Anthropoids',
```

```
            items: [
              {
                text: 'Apes',
                items: [
                  {
                    text: 'Lesser Apes'
                  },
                  {
                    text: 'Greater Apes'
                  }
                ]
              },
              {
                text: 'Monkeys'
              }
            ]
          }
        ]
      },
      {
        text: 'Prosimii'
      }
    ]
  };
});
```

How to do it...

As you might imagine, iteratively constructing a view or only partially using directives to accomplish this will become extremely messy very quickly. Instead, it would be better if you were able to create a directive that would seamlessly break apart the data recursively, and define and render the sub-HTML fragments cleanly. By cleverly using directives and the `$compile` service, this exact directive functionality is possible.

The ideal directive in this scenario will be able to handle the recursive object without any additional parameters or outside assistance in parsing and rendering the object. So, in the main view, your directive will look something like this:

```
<recursive value="nestedObject"></recursive>
```

The directive is accepting an isolate scope = binding to the parent scope object, which will remain structurally identical as the directive descends through the recursive object.

The $compile service

You will need to inject the $compile service in order to make the recursive directive work. The reason for this is that each level of the directive can instantiate directives inside it and convert them from an uncompiled template to real DOM material.

The angular.element() method

The angular.element() method can be thought of as the jQuery $() equivalent. It accepts a string template or DOM fragment and returns a jqLite object that can be modified, inserted, or compiled for your purposes. If the jQuery library is present when the application is initialized, AngularJS will use that instead of jqLite. If you use the AngularJS template cache, retrieved templates will already exist as if you had called the angular.element() method on the template text.

The $templateCache

Inside a directive, it's possible to create a template using angular.element() and a string of HTML similar to an underscore.js template. However, it's completely unnecessary and quite unwieldy to use compared to AngularJS templates. When you declare a template and register it with AngularJS, it can be accessed through the injected $templateCache, which acts as a key-value store for your templates.

The recursive template is as follows:

```
<script type="text/ng-template" id="recursive.html">
  <span>{{ val.text }}</span>
  <button ng-click="delSubtree()">delete</button>
  <ul ng-if="isParent" style="margin-left:30px">
    <li ng-repeat="item in val.items">
      <tree val="item" parent-data="val.items"></tree>
    </li>
  </ul>
</script>
```

The <span> and <button> elements are present at each instance of a node, and they present the data at that node as well as an interface to the click event (which we will define in a moment) that will destroy it and all its children.

Following these, the conditional <ul> element renders only if the isParent flag is set in the scope, and it repeats through the items array, recursing the child data and creating new instances of the directive. Here, you can see the full template definition of the directive:

```
<tree val="item" parent-data="val.items"></tree>
```

Not only does the directive take a `val` attribute for the local node data, but you can also see its `parent-data` attribute, which is the point of scope indirection that allows the tree structure. To make more sense of this, examine the following directive code:

```
(app.js)

.directive('tree', function($compile, $templateCache) {
  return {
    restrict: 'E',
    scope: {
      val: '=',
      parentData: '='
    },
    link: function(scope, el, attrs) {
      scope.isParent = angular.isArray(scope.val.items)
      scope.delSubtree = function() {
        if(scope.parentData) {
          scope.parentData.splice(
            scope.parentData.indexOf(scope.val),
            1
          );
        }
        scope.val={};
      }
      el.replaceWith(
        $compile(
          $templateCache.get('recursive.html')
        )(scope)
      );
    }
  };
});
```

With all of this, if you provide the recursive directive with the data object provided at the beginning of this recipe, it will result in the following (presented here without the auto-added AngularJS comments and directives):

```
(index.html - uncompiled)

<div ng-app="myApp">
  <div ng-controller="MainCtrl">
    <tree val="data"></tree>
  </div>

  <script type="text/ng-template" id="recursive.html">
```

```
      <span>{{ val.text }}</span>
      <button ng-click="deleteSubtree()">delete</button>
      <ul ng-if="isParent" style="margin-left:30px">
        <li ng-repeat="item in val.items">
          <tree val="item" parent-data="val.items"></tree>
        </li>
      </ul>
    </script>
</div>
```

The recursive nature of the directive templates enables nesting, and when compiled using the recursive data object located in the wrapping controller, it will compile into the following HTML:

```
(index.html - compiled)

<div ng-controller="MainController"> <span>Primates</span>
  <button ng-click="delSubtree()">delete</button>
  <ul ng-if="isParent" style="margin-left:30px">
    <li ng-repeat="item in val.items">
      <span>Anthropoidea</span>
      <button ng-click="delSubtree()">delete</button>
      <ul ng-if="isParent" style="margin-left:30px">
        <li ng-repeat="item in val.items">
          <span>New World Anthropoids</span>
          <button ng-click="delSubtree()">delete</button>
        </li>
        <li ng-repeat="item in val.items">
          <span>Old World Anthropoids</span>
          <button ng-click="delSubtree()">delete</button>
          <ul ng-if="isParent" style="margin-left:30px">
            <li ng-repeat="item in val.items">
              <span>Apes</span>
              <button ng-click="delSubtree()">delete</button>
              <ul ng-if="isParent" style="margin-left:30px">
                <li ng-repeat="item in val.items">
                  <span>Lesser Apes</span>
                  <button ng-click="delSubtree()">delete</button>
                </li>
                <li ng-repeat="item in val.items">
                  <span>Greater Apes</span>
                  <button ng-click="delSubtree()">delete</button>
                </li>
              </ul>
            </li>
```

```
          <li ng-repeat="item in val.items">
            <span>Monkeys</span>
            <button ng-click="delSubtree()">delete</button>
          </li>
        </ul>
      </li>
    </ul>
  </li>
  <li ng-repeat="item in val.items">
    <span>Prosimii</span>
    <button ng-click="delSubtree()">delete</button>
  </li>
</ul>
</div>
```

 JSFiddle: `http://jsfiddle.net/msfrisbie/ka46yx4u/`

How it works...

The definition of the isolate scope through the nested directives described in the previous section allows all or part of the recursive objects to be bound through `parentData` to the appropriate directive instance, all the while maintaining the nested connectedness afforded by the directive hierarchy. When a parent node is deleted, the lower directives are still bound to the data object and the removal propagates through cleanly.

The meatiest and most important part of this directive is, of course, the `link` function. Here, the `link` function determines whether the node has any children (which simply checks for the existence of an array in the local data node) and declares the deleting method, which simply removes the relevant portion from the recursive object and cleans up the local node. Up until this point, there haven't been any recursive calls, and there shouldn't need to be. If your directive is constructed correctly, AngularJS data binding and inherent template management will take care of the template cleanup for you. This, of course, leads into the final line of the `link` function, which is broken up here for readability:

```
el.replaceWith(
  $compile(
    $templateCache.get('recursive.html')
  )(scope)
);
```

Recall that in a `link` function, the second parameter is the jqLite-wrapped DOM object that the directive is linking—here, the `<tree>` element. This exposes to you a subset of jQuery object methods, including `replaceWith()`, which you will use here. The top-level instance of the directive will be replaced by the recursively-defined template, and this will carry down through the tree.

At this point, you should have an idea of how the recursive structure is coming together. The element parameter needs to be replaced with a recursively-compiled template, and for this, you will employ the `$compile` service. This service accepts a template as a parameter and returns a function that you will invoke with the current scope inside the directive's `link` function. The template is retrieved from `$templateCache` by the `recursive.html` key, and then it's compiled. When the compiler reaches the nested `<tree>` directive, the recursive directive is realized all the way down through the data in the recursive object.

There's more...

This recipe demonstrates the power of constructing a directive to convert a complex data object into a large DOM object. Relevant portions can be broken into individual templates, handled with distributed directive logic, and combined together in an elegant fashion to maximize modularity and reusability.

See also

- The *Optional nested directive controllers* recipe covers vertical communication between directives through their controller objects

2
Expanding Your Toolkit with Filters and Service Types

In this chapter, we will cover the following recipes:

- ▶ Using the `uppercase` and `lowercase` filters
- ▶ Using the `number` and `currency` filters
- ▶ Using the `date` filter
- ▶ Debugging using the `json` filter
- ▶ Using data filters outside the template
- ▶ Using built-in search filters
- ▶ Chaining filters
- ▶ Creating custom data filters
- ▶ Creating custom search filters
- ▶ Filtering with custom comparators
- ▶ Building a search filter from scratch
- ▶ Building a custom search filter expression from scratch
- ▶ Using service values and constants
- ▶ Using service factories
- ▶ Using services
- ▶ Using service providers
- ▶ Using service decorators

Introduction

In this chapter, you will learn how to effectively utilize AngularJS filters and services in your applications. Service types are essential tools required for code reuse, abstraction, and resource consumption in your application. Filters, however, are frequently glazed over in introductory courses as they are not considered integral to learning the framework basics. This is a pity as filters let you afford the ability to abstract and compartmentalize large chunks of application functionality cleanly.

All AngularJS filters perform the same class of operations on the data they are passed, but it is easier to think about filters in the context of a pseudo-dichotomy in which there are two kinds: data filters and search filters.

At a very high level, AngularJS data filters are merely tools that modulate JavaScript objects cleanly in the template. On the other half of the spectrum, search filters have the ability to select elements of an enumerable collection that match some of the criteria you have defined. They should be thought of as *black box* modifiers in your template—well-defined layers of indirection that keep your scopes free of messy data-parsing functions. They both enable your HTML code to be more declarative, and your code to be DRY.

Service types can be thought of as injectable singleton classes to be used throughout your application in order to house the utility functionality and maintain states. The AngularJS service types can appear as values, constants, factories, services, or providers.

Although filters and services are used very differently, a cunning developer can use them both as powerful tools for code abstraction.

Using the uppercase and lowercase filters

Two of the most basic built-in filters are `uppercase` and `lowercase` filters, and they can be used in the following fashion.

How to do it...

Suppose that you define the following controller in your application:

```
(app.js)

angular.module('myApp', [])
.controller('Ctrl', function ($scope) {
  $scope.data = {
    text: 'The QUICK brown Fox JUMPS over The LAZY dog',
    nums: '0123456789',
```

```
        specialChars: '!@#$%^&*()',
        whitespace: '    '
    };
});
```

You will then be able to use the filters in the template by passing them via the pipe operator, as follows:

```
(index.html)

<div ng-app="myApp">
  <div ng-controller="Ctrl">
    <p>{{ data.text | uppercase }}</p>
    <p>{{ data.nums | uppercase }}</p>
    <p>{{ data.specialChars | uppercase }}</p>
    <p>_{{ data.whitespace | uppercase }}_</p>
  </div>
</div>
```

The output rendered will be as follows:

```
THE QUICK BROWN FOX JUMPS OVER THE LAZY DOG
0123456789
!@#$%^&*()

 __    __
```

Similarly, the lowercase filter can be used with predictable results:

```
(index.html)

<div ng-app="myApp">
  <div ng-controller="Ctrl">
    <p>{{ data.text | lowercase }}</p>
    <p>{{ data.nums | lowercase }}</p>
    <p>{{ data.specialChars | lowercase }}</p>
    <p>_{{ data.whitespace | lowercase }}_</p>
  </div>
</div>
```

The output rendered will be as follows:

```
the quick brown fox jumps over the lazy dog
0123456789
!@#$%^&*()

 __    __
```

> JSFiddle: `http://jsfiddle.net/msfrisbie/vcuvxrom/`

How it works...

The `uppercase` and `lowercase` filters are essentially simple AngularJS wrappers used for native string methods `toUpperCase()` and `toLowerCase()` available in JavaScript. These filters ignore number characters, special characters, and whitespace when performing appropriate substitutions.

There's more...

As these filters are merely wrappers for native JavaScript methods, you almost certainly won't ever have a need to use them anywhere outside the template. Their primary utility is in their ability to be invoked in the template and their ability to chain themselves alongside other filters that might require them. For example, if you had created a search filter that only matched identical string matches in its results, you might want to pass a search string through a `lowercase` filter before passing it through the search comparator.

See also

▸ The *Chaining filters* recipe demonstrates how you would go about using `lowercase` filters in conjunction with other filters

Using the number and currency filters

AngularJS has some built-in filters that are less simple, such as `number` and `currency`; they can be used to format numbers into normalized strings. They also accept optional arguments that can further customize how the filters work.

Getting ready...

Suppose that you define the following controller in your application:

```
(app.js)

angular.module('myApp', [])
.controller('Ctrl', function ($scope) {
  $scope.data = {
    bignum: 1000000,
    num: 1.0,
```

```
        smallnum: 0.9999,
        tinynum: 0.0000001
    };
});
```

How to do it...

You can apply the `number` filter in your template, as follows:

```
(index.html)

<div ng-app="myApp">
  <div ng-controller="Ctrl">
    <p>{{ data.bignum | number }}</p>
    <p>{{ data.num | number }}</p>
    <p>{{ data.smallnum | number }}</p>
    <p>{{ data.tinynum | number }}</p>
  </div>
</div>
```

The output rendered will be as follows:

```
1,000,000
1
1.000
1e-7
```

This outcome might seem a bit arbitrary, but it demonstrates the next facet of filters examined here, which are arguments. Filters can take arguments to further customize the output. The `number` filter takes a `fractionSize` argument, which defines how many decimal places it will round to, defaulting to 3. This is shown in the following code:

```
(index.html)

<div ng-app="myApp">
  <div ng-controller="Ctrl">
    <!-- data | number : fractionSize(optional) -->
    <p>{{ data.smallnum | number : 4 }}</p>
    <p>{{ data.tinynum | number: 7 }}</p>
    <p>{{ 012345.6789 | number : 2 }}</p>
  </div>
</div>
```

The output rendered will be as follows:

```
0.9999
0.0000001
12,345.68
```

The `currency` filter is another AngularJS filter that takes an optional argument, `symbol`:

```
(index.html)
```

```html
<div ng-app="myApp">
  <div ng-controller="Ctrl">
    <!-- data | currency : symbol(optional) -->
    <p>{{ 1234.56 | currency }}</p>
    <p>{{ 0.02 | currency }}</p>
    <p>{{ 45682.78 | currency : "&#8364;" }}</p>
  </div>
</div>
```

The output rendered will be as follows:

```
$1,234.56
$0.02
€45,682.78
```

 JSFiddle: `http://jsfiddle.net/msfrisbie/Lcb33vnz/`

How it works...

JavaScript has a single format in which it stores numbers as 64-bit double precision floating point numbers. These AngularJS filters exist to neatly format this raw number format by examining the values passed to it and by deciding how to appropriately format it as a string. The `number` filter handles rounding, truncation, and compression in negative exponents. It optionally accepts the `fractionSize` argument, in order to allow you to customize the filter to your needs, something that greatly increases the utility of filters. The `currency` filter handles rounding and appending of the designated currency symbol. It optionally accepts the `symbol` argument, which will insert the provided symbol in front of the formatted number.

There's more...

Both of these filters inherently utilize the `$locale` service, which acts as a fallback for default arguments (for example, providing a `$` character for the `currency` filter in regions that use dollar, ordering of dates, and more). This service exists as a part of AngularJS's mission to act as a region agnostic framework.

See also...

▶ The *Chaining filters* recipe demonstrates how you will go about using these filters in conjunction with other filters

Using the date filter

The `date` filter is an extremely robust and customizable filter that can handle many different kinds of raw date strings and convert them into human readable versions. This is useful in situations when you want to let your server defer datetime processing to the client and just be able to pass it a Unix timestamp or an ISO date.

Getting ready...

Suppose, you have your controller set up in the following fashion:

```
(app.js)

angular.module('myApp', [])
.controller('Ctrl', function ($scope) {
  $scope.data = {
    unix: 1394787566535,
    iso: '2014-03-14T08:59:26Z',
    date: new Date(2014, 2, 14, 1, 59, 26, 535)
  };
});
```

How to do it...

All the date formats can be used seamlessly with the `date` filter inside the template, as follows:

```
(index.html)

<div ng-app="myApp">
  <div ng-controller="Ctrl">
    <p>{{ data.unix | date }}</p>
```

```
      <p>{{ data.iso | date }}</p>
      <p>{{ data.date | date }}</p>
    </div>
</div>
```

The output rendered will be as follows:

```
Mar 14, 2014
Mar 14, 2014
Mar 14, 2014
```

The `date` filter is heavily customizable, giving you the ability to generate a date and time representation using any piece of the datetime passed to it:

```
(index.html)

<div ng-app="myApp">
  <div ng-controller="Ctrl">
    <!-- AngularJS matches the expression components
    to datetime components, then stringifies as specified -->
    <p>{{ data.unix | date : "EEEE 'at' H:mma" }}</p>
    <p>{{ data.iso | date : "longDate" }}</p>
    <p>{{ data.date | date : "M/d H:m:s.sss" }}</p>
  </div>
</div>
```

This code uses various pieces of the `date` filter syntax to pull out elements from the datetime generated inside the filter, and assemble them together in the output string, the template for which is provided in the optional format argument. The output rendered will be as follows:

```
Friday at 1:59AM
March 14, 2014
3/14 1:59:26.535
```

 JSFiddle: `http://jsfiddle.net/msfrisbie/mvdqfv5z/`

How it works...

The `date` filter wraps a robust set of complex regular expressions inside the framework, which exists to parse the string passed to it into a normalized JavaScript `date` object. This `date` object is then broken apart and molded into the desired string format specified by the filter's argument syntax.

The AngularJS documentation at `https://docs.angularjs.org/api/ng/filter/date` provides the details of all the possible input and output formats required for date filters.

There's more...

The `date` filter provides you with two levels of indirection: normalized conversion from various datetime formats and normalized conversion into almost any human readable format. Note that in the absence of a provided time zone, the time zone assumed is the local time zone, which in this example is Pacific Daylight Time (UTC - 7), which is accommodated through the `$locale` service.

Debugging using the json filter

AngularJS provides you with a JSON conversion tool, the `json` filter, to serialize JavaScript objects into prettified JSON code. This filter isn't so much in use for production applications as it is used for real-time inspection of your scope objects.

Getting ready...

Suppose your controller is set up as follows with a prefilled `user` data object:

```
(app.js)

angular.module('myApp', [])
.controller('Ctrl', function ($scope) {
  $scope.user = {
    id: 123,
    name: {
      first: 'Jake',
      last: 'Hsu'
    },
    username: 'papatango',
    friendIds: [5, 13, 3, 1, 2, 8, 21],
    // properties prefixed with $$ will be excluded
    $$no_show: 'Hide me!'
  };
});
```

How to do it...

Your `user` object can be serialized in the template, as follows:

```
(index.html)

<div ng-app="myApp">
  <div ng-controller="Ctrl">
    <pre>{{ user | json }}</pre>
  </div>
</div>
```

The output will be rendered in HTML, as follows:

```
{
  "id": 123,
  "name": {
    "first": "Jake",
    "last": "Hsu"
  },
  "username": "papatango",
  "friendIds": [
    5,
    13,
    3,
    1,
    2,
    8,
    21
  ]
}
```

 JSFiddle: `http://jsfiddle.net/msfrisbie/yk0zxc9b/`

How it works...

The `json` filter simply wraps the `JSON.stringify()` method in JavaScript in order to provide you with an easy way to spit out formatted objects for inspection. When the filtered object is fed into a `<pre>` tag, the JSON string will be properly indented in the rendered template. Properties prefixed with `$$` will be skipped by the serializer as this notation is used internally in AngularJS as a private identifier.

There's more...

As AngularJS lets you afford two-way data binding in the template, you can see the filtered object update in real time in your template, as various interactions with your application change it; this is extremely useful for debugging.

Using data filters outside the template

Filters are built to perform template data processing, so their utilization outside the template will be infrequent. Nonetheless, AngularJS provides you with the ability to use filter functions via an injection of `$filter`.

Getting ready

Suppose that you have an application, as follows:

```
(app.js)

angular.module('myApp', [])
.controller('Ctrl', function ($scope) {
  $scope.val = 1234.56789;
});
```

How to do it...

In the view templates, the argument order is scrambled with the following format:

```
data | filter : optionalArgument
```

For this example, it would take the form in the template as follows:

```
<p>{{ val | number : 4 }}</p>
```

This will give the following result:

```
1,234.5679
```

In this example, it's cleanest to apply the filter in the view template, as the purpose of formatting the number is merely for readability. If, however, the `number` filter is needed to be used in a controller, `$filter` can be injected and used as follows:

```
(app.js)

angular.module('myApp', [])
```

```
.controller('Ctrl', function ($scope, $filter) {
    $scope.val = 1234.56789;
    $scope.filteredVal = $filter('number')($scope.val, 4);
});
```

With this, the values of `$scope.val` and `$scope.filteredVal` will be identical.

 JSFiddle: `http://jsfiddle.net/msfrisbie/9bzu85uu/`

How it works...

Although the syntax is very different compared to what is found in a template, using a dependency injected filter is functionally the same as applying it in the view template. The same filter method is invoked for both formats and both generate the same output.

There's more...

Although there are no cardinal sins committed by injecting `$filter` and using your filters that way, the syntax is awkward and verbose. Filters aren't really designed for that sort of use anyway. AngularJS is meant for building declarative templates, and that is exactly what data filters provide when used in templates—lightweight and flexible modulation functions for cleaning and organizing your data.

One of the primary use cases for using filters outside the template is when you are building a custom filter that uses one or more existing filters inside it. For example, you might want to use the `currency` filter inside a custom filter, which decides whether to use a $ or a ¢ prefix based on whether or not the amount is greater or less than $1.00.

Using built-in search filters

Search filters serve to evaluate individual elements in an enumerable object and return whether or not they belong in the resultant set. The returned value from the filter will also be an enumerable set with none, some, or all of the original values that were removed. AngularJS provides a rich suite of ways to filter an enumerable object.

Getting ready

Search filters return a subset of an enumerable object, so prepare a controller as follows, with a simple array of strings:

```
(app.js)

angular.module('myApp', [])
.controller('Ctrl', function ($scope) {
  $scope.users = [
    'Albert Pai',
    'Jake Hsu',
    'Jack Hanford',
    'Scott Robinson',
    'Diwank Singh'
  ];
});
```

How to do it...

The default search filter is used in the template in the same fashion as a data filter, but invoked with the pipe operator. It takes a mandatory argument, that is, the object that the filter will compare against.

The easiest way to test a search filter is by tying an input field to a model and using that model as the search filter argument, as follows:

```
(index.html)

<div ng-app="myApp">
  <div ng-controller="Ctrl">
    <input type="text" ng-model="search.val" />
  </div>
</div>
```

This model can then be applied in a search filter on an enumerable data object. The filter is most commonly applied inside an ng-repeat expression:

```
(index.html)

<div ng-app="myApp">
  <div ng-controller="Ctrl">
    <input type="text" ng-model="search.val" />
    <p ng-repeat="user in users | filter : search.val">
```

```
      {{ user }}
    </p>
  </div>
</div>
```

Entering `ja` will return the following output:

```
Jake Hsu
Jack Hanford
```

Entering `s` will return the following output:

```
Jake Hsu
Scott Robinson
Diwank Singh
```

Entering `a` will return the following output:

```
Albert Pai
Jake Hsu
Jack Hanford
Diwank Singh
```

 JSFiddle: `http://jsfiddle.net/msfrisbie/h1dbover/`

How it works...

With this setup, the string in the `search.val` model will be matched (case insensitive) against each element in the enumerable object and will only return the matches for the repeater to iterate through. This transformation occurs before the object is passed to the repeater, so the filter combined with AngularJS data binding results in a very impressive real-time, in-browser filtering system with minimal overhead.

See also

▸ The *Chaining filters* recipe demonstrates how to utilize a string search filter in conjunction with existing AngularJS string modulation filters

▸ The *Filtering with custom comparators* recipe demonstrates how to further customize the way an enumerable collection is compared to the reference object

Chaining filters

As AngularJS search filters simply reduce the modulation functions that return a subset of the object that is passed to it, it is possible to chain multiple filters together.

When filtering enumerable objects, AngularJS provides two built-in enumeration filters that are commonly used in conjunction with the search filters: `limitTo` and `orderBy`.

Getting ready

Suppose that your application contains a controller as follows with a simple array of objects containing a `name` string property:

(app.js)

```
angular.module('myApp', [])
.controller('Ctrl', function ($scope) {
  $scope.users = [
    {name: 'Albert Pai'},
    {name: 'Jake Hsu'},
    {name: 'Jack Hanford'},
    {name: 'Scott Robinson'},
    {name: 'Diwank Singh'}
  ];
});
```

In addition, suppose that the application template is set up as follows:

(index.html)

```
<div ng-app="myApp">
  <div ng-controller="Ctrl">
    <input type="text" ng-model="search.val" />
    <!-- simple repeater filtering against search.val -->
    <p ng-repeat="user in users | filter : search.val">
      {{ user.name }}
    </p>
  </div>
</div>
```

How to do it...

You can chain another filter following your first with an identical syntax by merely adding another pipe operator and the filter name with arguments. Here, you can see the setup to apply the `limitTo` filter to the matching results:

```
(index.html)

<p ng-repeat="user in users | filter : search.val | limitTo: 2">
  {{ user.name }}
</p>
```

Searching for h will result in the following output:

```
Jake Hsu
Jack Hanford
```

You can chain another filter, `orderBy`, which will sort the array, as follows:

```
(index.html)

<p ng-repeat="user in users | filter : search.val | orderBy: 'name' |
limitTo : 2">
  {{ user.name }}
</p>
```

Searching for h will result in the following output:

```
Diwank Singh
Jack Hanford
```

 JSFiddle: `http://jsfiddle.net/msfrisbie/ht3hfLrt/`

How it works...

AngularJS search filters are functions that return a Boolean, representing whether or not the particular element of the enumerable object belongs to the resultant set. For the array of string primitives in the preceding code, the filter performs a simple case-insensitive substring match operation against the provided matching string taken from the model bound to the `<input>` tag.

The subsequent chained filters `orderBy` and `limitTo` also take an enumerable object as an argument and perform an additional operation on it. In the preceding example, the filter first reduces the string array to a subset string array, which is first passed to the `orderBy` filter. This filter sorts the subset string array by the expression provided, which here is alphabetical order, as the argument is a string. This sorted array is then passed to the `limitTo` filter which truncates the sorted substring subset string array to the number of characters specified in the argument. This final array is then fed into the repeater in the template for rendering.

There's more...

It's worth mentioning that chained AngularJS filters are not necessarily commutative; the order in which filters are chained matters, as they are evaluated sequentially. In the last example, reversing the order of the chained filters (`limitTo` followed by `orderBy`) will truncate the subset string array and then sort only the truncated results. The proper way to think about this is to compare them to nested functions—similar to how `foo(bar(x))` is obviously not the same as `bar(foo(x))`, and `x | foo | bar` is not the same as `x | bar | foo`.

Creating custom data filters

At some point, the provided AngularJS data filters will not be enough to fill your needs, and you will need to create your own data filters. For example, assume that in an application that you are building, you have a region of the page that is limited in physical dimensions, but contains an arbitrary amount of text. You would like to truncate that text to a length which is guaranteed to fit in the limited space. A custom filter, as you might imagine, is perfect for this task.

How to do it...

The filter you wish to build accepts a string argument and returns another string. For now, the filter will truncate the string to 100 characters and append an ellipsis at the point of truncation:

```
(app.js)

angular.module('myApp', [])
.filter('simpletruncate', function () {
  // the text parameter
  return function (text) {
    var truncated = text.slice(0, 100);
    if (text.length > 100) {
      truncated += '...';
    }
    return truncated;
  };
});
```

This will be used in the template, as follows:

```
(index.html)

<div ng-app="myApp">
  <div ng-controller="Ctrl">
    <p>{{ myText | simpletruncate }}</p>
  </div>
</div>
```

This filter works well, but it feels a bit brittle. Instead of just defaulting to 100 characters and an ellipsis, the filter should also accept parameters that allow undefined input and optional definition of how many characters to truncate to and what the stop character(s) should be. It would be even better if the filter only cut off the text at a set of whitespace characters if possible:

```
(app.js)

angular.module('myApp', [])
.filter('regextruncate',function() {
  return function(text,limit,stoptext) {
    var regex = /\s/;
    if (!angular.isDefined(limit)) {
      limit = 100;
    }
    if (!angular.isDefined(stoptext)) {
      stoptext = '...';
    }
    limit = Math.min(limit,text.length);
    for(var i=0;i<limit;i++) {
      if(regex.exec(text[limit-i])
         && !regex.exec(text[(limit-i)-1])) {
        limit = limit-i;
        break;
      }
    }
    var truncated = text.slice(0, limit);
    if (text.length>limit) {
      truncated += stoptext;
    }
    return truncated;
  };
});
```

This will be used in the template as follows:

```
(index.html)

<div ng-app="myApp">
  <div ng-controller="Ctrl">
    <p>{{ myText | regextruncate : 150 : '???' }}</p>
  </div>
</div>
```

 JSFiddle: `http://jsfiddle.net/msfrisbie/a4ez926f/`

How it works...

The final version of the filter uses a simple whitespace-detecting regular expression to find the first point in the string that it can truncate. After setting the default values of `limit` and `stoptext`, the data filter iterates backwards through the relevant string values, watching for the first point at which it sees a non whitespace character followed by a whitespace character. This is the point at which it sets the truncation, and the string is broken apart, and then the relevant segment is returned with the appended `stoptext` statement.

These filter examples don't modify the model in any way, they are merely context-free data wrappers that package your model data neatly into a format that your template can easily digest. Each model change causes the filter to be invoked in order to keep the data in the template up-to-date, so the filter processing must be lightweight as it is assumed that the filter will be frequently invoked.

There's more...

A rich suite of data filters in your application will allow a cleaner decoupling of the presentation layer and model. The demonstration in this recipe was limited to the string primitive, but there is no reason you could not extend your filter logic to encompass and handle complex data objects in your application's models.

The entire purpose of filters is to improve readability and reusability, so if the construction and application of a custom filter enables you to do that, you are encouraged to do so.

Creating custom search filters

AngularJS search filters work exceedingly well out of the box, but you will quickly develop the desire to introduce some customization of how the filter actually relates the search object to the enumerable collection. This collection is frequently composed of complex data objects; a simple string comparison will not suffice, especially when you want to modify the rules by which matches are governed.

Searching against data objects is simply a matter of building the search object in the same mould as the enumerable collection objects.

Getting ready

Suppose, for example, your controller looks as follows:

```
(app.js)

angular.module('myApp', [])
.controller('Ctrl', function($scope) {
  $scope.users = [
    {
      firstName: 'John',
      lastName: 'Stockton'
    },
    {
      firstName: 'Michael',
      lastName: 'Jordan'
    }
  ];
});
```

How to do it...

When searching against this collection, in the case where the search filter is passed a string primitive, it will perform a wildcard search, as follows:

```
(index.html)

<div ng-app="myApp">
  <div ng-controller="Ctrl">
    <input ng-model="search" />
    <p ng-repeat="user in users | filter:search">
      {{ user.firstName}} {{ user.lastName }}
    </p>
  </div>
</div>
```

JSFiddle: `http://jsfiddle.net/msfrisbie/ghsa3nym/`

With this, if you were to enter `jo` in the input field, both `John Stockton` and `Michael Jordan` will be returned. When asked to compare a string primitive to an object, AngularJS has no choice but to compare the string to every field it can, and any objects that match are declared to be a part of the match-positive resultant set.

If instead you only want to compare against specific attributes of the enumerable collection, you can set the search object to have correlating attributes that should be matched against the collection attributes, as shown here:

```
(index.html)

<div ng-app="myApp">
  <div ng-controller="Ctrl">
    <input ng-model="search.firstName" />
    <p ng-repeat="user in users | filter:search">
      {{ user.firstName}} {{ user.lastName }}
    </p>
  </div>
</div>
```

JSFiddle: `http://jsfiddle.net/msfrisbie/72qucbhp/`

Now, if you were to enter `jo` in the input field, only `John Stockton` will be returned.

Filtering with custom comparators

If you want to search only for exact matches, vanilla wildcard filtering becomes problematic as the default comparator uses the search object to match against substrings in the collection object. Instead, you might want a way to specify exactly what constitutes a match between the reference object and enumerable collection.

Getting ready

Suppose that your controller contains the following data object:

```
(app.js)

angular.module('myApp', [])
```

```
.controller('Ctrl', function($scope) {
  $scope.users = [
    {
      firstName: 'John',
      lastName: 'Stockton',
      number: '12'
    },
    {
      firstName: 'Michael',
      lastName: 'Jordan',
      number: '23'
    },
    {
      firstName: 'Allen',
      lastName: 'Iverson',
      number: '3'
    }
  ];
});
```

How to do it...

Instead of using just a single search box, the application will use two search fields, one for the name and one for the number. Having a wildcard search for the first name and last name is more useful, but searching for wildcard numbers is not useful in this situation.

The search fields are constructed as follows:

```
(index.html)

<div ng-app="myApp">
  <div ng-controller="Ctrl">
    <input ng-model="search.$" />
    <input ng-model="search.number" />
    <p ng-repeat="user in users | filter:search">
      {{ user.firstName}} {{ user.lastName }}
    </p>
  </div>
</div>
```

The first input field appears with $; this is done merely to assign the wildcard search to the entire search object so that it does not interfere with other assigned search attributes. The second input field specifies that the application should only search against the collection's `number` attribute.

As expected, testing this code reveals that the `number` search field is performing a wildcard search, which is not desirable. To specify exact matches when searching, the filter takes an optional comparator argument that mandates how matches will be ascertained. A `true` value passed will enable exact matches:

```
(index.html)

<div ng-app="myApp">
  <div ng-controller="Ctrl">
    <input ng-model="search.$" required />
    <input ng-model="search.number" required />
    <p ng-repeat="user in users | filter:search:true">
      {{ user.firstName}} {{ user.lastName }}
    </p>
  </div>
</div>
```

With this setup, both inputs will create an AND filter to select data from the array with one or multiple criteria. The `required` statement will cause the model bound to it to reset to `undefined`, when the input is an empty string.

 JSFiddle: `http://jsfiddle.net/msfrisbie/on394so2/`

How it works...

The `comparator` argument will be resolved to a function in all cases. When passing in `true`, AngularJS will treat it as an alias for the following code:

```
function(actual, expected) {
  return angular.equals(expected, actual);
}
```

This will function as a strict comparison of the element in the enumerable collection and the reference object.

More generally, you can also pass in your own comparator function, which will return `true` or `false` based on whether or not `actual` matches `expected`. This will take the following form:

```
function(actual, expected) {
  // logic to determine if actual
  // should count as a match for expected
}
```

The functions from the comparator argument are the ones used to determine whether each piece of the enumerable collection belongs in the resultant subset.

See also

▶ The *Building a search filter from scratch* and *Building a custom search filter expression from scratch* recipes demonstrate alternate methods of architecting search filters to match your application's needs

Building a search filter from scratch

The provided search filters can serve your application's purposes only to a point. Eventually, you will need to construct a complete solution in order to filter an enumerable collection.

Getting ready

Suppose that your controller contains the following data object:

```
(app.js)

angular.module('myApp', [])
.controller('Ctrl', function($scope) {
  $scope.users = [
    {
      firstName: 'John',
      lastName: 'Stockton',
      number: '12'
    },
    {
      firstName: 'Michael',
      lastName: 'Jordan',
      number: '23'
    },
    {
      firstName: 'Allen',
      lastName: 'Iverson',
      number: '3'
    }
  ];
});
```

How to do it...

Suppose you wanted to create an OR filter for the name and number values. The brute force way to do this is to create an entirely new filter in order to replace the AngularJS filter. The filter takes an enumerable object and returns a subset of the object. Adding the following will do exactly that:

(app.js)

```
.filter('userSearch', function () {
  return function (users, search) {
    var matches = [];
    angular.forEach(users, function (user) {
      if (!angular.isDefined(users) ||
          !angular.isDefined(search)) {
        return false;
      }
      // initialize match conditions
      var nameMatch = false,
        numberMatch = false;
      if (angular.isDefined(search.name) &&
          search.name.length > 0) {
        // substring of first or last name will match
        if (angular.isDefined(user.firstName)) {
          nameMatch = nameMatch ||
          user.firstName.indexOf(search.name) > -1;
        }
        if (angular.isDefined(user.lastName)) {
          nameMatch = nameMatch ||
          user.lastName.indexOf(search.name) > -1;
        }
      }
      if (angular.isDefined(user.number) &&
          angular.isDefined(search.number)) {
        // only match if number is exact match
        numberMatch = user.number === search.number;
      }
      // either match should populate the results with user
      if (nameMatch || numberMatch) {
        matches.push(user);
      }
    });
    // this is the array that will be fed to the repeater
    return matches;
  };
});
```

This would then be used as follows:

```
(index.html)

<div ng-app="myApp">
  <div ng-controller="Ctrl">
    <input ng-model="search.name"
           required />
    <input ng-model="search.number"
           required />
    <p ng-repeat="user in users | userSearch : search">
      {{ user.firstName }} {{ user.lastName }}
    </p>
  </div>
</div>
```

 JSFiddle: `http://jsfiddle.net/msfrisbie/k4umoj3p/`

How it works...

Since this filter is built from scratch, it's constructed to handle all the edge cases of missing attributes and objects in the parameters. The filter performs substring lookups on the first and last name attributes and exact matches on number attributes. Once this is done, it performs the actual OR operation on the two results. However, having entirely rebuilt the search filter, it must return the entire collection subset.

There's more...

Rebuilding the filtering mechanism from top to bottom, as shown in this recipe, only makes sense if you need to significantly diverge from the existing filtering mechanism functionality.

See also

▶ The *Building a custom search filter expression from scratch* recipe shows you how to perform custom filtering while working within the existing search filter mechanisms

Building a custom search filter expression from scratch

Instead of reinventing the wheel, you can create a search filter expression that evaluates to `true` or `false` for each iteration in the enumerable collection.

How to do it...

The simplest way to do this is to define a function on your scope, as follows:

```
(app.js)

angular.module('myApp', [])
.controller('Ctrl', function ($scope) {
  $scope.users = [
    ...
  ];
  $scope.usermatch = function (user) {
    if (!angular.isDefined(user) ||
        !angular.isDefined($scope.search)) {
      return false;
    }
    var nameMatch = false,
      numberMatch = false;
    if (angular.isDefined($scope.search.name) &&
        $scope.search.name.length > 0) {
      if (angular.isDefined(user.firstName)) {
        nameMatch = nameMatch ||
          user.firstName.indexOf($scope.search.name) > -1;
      }
      if (angular.isDefined(user.lastName)) {
        nameMatch = nameMatch ||
          user.lastName.indexOf($scope.search.name) > -1;
      }
    }
    if (angular.isDefined(user.number) &&
        angular.isDefined($scope.search.number)) {
      numberMatch = user.number === $scope.search.number;
    }
    return nameMatch || numberMatch;
  };
});
```

Now, this can be passed to the built-in filter as follows:

```
(index.html)

<div ng-app="myApp">
  <div ng-controller="Ctrl">
    <input ng-model="search.name" required />
    <input ng-model="search.number" required />
    <p ng-repeat="user in users | filter:usermatch">
      {{ user.firstName }} {{ user.lastName }}
    </p>
  </div>
</div>
```

 JSFiddle: `http://jsfiddle.net/msfrisbie/76874ygr/`

In the Name search box, typing `Jo` now returns `Michael Jordan` and `John Stockton` and in the Number search box, typing `3` only returns `Allen Iverson`. Searching for both `Mi` and `3` will return `Michael Jordan` and `Allen Iverson`, as the filter constructed here is an OR filter. If you want to change it to an AND filter, you can simply change the return line to the following:

```
return nameMatch && numberMatch;
```

How it works...

All of these search filter techniques can be framed through a perspective that pays attention to what you are filtering. Search filters merely apply the question: "Does this fit my definition of a match?", over and over again. AngularJS's data binding causes this question to be asked to each member of the enumerable collection each time the object changes in content or population. The preceding recipes merely define how this question gets asked.

There's more...

Filters are merely applied JavaScript functions and the mechanisms by which they can be configured are flexible. Rarely in production applications will the built-in search filter infrastructure be sufficient, so it is advantageous to instead be able to mould exactly how the filter interprets a match.

Furthermore, as you begin to examine performance limitations, you will begin to consider ways to optimize repeaters and filters. If kept lightweight, filters are inexpensive and can be run hundreds of times in rapid succession without consequence. As complexity and data magnitude scale, filters can allow you to maintain a performant and responsive application.

Using service values and constants

AngularJS service types, at their core, are singleton containers used for unified resource access across your application. Sometimes, the resource access will just be a single JS object. For this, AngularJS offers service values and service constants.

How to do it...

Service values and service constants both act in a very similar way, but with one important difference.

Service value

The service value is the simplest of all service types. The `value` service acts as a key-value pair and can be injected and used as follows:

```
(app.js)

angular.module('myApp', [])
.controller('Ctrl', function($scope, MyValue) {
  $scope.data = MyValue;
  $scope.update = function() {
    MyValue.name = 'Brandon Marshall';
  };
})
.value('MyValue', {
  name: 'Tim Tebow',
  number: 15
});
```

An example of template use is as follows:

```
(index.html)

<div ng-app="myApp">
  <div ng-controller="Ctrl">
    <button ng-click="update()">Update</button>
    {{ data.name }} #{{ data.number }}
  </div>
</div>
```

 JSFiddle: `http://jsfiddle.net/msfrisbie/hs7uL1y0/`

You'll notice that AngularJS has no problem with you updating the service value. Since it is a singleton, any part of your application that injects the `value` service and reads/writes to it will be accessing the same data. Service values act like service factories (discussed in the *Using service factories* recipe) and cannot be injected into the providers or the `config()` phase of your application.

Service constant

Like service values, service constants also act as singleton key-value pairs. The important difference is that service constants act like service providers and can be injected into the `config()` phase and service providers. They can be used as follows:

```
(app.js)

angular.module('myApp', [])
.config(function(MyConstant) {
  // can't inject $log into config()
  console.log(MyConstant);
})
.controller('Ctrl', function($scope, MyConstant) {
  $scope.data = MyConstant;
  $scope.update = function() {
    MyConstant.name = 'Brandon Marshall';
  };
})
.constant('MyConstant', {
  name: 'Tim Tebow',
  number: 15
});
```

The template remains unchanged from the service value example.

 JSFiddle: `http://jsfiddle.net/msfrisbie/whaea0y1/`

How it works...

Service values and service constants act as read/write key-value pairs. The main difference is that you can choose one over the other based on whether you will need to have the data available to you when the application is being initialized.

▶ The *Using service providers* recipe provides details of the ancestor service type and how it relates to the service type life cycle

▶ The *Using service decorators* recipe demonstrates how a service type initialization can be intercepted for a just in time modification

Using service factories

A service factory is the simplest general purpose service type that allows you to use the singleton nature of AngularJS services with encapsulation.

How to do it...

The service factory's return value is what will be injected when the factory is listed as a dependency. A common and useful pattern is to define private data and functions outside this object, and define an API to them through a returned object. This is shown in the following code:

```
(app.js)

angular.module('myApp', [])
.controller('Ctrl', function($scope, MyFactory) {
  $scope.data = MyFactory.getPlayer();
  $scope.update = MyFactory.swapPlayer;
})
.factory('MyFactory', function() {
  // private variables and functions
  var player = {
    name: 'Peyton Manning',
    number: 18
  }, swap = function() {
    player.name = 'A.J. Green';
  };
  // public API
  return {
    getPlayer: function() {
      return player;
    },
    swapPlayer: function() {
      swap();
    }
  };
});
```

Since the service factory values are now bound to `$scope`, they can be used in the template normally, as follows:

```
(index.html)

<div ng-app="myApp">
  <div ng-controller="Ctrl">
    <button ng-click="update()">Update</button>
    {{ data.name }} #{{ data.number }}
  </div>
</div>
```

 JSFiddle: `http://jsfiddle.net/msfrisbie/5gydkrjw/`

How it works...

This example might feel a bit contrived, but it demonstrates the basic usage pattern that can be used with service factories for great effect. As with all service types, this is a singleton, so any modifications done by a component of the application will be reflected anywhere the factory is injected.

See also

- ▸ The *Using services* recipe shows how the sibling type of service factories is incorporated into applications
- ▸ The *Using service providers* recipe provides you with the details of the ancestor service type and how it relates to the service type life cycle
- ▸ The *Using service decorators* recipe demonstrates how service type initialization can be intercepted for a just in time modification

Using services

Services act in much the same way as service factories. Private data and methods can be defined and an API can be implemented on the service object through it.

How to do it...

A service is consumed in the same way as a factory. It differs in that the object to be injected is the controller itself. It can be used in the following way:

```
(app.js)

angular.module('myApp', [])
.controller('Ctrl', function($scope, MyService) {
  $scope.data = MyService.getPlayer();
  $scope.update = MyService.swapPlayer;
})
.service('MyService', function() {
  var player = {
    name: 'Philip Rivers',
    number: 17
  }, swap = function() {
    player.name = 'Alshon Jeffery';
  };
  this.getPlayer = function() {
    return player;
  };
  this.swapPlayer = function() {
    swap();
  };
});
```

When bound to $scope, the service interface is indistinguishable from a factory. This is shown here:

```
(index.html)

<div ng-app="myApp">
  <div ng-controller="Ctrl">
    <button ng-click="update()">Update</button>
    {{ data.name }} #{{ data.number }}
  </div>
</div>
```

 JSFiddle: http://jsfiddle.net/msfrisbie/5wn16dyk/

How it works...

Services invoke a constructor with the `new` operator, and the instantiated service object is the delivered injectable. Like a factory, it still exists as a singleton and the instantiation is deferred until the service is actually injected.

See also

- ▶ The *Using service factories* recipe shows how the sibling type of service is incorporated in applications
- ▶ The *Using service providers* recipe provides the details of the ancestor service type and how it relates to the service type life cycle
- ▶ The *Using service decorators* recipe demonstrates how service type initialization can be intercepted for a just in time modification

Using service providers

Service providers are the parent service type used for factories and services. They are the most configurable and extensible of the service types, and allow you to inspect and modify other service types during the application's initialization.

How to do it...

Service providers take a function parameter that returns an object that has a `$get` method. This method is what AngularJS will use to produce the injected value after the application has been initialized. The object wrapping the `$get` method is what will be supplied if the service provider is injected into the `config` phase. This can be implemented as follows:

```
(app.js)

angular.module('myApp', [])
.config(function(PlayerProvider) {
  // appending 'Provider' to the injectable
  // is an Angular config() provider convention
  PlayerProvider.configSwapPlayer();
  console.log(PlayerProvider.configGetPlayer());
})
.controller('Ctrl', function($scope, Player) {
  $scope.data = Player.getPlayer();
  $scope.update = Player.swapPlayer;
})
.provider('Player', function() {
```

```
  var player = {
    name: 'Aaron Rodgers',
    number: 12
  },  swap = function() {
    player.name = 'Tom Brady';
  };

  return {
    configSwapPlayer: function() {
      player.name = 'Andrew Luck';
    },
    configGetPlayer: function() {
      return player;
    },
    $get: function() {
      return {
        getPlayer: function() {
          return player;
        },
        swapPlayer: function() {
          swap();
        }
      };
    }
  };
});
```

When used this way, the provider appears to the controller as a normal service type, as follows:

```
(app.js)

  .controller('Ctrl', function($scope, Player) {
      $scope.data = Player.getPlayer();
      $scope.update = Player.swapPlayer;
  })

(index.html)

<div ng-app="myApp">
  <div ng-controller="Ctrl">
    <button ng-click="update()">Update</button>
    {{ data.name }} #{{ data.number }}
  </div>
</div>
```

JSFiddle: `http://jsfiddle.net/msfrisbie/49wjk54L/`

How it works...

Providers is the only service type that can be passed into a `config` function. Injecting a provider into the `config` function gives access to the wrapper object, and injecting a provider into an initialized application component will give you access to the return value of the `$get` method. This is useful when you need to configure aspects of a service type before it is used throughout the application.

There's more...

Providers can only be injected as their configured services in an initialized application. Similarly, types like service factories and services cannot be injected in a provider, as they will not yet exist during the `config` phase.

See also

▶ The *Using service decorators* recipe demonstrates how a service type initialization can be intercepted for a just in time modification

Using service decorators

An often overlooked aspect of AngularJS services is their ability to decorate service types in the initialization logic. This allows you to add or modify how factories or services will behave in the `config` phase before they are injected in the application.

How to do it...

In the `config` phase, the `$provide` service offers a decorator method that allows you to inject a service and modify its definition before it is formally instantiated. This is shown here:

```
(app.js)

angular.module('myApp', [])
.config(function($provide) {
  $provide.decorator('Player', function($delegate) {
    // $delegate is the Player service instance
```

```
      $delegate.setPlayer('Eli Manning');
      return $delegate;
  });
})
.controller('Ctrl', function($scope, Player) {
  $scope.data = Player.getPlayer();
  $scope.update = Player.swapPlayer;
})
.factory('Player', function() {
  var player = {
    number: 10
  },  swap = function() {
    player.name = 'DeSean Jackson';
  };

  return {
    setPlayer: function(newName) {
      player.name = newName;
    },
    getPlayer: function() {
      return player;
    },
    swapPlayer: function() {
      swap();
    }
  };
});
```

As you have merely modified a regular factory, it can be used in the template normally, as follows:

```
(index.html)

<div ng-app="myApp">
  <div ng-controller="Ctrl">
    <button ng-click="update()">Update</button>
    {{ data.name }} #{{ data.number }}
  </div>
</div>
```

 JSFiddle: http://jsfiddle.net/msfrisbie/cd3286rt/

How it works...

The decorator acts to intercept the creation of a service upon instantiation that allows you to modify or replace the service type as desired. This is especially useful when you are looking to cleanly monkeypatch a third-party library.

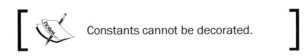 Constants cannot be decorated.

See also

> ▶ The *Using service providers* recipe provides details of the ancestor service type and how it relates to the service type life cycle

3
AngularJS Animations

In this chapter, we will cover the following recipes:

- Creating a simple fade in/out animation
- Replicating jQuery's `slideUp()` and `slideDown()` methods
- Creating enter animations with `ngIf`
- Creating leave and concurrent animations with `ngView`
- Creating move animations with `ngRepeat`
- Creating `addClass` animations with `ngShow`
- Creating `removeClass` animations with `ngClass`
- Staggering batched animations

Introduction

AngularJS incorporates its animation infrastructure as a separate module, `ngAnimate`. With this, you are able to tackle animating your application in several different ways, which are as follows:

- CSS3 transitions
- CSS3 animations
- JavaScript animations

Using any one of these three, you are able to fully animate your application in an extremely clean and modular fashion. In many cases, you will find that it is possible to add robust animations to your existing application using only the AngularJS class event progression and CSS definitions—no extra HTML or JS code is needed.

This chapter assumes that you are at least broadly familiar with the major topics involved in browser animations. We will focus more on how to integrate these animations into an AngularJS application without having to rely on jQuery or other animation libraries. As you will see in this chapter, there are a multitude of reasons why utilizing AngularJS/CSS animations is preferred to their respective counterparts in libraries such as jQuery.

For the sake of brevity, the recipes in this chapter will not include any vendor prefixes in the CSS class or animation definitions. Production applications should obviously include them for cross-browser compatibility, but in the context of this chapter, they are merely a distraction as AngularJS is unconcerned with the content of CSS definitions.

The ngAnimate module comes separately packaged in angular-animate.js. This file must be included alongside angular.js for the recipes in this chapter to work.

Creating a simple fade in/out animation

AngularJS animations work by integrating CSS animations into a directive class-based finite state machine. In other words, elements in AngularJS that serve to manipulate the DOM have defined class states that can be used to take full advantage of CSS animations, and the system moves between these states on well-defined events. This recipe will demonstrate how to make use of the directive finite state machine in order to create a simple fade in/out animation.

A **finite state machine** (**FSM**) is a computational system model defined by the states and transition conditions between them. The system can only exist in one state at any given time, and the system changes state when triggered by certain events. In the context of AngularJS animations, states are represented by the presence of CSS classes associated with the progress of a certain animation, and the events that trigger the state transformations are controlled by data binding and the directives controlling the classes.

Getting ready

As of AngularJS 1.2, animation comes as a completely separate module in AngularJS— ngAnimate. Your initial files should appear as follows:

```
(style.css)

.animated-container {
  padding: 20px;
```

```
    border: 5px solid black;
}

(index.html)

<div ng-app="myApp">
  <div ng-controller="Ctrl">
    <label>
      <button ng-click="boxHidden=!boxHidden">
        Toggle Visibility
      </button>
    </label>
    <div class="animated-container" ng-hide="boxHidden">
      Awesome text!
    </div>
  </div>
</div>

(app.js)

angular.module('myApp', ['ngAnimate'])
.controller('Ctrl', function($scope) {
  $scope.boxHidden = true;
});
```

You can see that the given code simply provides a button that instantly toggles the visibility of the styled `<div>` element.

How to do it...

There are several ways to accomplish a fade in/out animation, but the simplest is to use CSS transitions as they integrate very nicely into the AngularJS animation class state machine.

The animation CSS classes need to cover both cases, where the element is hidden and needs to fade in, and where the element is shown and needs to fade out. As is the case with CSS transitions, you need to define the initial state, the final state, and the transition parameters. This can be done as follows:

```
(style.css)

.animated-container {
  padding: 20px;
  border: 5px solid black;
}
```

```
.animated-container.ng-hide-add,
.animated-container.ng-hide-remove {
  transition: all linear 1s;
}
.animated-container.ng-hide-remove,
.animated-container.ng-hide-add.ng-hide-add-active {
  opacity: 0;
}
.animated-container.ng-hide-add,
.animated-container.ng-hide-remove.ng-hide-remove-active {
  opacity: 1;
}
```

 JSFiddle: `http://jsfiddle.net/msfrisbie/fqxwvyvj/`

These CSS classes cover the bi-directional transition to fade between `opacity: 0` and `opacity: 1` in 1 second. Clicking on the `<button>` element to toggle the visibility will work to trigger the fade in and fade out of the styled `<div>` element.

How it works...

Since CSS transitions are triggered by the change of relevant CSS classes, using the AngularJS class state machine allows you to animate when a directive manipulates the DOM. The show/hide state machine is cyclical and operates as shown in the following table (this is a simplified version of the full `ng-show`/`ng-hide` state machine, which is provided in detail in the *Creating addClass animations with ngShow* recipe):

Event	Directive state	Styled element classes	Element state
Initial state	ng-hide=true	animated-container ng-hide	display:none
boxHidden=false	ng-hide=false	animated-container ng-animate ng-hide-remove	opacity:0

Event	Directive state	Styled element classes	Element state

Time quanta elapses	`ng-hide=false`	`animated-container`
		
		`ng-animate`
		
		`ng-hide-remove`
		
		`ng-hide-remove-active`
			The animation is triggered; transition to `opacity:1` occurs

Animation completes	`ng-hide=false`	`animated-container`	`display:block`

`boxHidden=true`	`ng-hide=true`	`animated-container`
		
		`ng-animate`
		
		`ng-hide`
		
		`ng-hide-add`
			`opacity:1`

Time quanta elapses	`ng-hide=true`	`animated-container`
		
		`ng-animate`
		
		`ng-hide`
		
		`ng-hide-add`
		
		`ng-hide-add-active`
			The animation is triggered; transition to `opacity:0` occurs

Animation completes	`ng-hide=true`	`animated-container`
		
		`ng-hide`
			`display:none`

 The state machine shown in the preceding table is a simplified version of the actual animation state machine.

You can now see how the CSS classes utilize the animation class state machine to trigger the animation. When the directive state changes (in this case, the Boolean is negated), AngularJS applies sequential CSS classes to the element, intending them to be used as anchors for a CSS animation. Here, *Time quanta elapses* refers to the separate addition of `ng-hide-add` or `ng-hide-remove` followed by the `ng-hide-add-active` or `ng-hide-remove-active` classes. These classes are added sequentially and separately (this appears to be instantaneous, you will be unable to see the separation when watching the classes in a browser inspector), but the nature of the offset addition causes the CSS transition to be triggered properly.

In the case of moving from hidden to visible, the CSS styling defines a transition between the `.animated-container.ng-hide-add` selector and the `.animated-container.ng-hide-add.ng-hide-add-active` selector, with the transition definition attached under the `.animated-container.ng-hide-remove` selector.

In the case of moving from visible to hidden, the styling defines the opposite transition between the `.animated-container.ng-hide-add` selector and the `.animated-container.ng-hide-add.ng-hide-add-active` selector, with the transition definition attached under the `.animated-container.ng-hide-add` selector.

There's more...

As the class state machine is controlled entirely by the `ng-hide` directive, if you want to invert the animation (initially start as shown and then make the transition to hidden), all that is needed is the use of `ng-show` on the HTML element instead of `ng-hide`. These opposing directives will implement the class state machine appropriately for their definition, but will always use the `ng-hide` class as the default reference. In other words, using the `ng-show` directive will not utilize `ng-show-add` or `ng-show-remove` or anything of the sort; it will still be `ng-hide`, `ng-hide-add` or `ng-hide-remove`, and `ng-hide-add-active` or `ng-hide-remove-active`.

Keeping things clean

Since the animation starts as hidden, and you are loading the JS files at the bottom of the body, this is the perfect opportunity to utilize `ng-cloak` in order to prevent the styled `div` element from flashing before compilation. Modify your CSS and HTML as follows:

```
(style.css)

[ng\:cloak], [ng-cloak], [data-ng-cloak], [x-ng-cloak], .ng-cloak,
.x-ng-cloak {
  display: none !important;
}

(index.html)
...
<div class="animated-container" ng-show="boxHidden" ng-cloak>
  Awesome text!
</div>
```

No more boilerplate animation styling

Formerly, when animating `ng-hide` or `ng-show`, the display property needed to incorporate `display:block!important` during the animation states. As of AngularJS 1.3, this is no longer necessary; the `ngAnimate` module will handle this for you.

▶ The *Creating addClass animations with ngShow* and *Creating removeClass animations with ngClass* recipes go into further depth with the state machines that drive the directive animations

Replicating jQuery's slideUp() and slideDown() methods

jQuery provides a very useful pair of animation methods, `slideUp()` and `slideDown()`, which use JavaScript in order to accomplish the desired results. With the animation hooks provided for you by AngularJS, these animations can be accomplished with CSS.

Getting ready

Suppose that you want to slide a `<div>` element up and down in the following setup:

```
(index.html)

<div ng-app="myApp">
  <div ng-controller="Ctrl">
    <button ng-click="displayToggle=!displayToggle">
      Toggle Visibility
    </button>
    <div>Slide me up and down!</div>
  </div>
</div>

(app.js)
angular.module('myApp', ['ngAnimate'])
.controller('Ctrl', function($scope) {
  $scope.displayToggle = true;
});
```

How to do it...

A sliding animation requires truncation of the overflowing element and a transition involving the height of the element. The following implementation utilizes `ng-class`:

```
(style.css)

.container {
  overflow: hidden;
```

```
}
.slide-tile {
  transition: all 0.5s ease-in-out;
  width: 300px;
  line-height: 300px;
  text-align: center;
  border: 1px solid black;
  transform: translateY(0);
}
.slide-up {
  transform: translateY(-100%);
}
```

```
(index.html)
```

```html
<div ng-app="myApp">
  <div ng-controller="Ctrl">
    <button ng-click="displayToggle=!displayToggle">
      Toggle Visibility
    </button>
    <div class="container">
      <div class="slide-tile"
        ng-class="{'slide-up': !displayToggle}">
        Slide me up and down!
      </div>
    </div>
  </div>
</div>
```

 JSFiddle: `http://jsfiddle.net/msfrisbie/eqcs1dzr/`

A slightly more lightweight implementation is to tie the class definitions into the ng-show state machine:

```
(style.css)
```

```css
.container {
  overflow: hidden;
}
.slide-tile {
  transition: all 0.5s ease-in-out;
  width: 300px;
  line-height: 300px;
```

```
    text-align: center;
    border: 1px solid black;
    transform: translateY(0);
}
.slide-tile.ng-hide {
    transform: translateY(-100%);
}
```

(index.html)

```
<div ng-app="myApp">
    <div ng-controller="Ctrl">
        <button ng-click="displayToggle=!displayToggle">
            Toggle Visibility
        </button>
        <div class="container">
            <div class="slide-tile" ng-show="displayToggle">
                Slide me up and down!
            </div>
        </div>
    </div>
</div>
```

 JSFiddle: `http://jsfiddle.net/msfrisbie/bx01muha/`

How it works...

CSS transitions afford the convenience of a bi-directional animation as long as the endpoints and transitions are defined. For both of these implementations, the `translateY` CSS property is used to implement the sliding, and the hidden state (slide up for the `ng-class` implementation, and `ng-hide` for the `ng-show` implementation) is used as the concealed transition state endpoint.

See also

▶ The *Creating addClass animations with ngShow* and *Creating removeClass animations with ngClass* recipes go into further depth with the state machines that drive the directive animations

Creating enter animations with ngIf

AngularJS provides hooks to define a custom animation when a directive fires an `enter` event. The following directives will generate enter events:

- `ngIf`: This fires the `enter` event just after the `ngIf` contents change, and a new DOM element is created and injected into the `ngIf` container

- `ngInclude`: This fires the `enter` event when new content needs to be brought into the browser

- `ngRepeat`: This fires the `enter` event when a new item is added to the list or when an item is revealed after a filter

- `ngSwitch`: This fires the `enter` event after the `ngSwitch` contents change, and the matched child element is placed inside the container

- `ngView`: This fires the `enter` event when new content needs to be brought into the browser

- `ngMessage`: This fires the `enter` event when an inner message is attached

Getting ready

Suppose that you want to attach a fade-in animation to a piece of the DOM that has a `ng-if` directive attached to it. When the `ng-if` expression evaluates to `true`, the `enter` animation will trigger, as the template is brought into the page.

 The `ngIf` directive also has a complementary set of `leave` animation hooks, but those are not needed in this recipe and can be safely ignored if they are not being used.

The initial setup, before animation is implemented, can be structured as follows:

```
(index.html)

<div ng-app="myApp">
  <div ng-controller="Ctrl">
    <button ng-click="visible=!visible">Toggle</button>
    <span class="target" ng-if="visible">Bring me in!</span>
  </div>
</div>

(app.js)

angular.module('myApp', ['ngAnimate'])
.controller('Ctrl', function($scope) {
  $scope.visible = true;
});
```

The example in this recipe only uses `ngIf`, but it could have just as easily been performed with `ngInclude`, `ngRepeat`, `ngSwitch`, or `ngView`. All of the `enter` events fired for these directives involve content being introduced to the DOM in some way, so the animation hooks and procedures surrounding the animation definition can be handled in a more or less identical fashion.

How to do it...

When the button is clicked, this code instantaneously brings the `<div>` element with a `ngIf` expression attached to it into view as soon as the expression evaluates to `true`. However, with the inclusion of the `ngAnimate` module, AngularJS will add in animation hooks, upon which you can define an animation when the `<div>` element enters the page.

An animation can be defined by a CSS transition, CSS animation, or by JavaScript. The animation definition can be constructed in different ways. CSS transitions and CSS animations will use the `ng-enter` CSS class hooks to define the animation, whereas JavaScript animations will use the `ngAnimate` module's `enter()` method.

CSS3 transition

To animate with transitions, only the beginning and end state class styles need to be defined. This is shown here:

```
(style.css)

.target.ng-enter
{
  transition: all linear 1s;
  opacity: 0;
}
.target.ng-enter.ng-enter-active {
  opacity: 1;
}
```

JSFiddle: `http://jsfiddle.net/msfrisbie/zhuffnfj/`

CSS3 animation

Similar to CSS3 transition, it is relatively simple to accomplish the same animation with CSS keyframes. Since the animation is defined entirely within the keyframes, only a single class reference is needed in order to trigger the animation. This can be done as follows:

```
(style.css)

.target.ng-enter {
  animation: 1s target-enter;
}
@keyframes target-enter {
  from {
    opacity: 0;
  }
  to {
    opacity: 1;
  }
}
```

 JSFiddle: http://jsfiddle.net/msfrisbie/rp4mjgkL/

JavaScript animation

Animating with JavaScript requires that you manually add and remove the relevant CSS classes, as well as explicitly call the animations. Since AngularJS and jqLite objects don't have an animation method, you will need to use the jQuery object's `animate()` method:

```
(app.js)

angular.module('myApp', ['ngAnimate'])
.controller('Ctrl', function ($scope) {
  $scope.visible = false;
})
.animation('.target', function () {
  return {
    enter: function (element, done) {
      $(element)
      .css({
        'opacity': 0
      });
      $(element)
      .animate({
        'opacity': 1
```

```
    },
    1000,
    done);
  }
};
});
```

 JSFiddle: `http://jsfiddle.net/msfrisbie/2jt853no/`

How it works...

The `enter` animation behaves as a state machine. It cannot assume that either CSS transitions/animations or JavaScript animations are defined upon the `<div>` DOM element, and it must be able to apply all of them without creating conflicts. As a result, AngularJS will trigger the JavaScript animations and immediately begin the progression of the animation class sequence, which will trigger any CSS transitions/animations that might be defined upon them. In this way, both JavaScript and CSS animations can be used on the same DOM element simultaneously.

AngularJS uses a standard class naming convention for different states, which allows you to uniquely define each set of animations for the component being animated. The following set of tables define how the `enter` animation state machine operates.

The initial state of the animation components is defined as follows:

element	`[<span class="target" ng-if="visible">` `Bring me in!` `</span>,` `<!-- end ngIf: visible -->]`
parentElement	`[<div>` `...` `</div>]`
afterElement	`[<!-- ngIf: visible -->]`

The following table represents a full enter animation transition:

Event	DOM
The `$animate.enter()` method is called after the directive detects that `ng-if` evaluates to `true`	`<div>` `<!-- ngIf: visible -->` `</div>`

Event	DOM
The element is inserted into `parentElement` or beside `afterElement`	```<div> <!-- ngIf: visible --> <span class="target ng-if="visible"> Bring me in! </span> <!-- end ngIf: visible --> </div>```
The `$animate` service waits for a new digest cycle to begin animating; the `ng-animate` class is added	```<div> <!-- ngIf: visible --> <span class="target ng-animate" ng-if="visible"> Bring me in! </span> <!-- end ngIf: visible --> </div>```
The `$animate` service runs the JavaScript-defined animations detected on the element	No change in DOM
The `ng-enter` class is added to the element	```<div> <!-- ngIf: visible --> <span class="target ng-animate ng-enter" ng-if="visible"> Bring me in! </span> <!-- end ngIf: visible --> </div>```
The `$animate` service reads the element styles in order to get the CSS transition or CSS animation definition	No change in DOM
The `$animate` service blocks CSS transitions involving the element in order to ensure the `ng-enter` class styling is correctly applied without interference	No change in DOM
The `$animate` service waits for a single animation frame, which performs a reflow	No change in DOM
The `$animate` service removes the CSS transition block placed on the element	No change in DOM

Event	DOM

The `ng-enter-active` class is added; CSS transitions or CSS animations are triggered	```html
	<div>
	  <!-- ngIf: visible -->
	  <span class="target ng-animate
	ng-enter **ng-enter-active**"
	        ng-if="visible">
	    Bring me in!
	  </span>
	  <!-- end ngIf: visible -->
	</div>
	``

The `$animate` service waits for the animation to complete	No change in DOM

Animation completes; animation classes are stripped from the element	```html
	<div>
	  <!-- ngIf: visible -->
	  <span **class="target"**
	        ng-if="visible">
	    Bring me in!
	  </span>
	  <!-- end ngIf: visible -->
	</div>
	``

The `doneCallback()` method is fired (if provided)	No change in DOM

 Since it does not affect animation proceedings, this recipe intentionally ignores the presence of the `ng-scope` class, which in reality would be present on the DOM elements.

There's more...

JavaScript and CSS transitions/animations are executed in a parallel. Since they are defined independently, they can be run independently even though they can modify the same DOM element(s) entering the page.

See also

▶ The *Creating leave and concurrent animations with ngView* recipe provides the details of the complementary `leave` event

Creating leave and concurrent animations with ngView

AngularJS provides hooks used to define a custom animation when a directive fires a `leave` event. The following directives will generate `leave` events:

- `ngIf`: This fires the `leave` event just before the `ngIf` contents are removed from the DOM
- `ngInclude`: This fires the `leave` event when the existing included content needs to be animated away
- `ngRepeat`: This fires the `leave` event when an item is removed from the list or when an item is filtered out
- `ngSwitch`: This fires the `leave` event just after the `ngSwitch` contents change and just before the former contents are removed from the DOM
- `ngView`: This fires the `leave` event when the existing `ngView` content needs to be animated away
- `ngMessage`: This fires the `leave` event when an inner message is removed

Getting ready

Suppose that you want to attach a slide-in or slide-out animation to a piece of the DOM that exists inside the `ng-view` directive. Route changes that cause the content of `ng-view` to be altered will trigger an `enter` animation for the content about to be brought into the page, as well as trigger a `leave` animation for the content about to leave the page.

The initial setup, before animation is implemented, can be structured as follows:

```
(style.css)

.link-container {
  position: absolute;
  top: 320px;
}
.animate-container {
  position: absolute;
}
.animate-container div {
  width: 300px;
  text-align: center;
  line-height: 300px;
```

```
  border: 1px solid black;
}

(index.html)

<div ng-app="myApp">
  <ng-view class="animate-container"></ng-view>
  <div class="link-container">
    <a href="#/foo">Foo</a>
    <a href="#/bar">Bar</a>
  </div>

  <script type="text/ng-template" id="foo.html">
    <div>
      <span>Foo</span>
    </div>
  </script>
  <script type="text/ng-template" id="bar.html">
    <div>
      <span>Bar</span>
    </div>
  </script>
</div>

(app.js)

angular.module('myApp', ['ngAnimate', 'ngRoute'])
.config(function ($routeProvider) {
  $routeProvider
  .when('/bar', {
    templateUrl: 'bar.html'
  })
  .otherwise({
    templateUrl: 'foo.html'
  });
});
```

The example in this recipe only uses ngView, but it could have just as easily been performed with ngInclude, ngRepeat, ngSwitch, or ngIf. All the leave events fired for these directives involve content being removed from the DOM in some way, so the animation's hooks and procedures surrounding the animation definition can be handled in a more or less identical fashion. However, not all of these directives trigger enter and leave events concurrently.

How to do it...

When the route changes, AngularJS instantaneously injects the appropriate template into the `ng-view` directive. However, with the inclusion of the `ngAnimate` module, AngularJS will add in animation hooks, upon which you can define animations for how the templates will enter and leave the page.

An animation can be defined by a CSS transition, CSS animation, or by JavaScript. The animation definition can be constructed in different ways. CSS transitions and CSS animations will use the `ng-leave` CSS class hooks to define the animation, whereas JavaScript animations will use the `ngAnimate` directive's `leave()` method.

It is important to note here that `ng-view` triggers the `leave` and `enter` animations simultaneously. Therefore, your animation definitions must take this into account in order to prevent animation conflicts.

CSS3 transition

To animate with transitions, only the beginning and end state class styles need to be defined. Remember that the `enter` and `leave` animations begin at the same instant, so you must either define an animation that gracefully accounts for any overlap that might occur, or introduce a delay in animations in order to serialize them.

CSS transitions accept a transition-delay value, so serializing the animations is the easiest way to accomplish the desired animation here. Adding the following to the style sheet is all that is needed in order to define the slide-in or slide-out animation:

```
(style.css)

.animate-container.ng-enter {
  /* final value is the transition delay */
  transition: all 0.5s 0.5s;
}
.animate-container.ng-leave {
  transition: all 0.5s;
}
.animate-container.ng-enter,
.animate-container.ng-leave.ng-leave-active {
  top: -300px;
}
.animate-container.ng-leave,
.animate-container.ng-enter.ng-enter-active {
  top: 0px;
}
```

JSFiddle: http://jsfiddle.net/msfrisbie/y9de80ga/

CSS3 animation

Building this animation with CSS keyframes is also easy to accomplish. Keyframe percentages allow you to effectively delay the enter animation by a set length of time until the leave animation finishes. This can be done as follows:

```css
(style.css)

.animate-container.ng-enter {
  animation: 1s view-enter;
}
.animate-container.ng-leave {
  animation: 0.5s view-leave;
}
@keyframes view-enter {
  0%, 50% {
    top: -300px;
  }
  100% {
    top: 0px;
  }
}
@keyframes view-leave {
  0% {
    top: 0px;
  }
  100% {
    top: -300px;
  }
}
```

JSFiddle: http://jsfiddle.net/msfrisbie/penaakxy/

JavaScript animation

Animating with JavaScript requires that you manually add and remove the relevant CSS classes, as well as explicitly call the animations. Since AngularJS and jqLite objects don't have an animation method, you will need to use the jQuery object's `animate()` method. The delay between the serialized animations can be accomplished with the jQuery `delay()` method. The animation can be defined as follows:

```
(app.js)

angular.module('myApp', ['ngAnimate', 'ngRoute'])
.config(function ($routeProvider) {
  $routeProvider
  .when('/bar', {
    templateUrl: 'bar.html'
  })
  .otherwise({
    templateUrl: 'foo.html'
  });
})
.animation('.animate-container', function() {
  return {
    enter: function(element, done) {
      $(element)
      .css({
        'top': '-300px'
      });
      $(element)
      .delay(500)
      .animate({
        'top': '0px'
      }, 500, done);
    },
    leave: function(element, done) {
      $(element)
      .css({
        'top': '0px'
      });
      $(element)
      .animate({
        'top': '-300px'
      }, 500, done);
    }
  };
});
```

JSFiddle: `http://jsfiddle.net/msfrisbie/b4L35nrt/`

How it works...

The `leave` animation state machine has a good deal of parity with the `enter` animation. State machine class progressions work in a very similar way; sequentially adding the beginning and final animation hook classes in order to match the element coming in and out of existence. AngularJS uses the same standard class naming convention used by the `enter` animation for the different animation states. The following set of tables define how the `leave` animation state machine operates.

The initial state of the animation components is defined as follows:

element	`[<ng-view class="animate-container">`
	   `<div>`
	     `<span>Bar</span>`
	   `</div>`
	`</ng-view>]`

The following table represents a full leave animation transition:

Event	DOM

The `$animate.leave()` method is called when a new view needs to be introduced	`<ng-view class="animate-container">`
	   `<div>`
	     `<span>Bar</span>`
	   `</div>`
	`</ng-view>`

The `$animate` service runs the JavaScript-defined animations detected on the element; the `ng-animate` class is added	`<ng-view class="animate-container `**`ng-animate`**`">`
	   `<div>`
	     `<span>Bar</span>`
	   `</div>`
	`</ng-view>`

The `$animate` service waits for a new digest cycle to begin animating	No change in DOM

Event	DOM

The ng-leave class is added to the element	```<ng-view class="animate-container ng-animate ng-leave">```
	``` <div>```
	``` <span>Bar</span>```
	``` </div>```
	```</ng-view>```

The $animate service reads the element styles in order to get the CSS transition or CSS animation definition	No change in DOM
The $animate service blocks CSS transitions that involve the element in order to ensure that the ng-leave class styling is correctly applied without interference	No change in DOM
The $animate service waits for a single animation frame, which performs a reflow	No change in DOM
The $animate service removes the CSS transition block placed on the element	No change in DOM

The ng-leave-active class is added; CSS transitions or CSS animations are triggered	```<ng-view class="animate-container ng-animate ng-leave ng-leave-active">```
	``` <div>```
	``` <span>Bar</span>```
	``` </div>```
	```</ng-view>```

The $animate service waits for the animation to get completed	No change in DOM

The animation is complete; animation classes are stripped from the element	```<ng-view class="animate-container">```
	``` <div>```
	``` <span>Bar</span>```
	``` </div>```
	```</ng-view>```

The element is removed from DOM	```<ng-view class="animate-container">``` ```</ng-view>```
The doneCallback() method is fired (if provided)	No change in DOM

Since it does not affect the animation proceedings, this recipe intentionally ignores the presence of the ng-scope class, which in reality would be present in the DOM elements.

See also

▸ The *Creating enter animations with ngIf* recipe provides the details of the complementary enter event

Creating move animations with ngRepeat

AngularJS provides hooks to define a custom animation when a directive fires a move event. The only AngularJS directive that fires a move event by default is ngRepeat; it fires a move event when an adjacent item is filtered out causing a reorder or when the item contents are reordered.

Getting ready

Suppose that you want to attach a slide-in or slide-out animation to a piece of the DOM that exists inside the ng-view directive. Route changes that cause the content of ng-view to be altered will trigger an enter animation for the content about to be brought into the page, as well as trigger a leave animation for the content about to leave the page.

Suppose that you want to animate individual pieces of a list when they are initially added, moved, or removed. Additions and removals should slide in and out from the left-hand side, and move events should slide up and down.

The initial setup, before animation is implemented, can be structured as follows:

```
(style.css)

.animate-container {
  position: relative;
  margin-bottom: -1px;
  width: 300px;
  text-align: center;
  border: 1px solid black;
  line-height: 40px;
}
.repeat-container {
```

```
    position: absolute;
}


(index.html)

<div ng-app="myApp">
  <div ng-controller="Ctrl">
    <div style="repeat-container">
      <input ng-model="search.val" />
      <button ng-click="shuffle()">Shuffle</button>
      <div ng-repeat="el in arr | filter:search.val"
           class="animate-container">
        <span>{{ el }}</span>
      </div>
    </div>
  </div>
</div>


(app.js)

angular.module('myApp', ['ngAnimate'])
.controller('Ctrl', function($scope) {
  $scope.arr = [10,15,25,40,45];

  // implementation of Knuth in-place shuffle
  function knuthShuffle(a) {
    for(var i = a.length, j, k; i;
      j = Math.floor(Math.random() * i),
      k = a[--i],
      a[i] = a[j],
      a[j] = k);
    return a;
  }

  $scope.shuffle = function() {
    $scope.arr = knuthShuffle($scope.arr);
  };
});
```

 In this recipe, the ng-repeat search filter is implemented merely to provide the ability to add and remove elements from the list. As search filtering does not reorder the elements as defined by AngularJS (this will be explored later in this recipe), it will never generate move events.

How to do it...

When the order of the displayed iterable collection changes, AngularJS injects the appropriate template into the corresponding location in the list, and sibling elements whose indices have changed will instantaneously shift. However, with the inclusion of the `ngAnimate` module, AngularJS will add in animation hooks, upon which you can define animations for how the templates will move within the list.

The animation can be defined by a CSS transition, CSS animation, or by JavaScript. The animation definition can be constructed in different ways. CSS transitions and CSS animations will use the `ng-move` CSS class hooks in order to define the animation, whereas JavaScript animations will use the `ngAnimate` module's `move()` method.

It is important to note here that `ng-repeat` triggers `enter`, `leave`, and `move` animations simultaneously. Therefore, your animation definitions must take this into account to prevent animation conflicts.

CSS3 transition

To animate with transitions, you can utilize the animation hook class states to define the set of endpoints for each type of animation. Animations on each individual element in the collection will begin simultaneously, so you must define animations that gracefully account for any overlap that might occur.

Adding the following to the style sheet is all that is needed in order to define the slide-in or slide-out animation for the enter and leave events and a fade in for the move event:

```
(style.css)

.animate-container.ng-move {
  transition: all 1s;
  opacity: 0;
  max-height: 0;
}
.animate-container.ng-move-active {
  opacity: 1;
  max-height: 40px;
}
.animate-container.ng-enter {
  transition: left 0.5s, max-height 1s;
  left: -300px;
  max-height: 0;
}
.animate-container.ng-enter-active {
  left: 0px;
  max-height: 40px;
```

```
}
.animate-container.ng-leave {
  transition: left 0.5s, max-height 1s;
  left: 0px;
  max-height: 40px;
}
.animate-container.ng-leave-active {
  left: -300px;
  max-height: 0;
}
```

 JSFiddle: `http://jsfiddle.net/msfrisbie/f4puyv58/`

CSS3 animation

Building this animation with CSS keyframes allows you to have the advantage of being able to explicitly define the offset between animation segments, which allows you a cleaner enter/leave animation without tiles sweeping over each other. The enter and leave animations can take advantage of this by animating to full height before sliding into view. Add the following to the style sheet in order to define the desired animations:

```
(style.css)

.animate-container.ng-enter {
  animation: 0.5s item-enter;
}
.animate-container.ng-leave {
  animation: 0.5s item-leave;
}
.animate-container.ng-move {
  animation: 0.5s item-move;
}
@keyframes item-enter {
  0% {
    max-height: 0;
    left: -300px;
  }
  50% {
    max-height: 40px;
    left: -300px;
  }
  100% {
    max-height: 40px;
```

```
      left: 0px;
    }
  }
  @keyframes item-leave {
    0% {
      left: 0px;
      max-height: 40px;
    }
    50% {
      left: -300px;
      max-height: 40px;
    }
    100% {
      left: -300px;
      max-height: 0;
    }
  }
  @keyframes item-move {
    0% {
      opacity: 0;
      max-height: 0px;
    }
    100% {
      opacity: 1;
      max-height: 40px;
    }
  }
```

 JSFiddle: http://jsfiddle.net/msfrisbie/1632jm5g/

JavaScript animation

JavaScript animations are also relatively easy to define here, even though the desired effect has both serialized and parallel animation effects. This can be done as follows:

```
(app.js)

angular.module('myApp', ['ngAnimate'])
.controller('Ctrl', function($scope) {
  ...
})
.animation('.animate-container', function() {
  return {
```

```
        enter: function(element, done) {
          $(element)
          .css({
            'left': '-300px',
            'max-height': '0'
          });
          $(element)
          .animate({
            'max-height': '40px'
          }, 250)
          .animate({
            'left': '0px'
          }, 250, done);
        },
        leave: function(element, done) {
          $(element)
          .css({
            'left': '0px',
            'max-height': '40px'
          });
          $(element)
          .animate({
            'left': '-300px'
          }, 250)
          .animate({
            'max-height': '0'
          }, 250, done);
        },
        move: function(element, done) {
          $(element)
          .css({
            'opacity': '0',
            'max-height': '0'
          });
          $(element)
          .animate({
            'opacity': '1',
            'max-height': '40px'
          }, 500, done);
        }
      };
    });
```

JSFiddle: `http://jsfiddle.net/msfrisbie/rjaq5tqc/`

How it works...

The `move` animation state machine is very similar to the `enter` animation. State machine class progressions sequentially add the beginning and final animation hook classes in order to match the element that is being reintroduced into the list at its new index. AngularJS uses the same standard class naming convention used by the enter animation for different animation states.

 For the purpose of simplification, the following modifications and assumptions affect the content of the following state machine:

- The `ng-repeat` directive is assumed to be passed an array of [1,2]. The `move` event is triggered by the array's order being reversed to [2,1].

- The `ng-repeat` filter has been removed; a search filter cannot fire move events.

- The `ng-scope` and `ng-binding` directive classes have been removed from where they would normally occur, as they do not affect the state machine.

The following set of tables define how the `move` animation state machine operates.

The initial state of the animation components is defined as follows:

element	`[<div ng-repeat="el in arr"`
	`        class="animate-container">`
	`    <span>1</span>`
	`  </div>,`
	`  <!-- end ngRepeat: el in arr -->]`

parentElement	null
afterElement	`[<!-- ngRepeat: el in arr -->]`

The following table represents a full move animation transition:

Event	DOM

The `$animate.move()` method is invoked	```html
	<!-- ngRepeat: el in arr -->
	<div ng-repeat="el in arr"
	    class="animate-container">
	  <span>1</span>
	</div>
	<!-- end ngRepeat: el in arr -->
	<div ng-repeat="el in arr "
	    class="animate-container">
	  <span>2</span>
	</div>
	<!-- end ngRepeat: el in arr -->
	``

The element is moved into `parentElement` or beside `afterElement`	```html
	<!-- ngRepeat: el in arr -->
	<div ng-repeat="el in arr"
	    class="animate-container">
	  <span>2</span>
	</div>
	<!-- end ngRepeat: el in arr -->
	<div ng-repeat="el in arr "
	    class="animate-container">
	  <span>1</span>
	</div>
	<!-- end ngRepeat: el in arr -->
	``

The `$animate` service waits for a new digest cycle to begin animation; `ng-animate` is added	```html
	<!-- ngRepeat: el in arr -->
	<div ng-repeat="el in arr "
	    class="animate-container ng-
	animate">
	  <span>2</span>
	</div>
	<!-- end ngRepeat: el in arr -->
	<div ng-repeat="el in arr "
	    class="animate-container">
	  <span>1</span>
	</div>
	<!-- end ngRepeat: el in arr -->
	``

The `$animate` service runs the JavaScript-defined animations detected in the element	No change in DOM

Event	DOM

The `ng-move` directive is added to the element's classes	```html
	<!-- ngRepeat: el in arr -->
	<div ng-repeat="el in arr"
	     class="animate-container ng-
	animate **ng-move**">
	  <span>2</span>
	</div>
	<!-- end ngRepeat: el in arr -->
	<div ng-repeat="el in arr "
	     class="animate-container">
	  <span>1</span>
	</div>
	<!-- end ngRepeat: el in arr -->
	``

The `$animate` service reads the element styles in order to get the CSS transition or CSS animation definition	No change in DOM
The `$animate` service blocks CSS transitions that involve the element to ensure that the `ng-move` class styling is correctly applied without interference	No change in DOM
The `$animate` service waits for a single animation frame, which performs a reflow	No change in DOM
The `$animate` service removes the CSS transition block placed on the element	No change in DOM

The `ng-move-active` directive is added; CSS transitions or CSS animations are triggered	```html
	<!-- ngRepeat: el in arr -->
	<div ng-repeat="el in arr"
	     class="animate-container ng-
	animate ng-move **ng-move-active**">
	  <span>2</span>
	</div>
	<!-- end ngRepeat: el in arr -->
	<div ng-repeat="el in arr "
	     class="animate-container">
	  <span>1</span>
	</div>
	<!-- end ngRepeat: el in arr -->
	``

The `$animate` service waits for the animation to get completed	No change in DOM

Event	DOM
Animation is complete; animation classes are stripped from the element	```<!-- ngRepeat: el in arr --><div ng-repeat="el in arr" class="animate-container"> <span>2</span></div><!-- end ngRepeat: el in arr --><div ng-repeat="el in arr " class="animate-container"> <span>1</span></div><!-- end ngRepeat: el in arr -->```
The `doneCallback ()` method is fired (if provided)	No change in DOM

There's more...

The `move` animation's name can be a bit confusing as *move* implies a starting and ending location. A better way to think of it is as a secondary entrance animation used in order to demonstrate when new content is not being added to the list. You will notice that the `move` animation is triggered simultaneously for all the elements whose relative order in the list has changed, and that the animation triggers when it is in its new position.

Also note that even though the index of both elements changed, only one `move` animation was triggered. This is due to the way the movement within an enumerable collection is defined. AngularJS preserves the old ordering of the collection and compares its values in order to the entire new ordering, and all mismatches will fire `move` events. For example, if the old order is *1, 2, 3, 4, 5* and the new order is *5, 4, 2, 1, 3*, then the comparison strategy works as follows:

Comparison	Evaluation
`old[0] == new[0]`	False, fire the `move` event
`old[0] == new[1]`	False, fire the `move` event
`old[0] == new[2]`	False, fire the `move` event
`old[0] == new[3]`	True, increment the old order comparison index until an element, which was not yet seen, is reached (2 was already seen in the new order; skip to 3)
`old[2] == new[4]`	True

Astute developers will note that, with this order comparison implementation, a simple order shuffling will never mark the last element as "moved".

See also

▸ The *Staggering batched animations* recipe demonstrates how to introduce an animation delay between batched events in an `ngRepeat` context

Creating addClass animations with ngShow

AngularJS provides hooks used to define a custom animation when a directive fires an `addClass` event. The following directives will generate `addClass` events:

▸ ngShow: This fires the `addClass` event after the `ngShow` expression evaluates to a truthy value, and just before the contents are set to visible

▸ ngHide: This fires the `addClass` event after the `ngHide` expression evaluates to a non-truthy value, and just before the contents are set to visible

▸ ngClass: This fires the `addClass` event just before the class is applied to the element

▸ ngForm: This fires the `addClass` event to add validation classes

▸ ngModel: This fires the `addClass` event to add validation classes

▸ ngMessages: This is fired to add the `ng-active` class when one or more messages are visible, or to add the `ng-inactive` class when there are no messages

Getting ready

Suppose that you want to attach a fade-out animation to a piece of the DOM that has an `ng-show` directive. Remember that `ng-show` does not add or remove anything from the DOM; it merely toggles the CSS display property to set the visibility.

The initial setup, before animation is implemented, can be structured as follows:

```
(index.html)

<div ng-app="myApp">
  <div ng-controller="Ctrl">
    <button ng-click="displayToggle=!displayToggle">
      Toggle Visibility
    </button>
    <div class="animate-container" ng-show="displayToggle">
      Fade me out!
    </div>
  </div>
</div>
```

```
  </div>

  (app.js)

  angular.module('myApp', ['ngAnimate'])
  .controller('Ctrl',function($scope) {
    $scope.displayToggle = true;
  });
```

How to do it...

When the ng-show expression evaluates to false, the DOM element is immediately hidden. However, with the inclusion of the ngAnimate module, AngularJS will add in animation hooks, upon which you can define animations for how the element will be removed from the page.

The animation can be defined by a CSS transition, CSS animation, or by JavaScript. The animation definition can be constructed in different ways. CSS transitions and CSS animations will use the addClass CSS class hooks to define the animation, whereas JavaScript animations will use the ngAnimate directive's addClass() method.

CSS transitions

Animating a fade-in effect with CSS transitions simply requires attaching opposite opacity values when the ng-hide class is added. Remember that ng-show and ng-hide are merely toggling the presence of this ng-hide class through the use of the addClass and removeClass animation events. This can be done as follows:

```
  (style.css)

  .animate-container.ng-hide-add {
    transition: all linear 1s;
    opacity: 1;
  }
  .animate-container.ng-hide-add.ng-hide-add-active {
    opacity: 0;
  }
```

 JSFiddle: http://jsfiddle.net/msfrisbie/bewso5sd/

CSS animation

Animating with a CSS animation is just as simple as CSS transitions, as follows:

```
(style.css)

.animate-container.ng-hide-add {
  animation: 1s fade-out;
}
@keyframes fade-out {
  0% {
    opacity: 1;
  }
  100% {
    opacity: 0;
  }
}
```

 JSFiddle: `http://jsfiddle.net/msfrisbie/aez97r46/`

JavaScript animation

Animating with JavaScript requires that you manually add and remove the relevant CSS classes, as well as explicitly call the animations. Since AngularJS and jqLite objects don't have an animation method, you will need to use the jQuery object's `animate()` method. This can be done as follows:

```
(app.js)

angular.module('myApp', ['ngAnimate'])
.controller('Ctrl', function($scope) {
  $scope.displayToggle = true;
})
.animation('.animate-container', function() {
  return {
    addClass: function(element, className, done) {
      if (className==='ng-hide') {
        $(element)
        .removeClass('ng-hide')
        .css('opacity', 1)
        .animate(
          {'opacity': 0},
          1000,
          function() {
```

```
          $(element)
          .addClass('ng-hide')
          .css('opacity', 1);
          done();
      }
    );
  } else {
    done();
  }
 }
};
});
```

JSFiddle: `http://jsfiddle.net/msfrisbie/4taoda1e/`

Note that here, the `opacity` value is used for the animation, but is not the active class that hides the element. After its use in the animation, it must be reset to 1 in order to not interfere with the subsequent display toggling.

How it works...

Independent of what is defined in the actual class that is being added, `ngAnimate` provides animation hooks for the class that is being added to define animations. In the context of the `ng-show` directive, the `ng-hide` CSS class is defined implicitly within AngularJS, but the animation hooks are completely decoupled from the original class in order to provide a fresh animation definition interface. The following set of tables defines how the `addClass` animation state machine operates.

The initial state of the animation components is defined as follows:

element	`<div class="animate-container"`
	`     ng-show="displayToggle">`
	`Fade me out!`
	`</div>`
className	`'ng-hide'`

The following table represents a full `addClass` animation transition:

Event	DOM

The `$animate.`
`addClass(element, 'ng-`
`hide')` method is called
	```<div class="animate-container"```
	``` ng-show="displayToggle">```
	``` Fade me out!```
	```</div>```

The `$animate` service runs the JavaScript-defined animations detected on the element; `ng-animate` is added	```<div class="animate-container ng-```
	`animate"`
	``` ng-show="displayToggle">```
	``` Fade me out!```
	```</div>```

The `.ng-hide-add` class is added to the element	```<div class="animate-container ng-```
	```animate``` **`ng-hide-add"`**
	``` ng-show="displayToggle">```
	``` Fade me out!```
	```</div>```

The `$animate` service waits for a single animation frame (this performs a reflow)	No change in DOM

The `.ng-hide` and `.ng-hide-active` classes are added (this triggers the CSS transition/animation)	```<div class="animate-container ng-```
	```animate``` **`ng-hide`** ```ng-hide-add``` **`ng-hide-`**
	`add-active"`
	``` ng-show="displayToggle">```
	``` Fade me out!```
	```</div>```

The `$animate` service scans the element styles to get the CSS transition/animation duration and delay	No change in DOM
The `$animate` service waits for the animation to get completed (via events and timeout)	No change in DOM

The animation ends and all the generated CSS classes are removed from the element	```<div class="animate-container``` **`ng-`**
	`hide"`
	``` ng-show="displayToggle">```
	``` Fade me out!```
	```</div>```

The `ng-hide` class is kept on the element	No change in DOM
The `doneCallback()` callback is fired (if provided)	No change in DOM

- ▶ The *Creating removeClass animations with ngClass* recipe provides the details of the complementary `removeClass` event

Creating removeClass animations with ngClass

AngularJS provides hooks that can be used to define a custom animation when a directive fires a `removeClass` event. The following directives will generate `removeClass` events:

- ▶ `ngShow`: This fires the `removeClass` event after the `ngShow` expression evaluates to a non-truthy value, and just before the contents are set to hidden

- ▶ `ngHide`: This fires the `removeClass` event after the `ngHide` expression evaluates to a truthy value, and just before the contents are set to hidden

- ▶ `ngClass`: This fires the `removeClass` event just before the class is removed from the element

- ▶ `ngForm`: This fires the `removeClass` event to remove validation classes

- ▶ `ngModel`: This fires the `removeClass` event to remove validation classes

- ▶ `ngMessages`: This fires the `removeClass` event to remove the `ng-active` class when there are no messages, or to remove the `ng-inactive` class when one or more messages are visible

Getting ready

Suppose that you want to have a `div` element slide out of the view when a class is removed. Remember that `ng-class` does not add or remove any elements from the DOM; it merely adds or removes the classes defined within the directive expression.

The initial setup, before animation is implemented, can be structured as follows:

```
(style.css)

.container {
  background-color: black;
  width: 200px;
```

```
  height: 200px;
  overflow: hidden;
}
.prompt {
  position: absolute;
  margin: 10px;
  font-family: courier;
  color: lime;
}
.cover {
  position: relative;
  width: 200px;
  height: 200px;
  left: 200px;
  background-color: black;
}
.blackout {
  left: 0;
}
```

(index.html)

```
<div ng-app="myApp">
  <div ng-controller="Ctrl">
    <button ng-click="displayToggle=!displayToggle">
      Toggle Visibility
    </button>
    <div class="container">
      <span class="prompt">Wake up, Neo...</span>
      <div class="cover"
          ng-class="{blackout: displayToggle}">
      </div>
    </div>
  </div>
</div>
```

(app.js)

```
angular.module('myApp', ['ngAnimate'])
.controller('Ctrl', function($scope) {
  $scope.displayToggle = true;
});
```

How to do it...

When the `ng-class` value for `blackout` evaluates to `false`, it will immediately be stripped out. However, with the inclusion of the `ngAnimate` module, AngularJS will add in animation hooks, upon which you can define animations for how the class will be removed.

The animation can be defined by a CSS transition, CSS animation, or by JavaScript. The animation definition can be constructed in different ways. CSS transitions and CSS animations will use the `removeClass` CSS class hooks to define the animation, whereas JavaScript animations will use the `ngAnimate` directive's `removeClass()` method.

CSS transitions

Animating a slide-out effect with CSS transitions simply requires a transition that defines the left positioning distance. Remember that `ng-class` is merely toggling the presence of the `blackout` class through the use of the `addClass` and `removeClass` animation events. This can be done as follows:

```
(style.css)

.blackout-remove {
  left: 0;
}
.blackout-remove {
  transition: all 3s;
}
.blackout-remove-active {
  left: 200px;
}
```

 JSFiddle: `http://jsfiddle.net/msfrisbie/L6u4nzv7/`

CSS animation

Animating with a CSS animation is just as simple as CSS transitions, as follows:

```
(style.css)

.blackout-remove {
  animation: 1s slide-out;
}
@keyframes slide-out {
  0% {
    left: 0;
```

```
    }
    100% {
      left: 200px;
    }
  }
```

 JSFiddle: `http://jsfiddle.net/msfrisbie/oq5ha3zq/`

JavaScript animation

Animating with JavaScript requires that you manually add and remove the relevant CSS classes, as well as explicitly call the animations. Since AngularJS and jqLite objects don't have an animation method, you will need to use the jQuery object's `animate()` method. This can be done as follows:

```
(app.js)

angular.module('myApp', ['ngAnimate'])
.controller('Ctrl', function($scope) {
  $scope.displayToggle = true;
})
.animation('.blackout', function() {
  return {
    removeClass: function(element, className, done){
      if (className==='blackout') {
        $(element)
        .removeClass('blackout')
        .css('left', 0)
        .animate(
          {'left': '200px'},
          3000,
          function() {
            $(element).css('left','');
            done();
          }
        );
      } else {
        done();
      }
    }
  };
});
```

[JSFiddle: `http://jsfiddle.net/msfrisbie/4dnokg2o/`]

How it works...

The `ngAnimate` directive provides animation hooks for the class that is being removed in order to define animations independent of the actual class. In the context of this `ng-class` directive implementation, the `blackout` CSS class is defined explicitly, and the animation hooks build on top of this class name. The following set of tables defines how the `removeClass` animation state machine operates.

The animation components are defined as follows:

element	`<div class="cover blackout`
	`        ng-class="{blackout: displayToggle}">`
	`</div>`

className	`'blackout'`

The following table represents a full `removeClass` animation transition:

Event	DOM

The `$animate.`
`removeClass(element,`
`'blackout')` method is called
	`<div class="cover blackout"`
	`        ng-class="{blackout:`
	`displayToggle}">`
	`</div>`

The `$animate` service runs the JavaScript-defined animations detected in the element; `ng-animate` is added	`<div class="cover blackout `**`ng-`**
	`animate``"`
	`        ng-class="{blackout:`
	`displayToggle}">`
	`</div>`

The `.blackout-remove` class is added to the element	`<div class="cover blackout ng-`
	`animate `**`blackout-remove`**`"`
	`        ng-class="{blackout:`
	`displayToggle}">`
	`</div>`

The `$animate` service waits for a single animation frame (this performs a reflow)	No change in DOM

Event	DOM
The `.blackout-remove-active` class is added and `.blackout` is removed (this triggers the CSS transition/animation)	```<div class="cover ng-animate blackout-remove blackout-remove-active" ng-class="{blackout: displayToggle}"> </div>```
The `$animate` service scans the element styles to get the CSS transition/animation duration and delay	No change in DOM
The `$animate` service waits for the animation to get completed (via events and timeout)	No change in DOM
The animation ends and all the generated CSS classes are removed from the element	```<div class="cover" ng-class="{blackout: displayToggle}"> </div>```
The `doneCallback()` callback is fired (if provided)	No change in DOM

See also

▸ The *Creating addClass animations with ngShow* recipe provides the details of the complementary `addClass` event

Staggering batched animations

AngularJS incorporates native support for staggering animations that happen as a batch. This will almost exclusively occur in the context of `ng-repeat`.

Getting ready

Suppose that you have an animated `ng-repeat` implementation, as follows:

```
(style.css)

.container {
  line-height: 30px;
}
.container.ng-enter,
.container.ng-leave,
.container.ng-move {
```

```css
    transition: all linear 0.2s;

}
.container.ng-enter,
.container.ng-leave.ng-leave-active,
.container.ng-move {
  opacity: 0;
  max-height: 0;
}
.container.ng-enter.ng-enter-active,
.container.ng-leave,
.container.ng-move.ng-move-active {
  opacity: 1;
  max-height: 30px;
}
```

(index.html)

```html
<div ng-app="myApp">
  <div ng-controller="Ctrl">
    <input ng-model="search" />
    <div ng-repeat="name in names | filter:search"
        class="container">
      {{ name }}
    </div>
  </div>
</div>
```

(app.js)

```javascript
angular.module('myApp', ['ngAnimate'])
.controller('Ctrl', function($scope) {
  $scope.names = [
    'Jake',
    'Henry',
    'Roger',
    'Joe',
    'Robert',
    'John'
  ];
});
```

How to do it...

Since the animation is accomplished through the use of CSS transitions, you can tap into the CSS class staggering that is afforded to you by adding the following to the style sheet:

```
(style.css)

.container.ng-enter-stagger,
.container.ng-leave-stagger,
.container.ng-move-stagger {
  transition-delay: 0.2s;
  transition-duration: 0;
}
```

 JSFiddle: `http://jsfiddle.net/msfrisbie/emxsze4q/`

How it works...

For the example dataset, filtering with J will cause multiple elements to be removed, as well as multiple elements to change their index. All of these changes correspond to an animation event. Since these animations occur simultaneously, AngularJS can take advantage of the fact that animations are queued up and executed in batches within a single reflow to compensate for the fact that reflows are computationally expensive.

The `-stagger` classes essentially act as shims for successive animations. Instead of running all the animations in parallel, they are run serially, delimited by the additional stagger transition.

There's more...

It is also possible to stagger animations using keyframes. This can be accomplished as follows:

```
(style.css)

.container.ng-enter-stagger,
.container.ng-leave-stagger,
.container.ng-move-stagger {
  animation-delay: 0.2s;
  animation-duration: 0;
}
.container.ng-leave {
  animation: 0.5s repeat-leave;
```

```
    }
    .container.ng-enter {
      animation: 0.5s repeat-enter;
    }
    .container.ng-move {
      animation: 0.5s repeat-move;
    }
    @keyframes repeat-enter {
      from {
        opacity: 0;
        max-height: 0;
      }
      to {
        opacity: 1;
        max-height: 30px;
      }
    }
    @keyframes repeat-leave {
      from {
        opacity: 1;
        max-height: 30px;
      }
      to {
        opacity: 0;
        max-height: 0;
      }
    }
    @keyframes repeat-move {
      from {
        opacity: 0;
        max-height: 0;
      }
      to {
        opacity: 1;
        max-height: 30px;
      }
    }
```

 JSFiddle: http://jsfiddle.net/msfrisbie/bbetcp1m/

See also

▶ The *Creating move animations with ngRepeat* recipe goes through all the intricacies of animating an `ngRepeat` directive's events

4
Sculpting and Organizing your Application

In this chapter, we will cover the following recipes:

- ▶ Manually bootstrapping an application
- ▶ Using safe `$apply`
- ▶ Application file and module organization
- ▶ Hiding AngularJS from the user
- ▶ Managing application templates
- ▶ The "Controller as" syntax

Introduction

In this chapter, you will discover strategies to keep your application clean—visually, structurally, and organizationally.

Manually bootstrapping an application

When initializing an AngularJS application, very frequently you will allow the framework to do it transparently with the `ng-app` directive. When attached to a DOM node, the application will be automatically initialized upon the `DOMContentLoaded` event, or when the framework script is evaluated and the `document.readyState === 'complete'` statement becomes true. The application parses the DOM for the `ng-app` directive, which becomes the root element of the application. It will then begin initializing itself and compiling the application template. However, in some scenarios, you will want more control over when this initialization occurs, and AngularJS provides you with the ability to do this with `angular.bootstrap()`. Some examples of this include the following:

- ▶ Your application uses script loaders
- ▶ You want to modify the template before AngularJS begins compilation
- ▶ You want to use multiple AngularJS applications on the same page

Getting ready

When manually bootstrapping, the application will no longer use the `ng-app` directive. Suppose that this is your application template:

```
(index.html)

<!doctype html>
<html>
  <body>
    <div ng-controller="Ctrl">
      {{ mydata }}
    </div>
    <script src="angular.js"></script>
    <script src="app.js"></script>
  </body>
</html>

(app.js)

angular.module('myApp', [])
.controller('Ctrl', function($scope) {
  $scope.mydata = 'Some scope data';
});
```

How to do it...

The AngularJS initialization needs to be triggered by an event after the `angular.js` file is loaded, and it must be directed to a DOM element to be used as the root of the application. This can be accomplished in the following way:

```
(app.js)

angular.module('myApp', [])
.controller('Ctrl', function($scope) {
  $scope.mydata = 'Some scope data';
});

angular.element(document).ready(function() {
  angular.bootstrap(document, ['myApp']);
});
```

 JSFiddle: `http://jsfiddle.net/msfrisbie/5nfgyxsz/`

How it works...

The `angular.bootstrap()` method is used to link an existing application module to the designated DOM root node. In this example, the jqLite `ready()` method is passed a callback, which indicates that the browser's `document` object should be used as the root node of the `myApp` application module. If you were to use `ng-app` to auto-bootstrap, the following would roughly be the equivalent:

```
(index.html)

<!doctype html>
<html ng-app="myApp">
  <body>
    <div ng-controller="Ctrl">
      {{ mydata }}
    </div>
    <script src="angular.js"></script>
    <script src="app.js"></script>
  </body>
</html>
```

There's more...

By no means are you required to use the `<html>` element as the root of your application. You can just as easily attach the application to an inner DOM element if your application only needed to manage a subset of the DOM. This can be done as follows:

(index.html)

```
<!doctype html>
<html ng-app="myApp">
  <body>
    <div id="child">
      <div ng-controller="Ctrl">
        {{ mydata }}
      </div>
    </div>
    <script src="angular.js"></script>
    <script src="app.js"></script>
  </body>
</html>
```

(app.js)

```
angular.module('myApp', [])
.controller('Ctrl', function($scope) {
  $scope.mydata = 'Some scope data';
});

angular.element(document).ready(function() {
  angular.bootstrap(document.getElementById('child'), ['myApp']);
});
```

 JSFiddle: `http://jsfiddle.net/msfrisbie/k4nn5Lha/`

Using safe $apply

In the course of developing AngularJS applications, you will become very familiar with `$apply()` and its implications. The `$apply()` function cannot be invoked while the `$apply()` phase is already in progress without causing AngularJS to raise an exception. While in simpler applications, this problem can be solved by being careful and methodical about where you invoke `$apply()`; however, this becomes increasingly more difficult when applications incorporate third-party extensions with high DOM event density. The resulting problem is one where the necessity of invoking `$apply` is indeterminate.

As it is entirely possible to ascertain the state of the application when `$apply()` might need to be invoked, you can create a wrapper for `$apply()` to ascertain the state of the application, and conditionally invoke `$apply()` only when not in the `$apply` phase, essentially creating an idempotent `$apply()` method.

> This recipe contains content that the AngularJS wiki considers an anti-pattern, but it proffers an interesting discussion on the application life cycle as well as architecting scope utilities. As consolation, it includes a solution that is more idiomatic.

Getting ready

Suppose that this is your application:

```
(index.html)

<div ng-app="myApp">
  <div ng-controller="Ctrl">
    <button ng-click="increment()">Increment</button>
    {{ val }}
  </div>
</div>

(app.js)

angular.module('myApp', [])
.controller('MainController', function($scope) {
  $scope.val = 0;

  $scope.increment = function() {
```

```
        $scope.val++;
    };

    setInterval(function() {
      $scope.increment();
    }, 1000);
  });
```

 AngularJS has its own `$interval` service that would ameliorate the problem with this code, but this recipe is trying to demonstrate a scenario where `safeApply()` might come in handy.

How to do it...

In this example, the use of `setInterval()` means that a DOM event is occurring and AngularJS is not paying attention to it or what it does. The model is correctly being modified, but AngularJS's data binding is not propagating that change to the view. The button click, however, is using a directive that starts the `$apply` phase. This would be fine; however, as it presently exists, clicking the button will update the DOM, but the `setInterval()` callback will not.

Worse yet, incorporating a call to `$scope.$apply()` inside the `increment()` method does not solve the problem. This is because when the button is clicked, the method will attempt to invoke `$apply()` while already in the `$apply` phase, which as mentioned before, will cause an exception to be raised. The `setInterval()` callback, however, will function properly.

The ideal solution is one where you are able to reuse the same method for both events, but `$apply()` will be conditionally invoked only when it is needed. The most trivial and straightforward method of achieving this is to attach a `safeApply()` method to the parent controller scope of the application and let inheritance propagate it throughout your application. This can be done as follows:

```
(app.js)

angular.module('myApp', [])
.controller('Ctrl', function ($scope) {
  $scope.safeApply = function (func) {
    var currentPhase = this.$root.$$phase;

    // determine if already in $apply/$digest phase
    if (currentPhase === '$apply' ||
      currentPhase === '$digest') {
```

```
    // already inside $apply/$digest phase

    // if safeApply() was passed a function, invoke it
    if (typeof func === 'function') {
      func();
    }
  } else {
    // not inside $apply/$digest phase, safe to invoke $apply
    this.$apply(func);
  }
};

$scope.val = 0;

// method that may or may not be called from somewhere
// that will not trigger a $digest
$scope.increment = function () {
  $scope.val++;
  $scope.safeApply();
};

// application component that modifies the model without
// triggering a $digest
setInterval(function () {
  $scope.increment();
}, 1000);
});
```

 JSFiddle: `http://jsfiddle.net/msfrisbie/pnhmo2gx/`

How it works...

The current phase of the application can be determined by reading the $$phase attribute of the root scope of the application. If it is either in the $apply or $digest phase, it should not invoke $apply(). The reason for this is that $scope.$digest() is the actual method that will check to see whether any binding values have changed, but this should only be called after the non-AngularJS events have occurred. The $scope.$apply() method does this for you, and it will invoke $digest() only after evaluating any function passed to it. Thus, inside the safeApply() method, it should only invoke $apply() if the application is not in either of these phases.

There's more...

The preceding example will work fine as long as all scopes that want to use safeApply() inherit from the controller scope on which it is defined. Even so, controllers are initialized relatively late in the application's bootstrap process, so safeApply() cannot be invoked until this point. On top of this, defining something like safeApply() inside a controller introduces a bit of code smell, as you would ideally like a method of this persuasion to be implicitly available throughout the entire application without relegating it to a specific controller.

A much more robust way of doing this is to decorate $rootScope of the application with the method during the config phase. This ensures that it will be available to any services, controllers, or directives that try to use it. This can be accomplished in the following fashion:

```
(app.js)

angular.module('myApp', [])
.config(function($provide) {
  // define decorator for $rootScope service
  return $provide.decorator('$rootScope', function($delegate) {
    // $delegate acts as the $rootScope instance
    $delegate.safeApply = function(func) {
      var currentPhase = $delegate.$$phase;

      // determine if already in $apply/$digest phase
      if (currentPhase === "$apply" ||
        currentPhase === "$digest") {
        // already inside $apply/$digest phase

        // if safeApply() was passed a function, invoke it
        if (typeof func === 'function') {
          func();
        }
      }
      else {
        // not inside $apply/$digest phase,
        // safe to invoke $apply
        $delegate.$apply(func);
      }
    };
    return $delegate;
  });
})
.controller('Ctrl', function ($scope) {
```

```
  $scope.val = 0;

  // method that may or may not be called from somewhere
  // that will not trigger a $digest
  $scope.increment = function () {
    $scope.val++;
    $scope.safeApply();
  };

  // application component that modifies the model without
  // triggering a $digest
  setInterval(function () {
    $scope.increment();
  }, 1000);
});
```

 JSFiddle: `http://jsfiddle.net/msfrisbie/a0xcn9y4/`

Anti-pattern awareness

The AngularJS wiki notes that if your application needs to use a construct such as `safeApply()`, then the location where you are invoking `$scope.$apply()` isn't high enough in the call stack. This is true, and if you can avoid using `safeApply()`, you should do so. That being said, it is easy to think up a number of scenarios similar to this recipe's example where using `safeApply()` allows your code to remain DRY and concise, and for smaller applications, perhaps this is acceptable.

By the same token, the rigorous developer will not be satisfied with this and will desire an idiomatic solution to this problem aside from laborious code refactoring. One solution is to use `$timeout`, as shown here:

```
(app.js)

angular.module('myApp', [])
.controller('Ctrl', function ($scope, $timeout) {
  $scope.val = 0;

  // method that may or may not be called from somewhere
  // that will not trigger a $digest
  $scope.increment = function () {
    // wraps model modification in $timeout promise
    $timeout(function() {
      $scope.val++;
```

```
    });
  };

  // application component that modifies the model without
  // triggering a $digest
  setInterval(function () {
    $scope.increment();
  }, 1000);
});
```

 JSFiddle: `http://jsfiddle.net/msfrisbie/sagmbkft/`

The `$timeout` wrapper is the AngularJS wrapper for `window.setTimeout`. What this does is effectively schedule the model modification inside a promise that will be resolved as soon as possible and when `$apply` can be invoked without consequence. In most cases, this solution is acceptable as long as the deferred `$apply` phase does not affect other portions of the application.

Application file and module organization

Few things are less enjoyable than working on a project where the organization of the application files and modules is garbage, especially if the application is written by people other than you. Keeping your application file tree and module hierarchy clean and tidy will save you and whoever is reading and using your code lots of time in the long run.

Getting ready

Assume that an application you are working on is a generic e-commerce site, with many users who can view and purchase products, leave reviews, and so on.

How to do it...

There are several guidelines that can be followed to yield extremely tight and clean applications that are able to scale without bloating.

One module, one file, and one name

This might seem obvious, but the benefits of following the one module, one file, and one name approach are plentiful:

  ▸ Keep only one module per file. A module can be extended in other files in the subfiles and subdirectories as necessary, but `angular.module('my-module')` should only ever appear once. A file should not contain all or part of the two different modules.

  ▸ Name your files after your modules. It should be easy to figure out what to expect when opening `inventory-controller.js`.

  ▸ Module names should reflect the hierarchy in which it exists. The module in `/inventory/inventory-controller.js` should reflect its location in the hierarchy by being named something along the lines of `inventory.controller`.

Keep your related files close, keep your unit tests closer

Proper locality and organization of test files is not always obvious. Rigorously following this style guide is not mandatory, but choosing a unified naming and organization convention will save you a lot of headaches later on. This approach entails the following:

  ▸ Name your unit test files by appending `_test` to whatever module file it is testing. The `inventory-controller.js` module will have its unit tests located in `inventory-controller_test.js`.

  ▸ Keep unit tests in the same folder as the JS file they are testing. This will encourage you to write your tests as you develop the application. Additionally, you won't need to spend time mirroring your test directory structure to that of your application directory (see *Chapter 6, Testing in AngularJS*, for more information on testing procedures).

Group by feature, not by component type

Applications that group by component type (all directives in one place and all controllers in another) will scale poorly. The file and module locality should reflect that which appears in AngularJS dependencies. This includes the following:

  ▸ Grouping by feature allows your file and module structure to imitate how the application code is connected. As the application begins to scale, it is cleaner and makes more sense for code that is more closely related in execution to have matching spatial locality.

  ▸ Feature grouping also allows nested directories of functionality within larger features.

Don't fight reusability

Some parts of your application will be used almost everywhere and some parts will only be used once. Your application structure should reflect this. This approach includes the following:

- ▸ Keep common unspecialized components that are used throughout the application inside a `components/` directory. This directory can also hold common asset files and other shared application pieces.

- ▸ Directives, services, and filters are all application components that can potentially see a lot of reuse. Don't hesitate to house them in the `components/` directory if it makes sense to do so.

An example directory structure

With the tips mentioned in the preceding section, the e-commerce application will look something like this:

```
ng-commerce/
   index.html
   app.js
   app-controller.js
   app-controller_test.js
   components/
      login/
         login.js
         login-controller.js
         login-controller_test.js
         login-directive.js
         login-directive_test.js
         login.css
         login.tpl.html
      search/
         search.js
         search-directive.js
         search-directive_test.js
         search-filter.js
         search-filter_test.js
         search.css
         search.tpl.html
   shopping-cart/
      checkout/
         checkout.js
         checkout-conroller.js
         checkout-controller_test.js
         checkout-directive.js
         checkout-directive_test.js
```

```
        checkout.tpl.html
        checkout.css
    shopping-cart.js
    shopping-cart-controller.js
    shopping-cart-controller_test.js
    shopping-cart.tpl.html
    shopping-cart.css
```

The `app.js` file is the top-level configuration file, complete with route definitions and initialization logic. JS files matching their directory names are the combinatorial files that bind all the directory modules together.

CSS files provide styling that is only used by that component in that directory. Templates also follow this convention.

Hiding AngularJS from the user

As unique and elegant as AngularJS is, the reality of the situation is that it is a framework that lives inside asynchronously executed client-side code, and this requires some considerations. One of these considerations is the first-time delivery initialization latency. Especially when your application JS files are located at the end of the page, you might experience a phenomenon called "template flashing," where the uncompiled template is presented to the user before AngularJS bootstraps and compiles the page. This can be elegantly prevented using `ng-cloak`.

Getting ready

Suppose that this is your application:

```
(index.html)

<body>
  {{ youShouldntSeeThisBecauseItIsUndefined }}
</body>
```

How to do it...

The solution is to simply declare sections of the DOM that the browser should treat as hidden until AngularJS tells it otherwise. This can be accomplished with the `ng-cloak` directive, as follows:

```
(app.css)

/* this css rule is provided in the angular.js file, but
if AngularJS is not included in <head>, you must
```

```
define this style yourself */

[ng\:cloak], [ng-cloak], [data-ng-cloak], [x-ng-cloak], .ng-cloak,
.x-ng-cloak {
  display: none !important;
}


(index.html)

<body ng-cloak>
  {{ youShouldntSeeThisBecauseItIsUndefined }}
</body>
```

 JSFiddle: `http://jsfiddle.net/msfrisbie/6tnxoozn/`

How it works...

Any section with `ng-cloak` initially applied to it will be hidden by the browser. AngularJS will delete the `ng-cloak` directive when it begins to compile the application template, so the page will only be revealed once compilation is complete, effectively shielding the user from the uncompiled template. In this case, as the entire `<body>` element has the `ng-cloak` directive, the user will be presented with a blank page until AngularJS is initialized and compiles the page.

There's more...

It might not behoove you to cloak the entire application until it's ready. First, if you only need to compile a subset or subsets of a page, you should take advantage of that by compartmentalizing `ng-cloak` to those sections. Often, it's better to present the user with something while the page is being assembled than with a blank screen. Second, breaking `ng-cloak` apart into multiple locations will allow the page to progressively render each component it must compile. This will probably give the feeling of a faster load as you are presenting compiled pieces of the view as they become available instead of waiting for everything to be ready.

Managing application templates

As is to be expected with a single-page application, you will be managing a large number of templates in your application. AngularJS has several template management solutions baked into it, which offer a range of ways for your application to handle template delivery.

Getting ready

Suppose you are using the following template in your application:

```
<div class="btn-group">
  #{{ player.number }} {{ player.name }}
</div>
```

The content of the template is unimportant; it is merely to demonstrate that this template has HTML and uncompiled AngularJS content inside it.

Additionally, assume you have the following directive that is trying to use the preceding template:

```
(app.js)

angular.module('myApp', [])
.directive('playerBox', function() {
  return {
    link: function(scope) {
      scope.player = {
        name: 'Jimmy Butler',
        number: 21
      };
    }
  };
});
```

The top-level template will look as follows:

```
(index.html)

<div ng-app="myApp">
  <player-box></player-box>
</div>
```

How to do it...

There are four primary ways to provide the directive with the template's HTML. All of these will feed the template into `$templateCache`, which is where the directive and other components tasked with locating a template will search first.

The string template

AngularJS is capable of generating a template from a string of uncompiled HTML. This can be accomplished as follows:

```
(app.js)

angular.module('myApp', [])
.directive('playerBox', function() {
  return {
    template: '<div>' +
              ' #{{ player.number }} {{ player.name }}' +
              '</div>',
    link: function(scope) {
      scope.player = {
        name: 'Jimmy Butler',
        number: 21
      };
    }
  };
});
```

 JSFiddle: http://jsfiddle.net/msfrisbie/8ct0u33z/

Remote server templates

When the component cannot find a template in `$templateCache`, it will make a request to the corresponding location on the server. This template will then receive an entry in `$templateCache`, which can be used as follows:

```
(app.js)

angular.module('myApp', [])
.directive('playerBox', function() {
  return {
    // will attempt to acquire the template at this relative URL
    templateUrl: '/static/js/templates/player-box.html',
    link: function(scope) {
```

```
      scope.player = {
        name: 'Jimmy Butler',
        number: 21
      };
    }
  };
});
```

On the server, your file directory structure will look something like the following:

```
yourApp/
  static/
    js/
      templates/
        player-box.html
```

Inline templates using ng-template

It is also possible to serve and register the templates along with another template. HTML inside `<script>` tags with `type="text/ng-template"` and the `id` attribute set to the key for `$templateCache` will be registered and available in your application. This can be done as follows:

```
(app.js)

angular.module('myApp', [])
.directive('playerBox', function() {
  return {
    templateUrl: 'player-box.html',
    link: function(scope) {
      scope.player = {
        name: 'Jimmy Butler',
        number: 21
      };
    }
  };
});

(index.html)

<div ng-app="myApp">
  <player-box></player-box>

  <script type="text/ng-template" id="player-box.html">
    <div>
      #{{ player.number }} {{ player.name }}
    </div>
  </script>
</div>
```

JSFiddle: `http://jsfiddle.net/msfrisbie/kg95bn9g/`

Pre-defined templates in the cache

Even cleaner is the ability to directly insert your templates into `$templateCache` on application startup. This can be done as follows:

```
(app.js)

angular.module('myApp', [])
.run(function($templateCache) {
  $templateCache.put(
    // the template key
    'player-box.html',
    // the template markup
    '<div>' +
    '  #{{ player.number }} {{ player.name }}' +
    '</div>'
  );
})
.directive('playerBox', function() {
  return {
    templateUrl: 'player-box.html',
    link: function(scope) {
      scope.player = {
        name: 'Jimmy Butler',
        number: 21
      };
    }
  };
});
```

 JSFiddle: `http://jsfiddle.net/msfrisbie/mp79srjf/`

How it works...

All these denominations of template definitions are different flavors of the same thing: uncompiled templates are accumulated and served from within `$templateCache`. The only real decision to be made is how you want it to affect your development flow and where you want to expose the latency.

Accessing the templates from a remote server ensures that you aren't delivering content to the user that they won't need, but when different pieces of the application are rendering, they will all need to generate requests for templates from the server. This can make your application sluggish at times. On the other hand, delivering all the templates with the initial application load can slow things down quite a bit, so it's important to make informed decisions on which part of your application flow is more latency-tolerant.

There's more...

The last method of defining templates is provided in a popular Grunt extension, called `grunt-angular-templates`. During the application build, this extension will automatically locate your templates and interpolate them into your `index.html` file as JavaScript string templates, registering them in `$templateCache`. Managing your application with build tools such as Grunt has huge and obvious benefits, and this recipe is no exception.

The "Controller as" syntax

AngularJS 1.2 introduced the ability to namespace your controller methods using the "controller as" syntax. This allows you to abstract `$scope` in controllers and provide more contextual information in the template.

Getting ready

Suppose you had a simple application set up as follows:

```
(index.html)

<div ng-app="myApp">
  <div ng-controller="Ctrl">
    {{ data }}
  </div>
</div>

(app.js)

angular.module('myApp', [])
.controller('Ctrl', function($scope) {
  $scope.data = "This is string data";
});
```

How to do it...

The simplest way to take advantage of the "controller as" syntax is inside the `ng-controller` directive in a template. This allows you to namespace pieces of data in the view, which should feel good to you as more declarative views are the AngularJS way. The initial example can be refactored to appear as follows:

```
(index.html)
```

```html
<div ng-app="myApp">
  <div ng-controller="Ctrl as MyCtrl">
    {{ MyCtrl.data }}
  </div>
</div>
```

```
(app.js)
```

```javascript
angular.module('myApp', [])
.controller('Ctrl', function() {
  this.data = "This is string data";
});
```

 JSFiddle: `http://jsfiddle.net/msfrisbie/yh3r2t6r/`

Note that there is no longer a need to inject `$scope`, as you are instead attaching the string attribute to the controller object.

This syntax can also be extended for use in directives. Suppose the application was retooled to exist as follows:

```
(index.html)
```

```html
<div ng-app="myApp">
  <foo-directive></foo-directive>
</div>
```

```
(app.js)
```

```javascript
angular.module('myApp', [])
```

```
.directive('fooDirective', function() {
  return {
    restrict: 'E',
    template: '<div>{{ data }}</div>',
    controller: function($scope) {
      $scope.data = 'This is controller scope data';
    }
  };
});
```

This works, but the "controller as" syntactic sugar can be applied here to make the content of the directive template a little less ambiguous:

```
(app.js)

angular.module('myApp', [])
.directive('fooDirective', function() {
  return {
    restrict: 'E',
    template: '<div>{{ fooController.data }}</div>',
    controller: function() {
      this.data = 'This is controller data';
    },
    controllerAs: 'fooController'
  }
});
```

 JSFiddle: http://jsfiddle.net/msfrisbie/7uobd20v/

How it works...

Using the "controller as" syntax allows you to directly reference the controller object within the template. By doing this, you are able to assign attributes to the controller object itself rather than to $scope.

There's more...

There are a couple of main benefits of using this style, which are as follows:

- You get more information in the view. By using this syntax, you are able to directly infer the source of the object from only the template, which is something you could not do before.

- You are able to define directive controllers anonymously and define them where you choose. Being able to rebrand a function object in a directive allows a lot of flexibility in the application structure and locality of definition.

- Testing is easier. Controllers defined in this way by nature are easier to set up, as injecting `$scope` into controllers means that unit tests need some boilerplate initialization.

5
Working with the Scope and Model

In this chapter, we will cover the following recipes:

- ▸ Configuring and using AngularJS events
- ▸ Managing `$scope` inheritance
- ▸ Working with AngularJS forms
- ▸ Working with `<select>` and `ngOptions`
- ▸ Building an event bus

Introduction

AngularJS provides faculties to manage data alteration throughout the application, largely based around the model modification architecture. AngularJS' powerful data binding affords you the ability to build robust tools on top of the architecture as well as channels of communication that can efficiently reach throughout the application.

Configuring and using AngularJS events

AngularJS offers a powerful event infrastructure that affords you the ability to control the application in scenarios where data binding might not be suitable or pragmatic. Even with a rigorously organized application topology, there are lots of applications for events in AngularJS.

How to do it...

AngularJS events are identified by strings and carry with them a payload that can take the form of an object, a function, or a primitive. The event can either be delivered via a parent scope that invokes `$scope.$broadcast()`, or a child scope (or the same scope) that invokes `$scope.$emit()`.

The `$scope.$on()` method can be used anywhere a scope object can be used, as shown here:

```
(app.js)

angular.module('myApp', [])
.controller('Ctrl', function($scope, $log) {
  $scope.$on('myEvent', function(event, data) {
    $log.log(event.name + ' observed with payload ', data);
  });
});
```

Broadcasting an event

The `$scope.$broadcast()` method triggers the event in itself and all child scopes. The 1.2.7 release of AngularJS introduced an optimization for `$scope.$broadcast()`, but since this action will still bubble down through the scope hierarchy to reach the listening child scopes, it is possible to introduce performance problems if this is overused. Broadcasting can be implemented as follows:

```
(app.js)

angular.module('myApp', [])
.directive('myListener', function($log) {
  return {
    restrict: 'E',
    // each directive should be given its own scope
    scope: true,
    link: function(scope, el, attrs) {
      // method to generate event
      scope.sendDown = function() {
        scope.$broadcast('myEvent', {origin: attrs.local});
      };
      // method to listen for event
      scope.$on('myEvent', function(event, data) {
        $log.log(
          event.name +
          ' observed in ' +
          attrs.local +
```

```
          ', originated from ' +
          data.origin
       );
     });
   }
 };
});
```

(index.html)

```
<div ng-app="myApp">
  <my-listener local="outer">
    <button ng-click="sendDown()">Send Down</button>
    <my-listener local="middle">
      <my-listener local="first inner"></my-listener>
      <my-listener local="second inner"></my-listener>
    </my-listener>
  </my-listener>
</div>
```

In this setup, clicking on the **Send Down** button will log the following in the browser console:

```
myEvent observed in outer, originated from outer
myEvent observed in middle, originated from outer
myEvent observed in first inner, originated from outer
myEvent observed in second inner, originated from outer
```

 JSFiddle: `http://jsfiddle.net/msfrisbie/dn0zjep9/`

Emitting an event

As you might expect, `$scope.$emit()` does the opposite of `$scope.$broadcast()`. It will trigger all listeners of the event that exist within that same scope, or any of the parent scopes along the prototype chain, all the way up to `$rootScope`. This can be implemented as follows:

(app.js)

```
angular.module('myApp', [])
.directive('myListener', function($log) {
  return {
    restrict: 'E',
    // each directive should be given its own scope
    scope: true,
```

```
    link: function(scope, el, attrs) {
      // method to generate event
      scope.sendUp = function() {
        scope.$emit('myEvent', {origin: attrs.local});
      };
      // method to listen for event
      scope.$on('myEvent', function(event, data) {
        $log.log(
          event.name +
          ' observed in ' +
          attrs.local +
          ', originated from ' +
          data.origin
        );
      });
    }
  };
});
```

```
(index.html)
```

```html
<div ng-app="myApp">
  <my-listener local="outer">
    <my-listener local="middle">
      <my-listener local="first inner">
        <button ng-click="sendUp()">
          Send First Up
        </button>
      </my-listener>
      <my-listener local="second inner">
        <button ng-click="sendUp()">
          Send Second Up
        </button>
      </my-listener>
    </my-listener>
  </my-listener>
</div>
```

In this example, clicking on the **Send First Up** button will log the following to the browser console:

```
myEvent observed in first inner, originated from first inner
myEvent observed in middle, originated from first inner
myEvent observed in outer, originated from first inner
```

Clicking on the **Send Second Up** button will log the following to the browser console:

```
myEvent observed in second inner, originated from second inner
myEvent observed in middle, originated from second inner
myEvent observed in outer, originated from second inner
```

 JSFiddle: `http://jsfiddle.net/msfrisbie/a344o7vo/`

Deregistering an event listener

Similar to `$scope.$watch()`, once an event listener is created, it will last the lifetime of the scope object they are added in. The `$scope.$on()` method returns the deregistration function, which must be captured upon declaration. Invoking this deregistration function will prevent the scope from evaluating the callback function for this event. This can be toggled with a setup/teardown pattern, as follows:

```
(app.js)

angular.module('myApp', [])
.controller('Ctrl', function($scope, $log) {
  $scope.setup = function() {
    $scope.teardown = $scope.$on('myEvent',function(event, data) {
      $log.log(event.name + ' observed with payload ', data);
    });
  };
});
```

Invoking `$scope.setup()` will initialize the event binding, and invoking `$scope.teardown()` will destroy that binding.

Managing $scope inheritance

Scopes in AngularJS are bound to the same rules of prototypical inheritance as plain old JavaScript objects. When wielded properly, they can be used very effectively in your application, but there are some "gotchas" to be aware of that can be avoided by adhering to best practices.

Getting ready

Suppose that your application contained the following:

```
(app.js)

angular.module('myApp', [])
.controller('Ctrl', function() {})

(index.html)

<div ng-app="myApp">
  <div ng-controller="Ctrl" ng-init="data=123">
    <input ng-model="data" />
    <div ng-controller="Ctrl">
      <input ng-model="data" />
    </div>
    <div ng-controller="Ctrl">
      <input ng-model="data" />
    </div>
  </div>
</div>
```

How to do it...

In the current setup, the $scope instances in the nested Ctrl instances will prototypically inherit from the parent Ctrl $scope. When the page is loaded, all three inputs will be filled with 123, and when you change the value of the parent Ctrl <input>, both inputs bound to the child $scope instances will update in turn, as all three are bound to the same object. However, when you change the values of either input bound to a child $scope object, the other inputs will not reflect that value, and the data binding from that input is broken until the application is reloaded.

To fix this, simply add an object that is nested to any primitive types on your scope. This can be accomplished in the following fashion:

```
(index.html)

<div ng-app="myApp">
  <div ng-controller="Ctrl" ng-init="data.value=123">
    <input ng-model="data.value" />
    <div ng-controller="Ctrl">
      <input ng-model="data.value" />
    </div>
    <div ng-controller="Ctrl">
```

```
      <input ng-model="data.value" />
    </div>
  </div>
</div>
```

 JSFiddle: `http://jsfiddle.net/msfrisbie/obe24zet/`

Now, any of the three inputs can be altered, and the change will reflect in the other two. All three remain bound to the same $scope object in the parent Ctrl $scope object.

The rule of thumb is to always maintain one layer of object indirection for anything (especially primitive types) in your scope if you are relying on the $scope inheritance in any way. This is colloquially referred to as "always using a dot."

How it works...

When the value of a $scope property is altered from an input, this performs an assignment on the $scope property to which it is bound. As is the case with prototypical inheritance, assignment to an object property will follow the prototype chain all the way up to the original instance, but assignment to a primitive will create a new instance of the primitive in the local $scope property. In the preceding example, before the .value fix was added, the new local instance was detached from the ancestral value, which resulted in the dual $scope property values.

There's more...

The following two examples are considered to be bad practice (for hopefully obvious reasons), and it is much easier to just maintain at least one level of object indirection for any data that needs to be inherited down through the application's $scope tree.

It's possible to reestablish this inheritance by removing the primitive property from the local $scope object:

```
(app.js)

angular.module('myApp', [])
.controller('outerCtrl', function($scope) {
  $scope.data = 123;
})
.controller('innerCtrl', function($scope) {
  $scope.reattach = function() {
    delete($scope.data);
  };
```

```
});

(index.html)

<div ng-app="myApp">
  <div ng-controller="outerCtrl">
    <input ng-model="data" />
    <div ng-controller="innerCtrl">
      <input ng-model="data" />
    </div>
    <div ng-controller="innerCtrl">
      <input ng-model="data" />
      <button ng-click="reattach()">Reattach</button>
    </div>
  </div>
</div>
```

 JSFiddle: `http://jsfiddle.net/msfrisbie/r33nekbg/`

It is also possible to directly access the parent `$scope` object using `$scope.$parent` and ignore the inheritance completely. This can be done as follows:

```
(app.js)

angular.module('myApp', [])
.controller('Ctrl', function() {});

(index.html)

<div ng-app="myApp">
  <div ng-controller="Ctrl" ng-init="data=123">
    <input ng-model="data" />
    <div ng-controller="Ctrl">
      <input ng-model="$parent.data" />
    </div>
    <div ng-controller="Ctrl">
      <input ng-model="$parent.data" />
    </div>
  </div>
</div>
```

Troublemaker built-in directives

The preceding examples explicitly demonstrate nested scopes that prototypically inherit from the parent $scope object. In a real application, this would likely be very easy to detect and debug. However, AngularJS comes bundled with a number of built-in directives that silently create their own scopes, and if prototypical scope inheritance is not heeded, this can cause problems. There are six built-in directives that create their own scope: ngController, ngInclude, ngView, ngRepeat, ngIf, and ngSwitch.

The following examples will interpolate the $scope $id into the template to demonstrate the creation of a new scope.

ngController

The use of ngController should be obvious, as your controller logic relies on attaching functions and data to the new child scope created by the ngController directive.

ngInclude

Irrespective of the HTML content of whatever is being included, ng-include will wrap it inside a new scope. As ng-include is normally used to insert monolithic application components that do not depend on their surroundings, it is less likely that you would run into the $scope inheritance problems using it.

The following is an incorrect solution:

```
(app.js)

angular.module('myApp', [])
.controller('Ctrl', function($scope) {
  $scope.data = 123;
});

(index.html)

<div ng-app="myApp">
  <div ng-controller="Ctrl">
    Scope id: {{ $id }}
    <input ng-model="data " />
    <ng-include src="'innerTemplate.html'"></ng-include>
  </div>

  <script type="text/ng-template" id="innerTemplate.html">
    <div>
      Scope id: {{ $id }}
      <input ng-model="data " />
    </div>
  </script>
</div>
```

The new scope inside the compiled `ng-include` directive inherits from the controller `$scope`, but binding to its primitive value sets up the same problem.

The following is the correct solution:

```
(app.js)

angular.module('myApp', [])
.controller('Ctrl', function($scope) {
  $scope.data = {
    val: 123
  };
});

(index.html)

<div ng-app="myApp">
  <div ng-controller="Ctrl">
    Scope id: {{ $id }}
    <input ng-model="data.val" />
    <ng-include src="'innerTemplate.html'"></ng-include>
  </div>

  <script type="text/ng-template" id="innerTemplate.html">
    <div>
      Scope id: {{ $id }}
      <input ng-model="data.val" />
    </div>
  </script>
</div>
```

 JSFiddle: `http://jsfiddle.net/msfrisbie/c8nLk676/`

ngView

With respect to prototypal inheritance, `ng-view` operates identically to `ng-include`. The inserted compiled template is provided its own new child `$scope`, and correctly inheriting from the parent `$scope` can be accomplished in the exact same fashion.

ngRepeat

The ngRepeat directive is the most problematic directive when it comes to incorrectly managing the `$scope` inheritance. Each element that the repeater creates is given its own scope, and modifications to these child scopes (such as inline editing of data in a list) will not affect the original object if it is bound to primitives.

The following is an incorrect solution:

```
(app.js)

angular.module('myApp', [])
.controller('Ctrl', function($scope) {
  $scope.names = [
    'Alshon Jeffrey',
    'Brandon Marshall',
    'Matt Forte',
    'Martellus Bennett',
    'Jay Cutler'
  ];
});
```

```
(index.html)

<div ng-app="myApp">
  <div ng-controller="Ctrl">
    Scope id: {{ $id }}
    <pre>{{ names | json }}</pre>
    <div ng-repeat="name in names">
      Scope id: {{ $id }}
      <input ng-model="name" />
    </div>
  </div>
</div>
```

As described earlier, changing the value of the input fields only serves to modify the instance of the primitive in the child scope, not the original object. One way to fix this is to restructure the data object so that instead of iterating through primitive types, it iterates through objects wrapping the primitive types.

The following is the correct solution:

```
(app.js)

angular.module('myApp', [])
.controller('Ctrl', function($scope) {
  $scope.players = [
    { name: 'Alshon Jeffrey' },
    { name: 'Brandon Marshall' },
    { name: 'Matt Forte' },
    { name: 'Martellus Bennett' },
    { name: 'Jay Cutler' }
```

```
  ];
});
```

```
(index.html)
```

```html
<div ng-app="myApp">
  <div ng-controller="Ctrl">
    Scope id: {{ $id }}
    <pre>{{ players | json }}</pre>
    <div ng-repeat="player in players">
      Scope id: {{ $id }}
      <input ng-model="player.name" />
    </div>
  </div>
</div>
```

 JSFiddle: http://jsfiddle.net/msfrisbie/zesj1gb6/

With this, the original array is being modified properly, and all is right with the world. However, sometimes restructuring an object is not a feasible solution for an application. In this case, changing an array of strings to an array of objects seems like an odd workaround. Ideally, you would prefer to be able to iterate through the string array without modifying it first. Using track by as part of the ng-repeat expression, this is possible.

The following is also a correct solution:

```
(app.js)
```

```javascript
angular.module('myApp', [])
.controller('Ctrl', function($scope) {
  $scope.players = [
    'Alshon Jeffrey',
    'Brandon Marshall',
    'Matt Forte',
    'Martellus Bennett',
    'Jay Cutler'
  ];
});
```

```
(index.html)
```

```html
<div ng-app="myApp">
  <div ng-controller="Ctrl">
```

```
   Scope id: {{ $id }}
   <pre>{{ players | json }}</pre>
   <div ng-repeat="player in players track by $index">
     Scope id: {{ $id }}
     <input ng-model="players[$index]" />
   </div>
  </div>
</div>
```

 JSFiddle: `http://jsfiddle.net/msfrisbie/ovas398h/`

Now, even though the repeater is iterating through the `players` array elements, as the child `$scope` objects created for each element will still prototypically inherit the players array, it simply binds to the respective element in the array using the `$index` repeater.

As primitive types are immutable in JavaScript, altering a primitive element in the array will replace it entirely. When this replacement occurs, as a vanilla utilization of `ng-repeat` identifies array elements by their string value, `ng-repeat` thinks a new element has been added, and the entire array will re-render—a functionality which is obviously undesirable for usability and performance reasons. The `track by $index` clause in the `ng-repeat` expression solves this problem by identifying array elements by their index rather than their string value, which prevents constant re-rendering.

ngIf

As the `ng-if` directive destroys the DOM content nested inside it every time its expression evaluates as `false`, it will re-inherit the parent `$scope` object every time the inner content is compiled. If anything inside the `ng-if` element directive inherits incorrectly from the parent `$scope` object, the child `$scope` data will be wiped out every time recompilation occurs.

The following is an incorrect solution:

```
(app.js)

angular.module('myApp', [])
.controller('Ctrl', function($scope) {
  $scope.data 123;
  $scope.show = false;
});

(index.html)

<div ng-app="myApp">
  <div ng-controller="Ctrl">
    Scope id: {{ $id }}
```

```
      <input ng-model="data " />
      <input type="checkbox" ng-model="show" />
      <div ng-if="show">
        Scope id: {{ $id }}
        <input ng-model="data " />
      </div>
    </div>
</div>
```

Every time the checkbox is toggled, the newly created child $scope object will re-inherit from the parent $scope object and wipe out the existing data. This is obviously undesirable in many scenarios. Instead, the simple utilization of one level of object indirection solves this problem.

The following is the correct solution:

```
(app.js)

angular.module('myApp', [])
.controller('Ctrl', function($scope) {
  $scope.data = {
    val: 123
  };
  $scope.show = false;
});
```

```
(index.html)

<div ng-app="myApp">
  <div ng-controller="Ctrl">
    Scope id: {{ $id }}
    <input ng-model="data.val" />
    <input type="checkbox" ng-model="show" />
    <div ng-if="show">
      Scope id: {{ $id }}
      <input ng-model="data.val" />
    </div>
  </div>
</div>
```

 JSFiddle: http://jsfiddle.net/msfrisbie/hq7r5frm/

ngSwitch

The ngSwitch directive acts much in the same way as if you were to combine several ngIf statements together. If anything inside the active ng-switch $scope inherits incorrectly from the parent $scope object, the child $scope data will be wiped out every time recompilation occurs when the watched switch value is altered.

The following is an incorrect solution:

```
(app.js)

angular.module('myApp', [])
.controller('Ctrl', function($scope) {
  $scope.data = 123;
});

(index.html)

<div ng-app="myApp">
  <div ng-controller="Ctrl">
    Scope id: {{ $id }}
    <input ng-model="data " />
    <div ng-switch on="data ">
      <div ng-switch-when="123">
        Scope id: {{ $id }}
        <input ng-model="data " />
      </div>
      <div ng-switch-default>
        Scope id: {{ $id }}
        Default
      </div>
    </div>
  </div>
</div>
```

In this example, when the outer <input> tag is set to the matching value 123, the inner <input> tag nested in ng-switch will inherit that value, as expected. However, when altering the inner input, it doesn't modify the inherited value as the prototypical inheritance chain is broken.

The following is the correct solution:

```
(app.js)

angular.module('myApp', [])
.controller('Ctrl', function($scope) {
  $scope.data = {
```

```
      val: 123
   };
});
```

```
(index.html)
```

```
<div ng-app="myApp">
  <div ng-controller="Ctrl">
    Scope id: {{ $id }}
    <input ng-model="data.val" />
    <div ng-switch on="data.val">
      <div ng-switch-when="123">
        Scope id: {{ $id }}
        <input ng-model="data.val" />
      </div>
      <div ng-switch-default>
        Scope id: {{ $id }}
        Default
      </div>
    </div>
  </div>
</div>
```

 JSFiddle: `http://jsfiddle.net/msfrisbie/8kh41wdm/`

Working with AngularJS forms

AngularJS offers close integration with HTML form elements in the form of directives to afford you the ability to build animated and styled form pages, complete with validation, quickly and easily.

How to do it...

AngularJS forms exist inside the `<form>` tag, which corresponds to a native AngularJS directive, as shown in the following code. The `novalidate` attribute instructs the browser to ignore its native form validation:

```
<form novalidate>
  <!-- form inputs -->
</form>
```

Your HTML input elements will reside inside the `<form>` tags. Each instance of the `<form>` tag creates a `FormController`, which keeps track of all its controls and nested forms. The entire AngularJS form infrastructure is built on top of this.

 As browsers don't allow nested form tags, `ng-form` should be used to nest forms.

What the form offers you

Suppose you have a controller; a form in your application is as follows:

```
<div ng-controller="Ctrl">
  <form novalidate name="myform">
    <input name="myinput" ng-model="formdata.myinput" />
  </form>
</div>
```

With this, `Ctrl $scope` is provided a constructor for the `FormController` as `$scope.myform`, which contains a lot of useful attributes and functions. The individual form entries for each input can be accessed as child `FormController` objects on the parent `FormController` object; for example, `$scope.myform.myinput` is the `FormController` object for the text input.

 The inputs must be coupled with an `ng-model` directive for the state and validation bindings to work.

Tracking the form state

Inputs and forms are provided with their own controllers, and AngularJS tracks the state of both the individual inputs and the entire form using a pristine/dirty dichotomy. "Pristine" refers to the state in which inputs are set to their default values, and "dirty" refers to any modifying action taken on the model corresponding to the inputs. The "pristine" state of the entire form is a logical AND result of all the input pristine states or a NOR result of all the dirty states; by its inverted definition, the "dirty" state of the entire form represents an OR result of all the dirty states or a NAND result of all the pristine states.

 JSFiddle: `http://jsfiddle.net/msfrisbie/trjfzdwc/`

These states can be used in several different ways.

Both the `<form>` and `<input>` elements have the CSS classes, `ng-pristine` and `ng-dirty`, automatically applied to them based on the state the form is in. These CSS classes can be used to style the inputs based on their state, as follows:

```
form.ng-pristine {
}
input.ng-pristine {
}
form.ng-dirty {
}
input.ng-dirty {
}
```

All instances of the `FormController` and the `ngModelController` instances inside it have the `$pristine` and `$dirty` Boolean properties available. These can be used in the controller business logic or to control the user flow through the form.

The following example shows **Enter a value** until the input has been modified:

```
(app.js)

angular.module('myApp', [])
.controller('Ctrl', function($scope) {
  $scope.$watch('myform.myinput.$pristine', function(newval) {
    $scope.isPristine = newval;
  });
});

(index.html)

<div ng-app="myApp">
  <div ng-controller="Ctrl">
    <form novalidate name="myform">
      <input name="myinput" ng-model="formdata.myinput" />
    </form>
    <div ng-show="isPristine">
      Enter a value
    </div>
  </div>
</div>
```

 JSFiddle: `http://jsfiddle.net/msfrisbie/unxbyun2/`

Alternately, as the form object is attached to the scope, it is possible to directly detect whether the input is pristine in the view:

```
(index.html)

<div ng-app="myApp">
  <div ng-controller="Ctrl">
    <form novalidate name="myform">
      <input name="myinput" ng-model="formdata.myinput" />
      <div ng-show="myform.myinput.$pristine">
        Enter a value
      </div>
    </form>
  </div>
</div>
```

 JSFiddle: http://jsfiddle.net/msfrisbie/pr3L1e2b/

It's also possible to force a form or input into a pristine or dirty state using the `$setDirty()` or `$setPristine()` methods. This has no bearing on what exists inside the inputs at that point in time; it simply overrides the Booleans values, `$pristine` and `$dirty`, and sets the corresponding CSS class, `ng-pristine` or `ng-dirty`. Invoking these methods will propagate to any parent forms.

Validating the form

Similar to the pristine/dirty dichotomy, AngularJS forms also have a valid/invalid dichotomy. Input fields in a form can be assigned validation rules that must be satisfied for the form to be valid. AngularJS tracks the validity of both the individual inputs and the entire form using the valid/invalid dichotomy. "Valid" refers to the state in which the inputs satisfy all validation requirements assigned to it, and "invalid" refers to an input that fails one or more validation requirements. The "valid" state of the entire form is a logical AND result of all the input valid states or a NOR result of all the invalid states; by its inverted definition, the "invalid" state of the entire form represents an OR result of all the invalid states or a NAND result of all the valid states.

 JSFiddle: http://jsfiddle.net/msfrisbie/ejpsrfgz/

Similar to pristine and dirty, both the `<form>` and `<input>` elements have the CSS classes, `ng-valid` and `ng-invalid`, automatically applied to them based on the state the form is in. These CSS classes can be used to style the inputs based on their state, as follows:

```
form.ng-valid {
}
input.ng-valid {
}
form.ng-invalid {
}
input.ng-invalid {
}
```

All instances of `FormController` and the `ngModelController` instances inside it have the `$valid` and `$invalid` Boolean attributes available. These can be used in the controller business logic or to control the user flow through the form.

The following example shows **Input field cannot be blank** while the input field is empty:

```
(app.js)

angular.module('myApp', [])
.controller('Ctrl', function($scope) {
  $scope.$watch('myform.myinput.$invalid', function(newval) {
    $scope.isInvalid = newval;
  });
});

(index.html)

<div ng-app="myApp">
  <div ng-controller="Ctrl">
    <form novalidate name="myform">
      <input name="myinput"
             ng-model="formdata.myinput"
             required />
    </form>
    <div ng-show="isInvalid">
      Input field cannot be blank
    </div>
  </div>
</div>
```

 JSFiddle: `http://jsfiddle.net/msfrisbie/40bdaey4/`

Alternately, as the form object is attached to the scope, it is possible to directly detect whether the input is valid in the view:

```
(app.js)

angular.module('myApp', [])
.controller('Ctrl', function() {});

(index.html)

<div ng-app="myApp">
  <div ng-controller="Ctrl">
    <form novalidate name="myform">
      <input name="myinput"
             ng-model="formdata.myinput"
             required />
      <div ng-show="myform.myinput.$invalid">
        Input field cannot be blank
      </div>
    </form>
  </div>
</div>
```

 JSFiddle: `http://jsfiddle.net/msfrisbie/bc2hn05p/`

Built-in and custom validators

AngularJS comes bundled with the following basic validators:

- `email`
- `max`
- `maxlength`
- `min`
- `minlength`
- `number`
- `pattern`
- `required`
- `url`

While they are useful and largely self-explanatory, you'll likely want to build a custom validator. To do this, you'll need to construct a directive that will watch the model value of that input field, perform some analysis of it, and manually set the validity of that field using the $setValidity() method.

 As part of the 1.3 release, there is now an alternate method of creating custom form validators. See the *Creating and integrating custom form validators* recipe in *Chapter 9, What's New in AngularJS 1.3*.

The following example creates a custom validator that checks whether an input field is a prime number:

```
(app.js)

angular.module('myApp', [])
.directive('ensurePrime', function() {
  return {
    require: 'ngModel',
    link: function(scope, element, attrs, ctrl) {
      function isPrime(n) {
        if (n<2) {
          return false;
        }

        var m = Math.sqrt(n);

        for (var i=2; i<=m; i++) {
          if (n%i === 0) {
            return false;
          }
        }
        return true;
      }

      scope.$watch(attrs.ngModel, function(newval) {
        if (isPrime(newval)) {
          ctrl.$setValidity('prime', true);
        }
        else {
          ctrl.$setValidity('prime', false);
        }
      });
    }
  };
```

```
});

(index.html)

<div ng-app="myApp">
  <form novalidate name="myform">
    <input type="number"
           ensure-prime name="myinput"
           ng-model="formdata.myinput"
           required />
  </form>
  <div ng-show="myform.myinput.$invalid">
    Input field must be a prime number
  </div>
</div>
```

 JSFiddle: `http://jsfiddle.net/msfrisbie/7mhqvgcp/`

How it works...

AngularJS forms tap into the existing data binding architecture to determine the form state and validation state. The `FormController` instances tied to the form and the input inside it provide a very pleasant, modular way of managing the form flow.

Working with <select> and ngOptions

AngularJS provides an `ngOptions` directive to populate the `<select>` elements in your application. Although this is at first glance a trivial matter, `ngOptions` utilizes a convoluted `comprehension_expression` that can populate the dropdown from a data object in a variety of ways.

Getting ready

Assume that your application is as follows:

```
(app.js)

angular.module('myApp', [])
.controller('Ctrl', function($scope) {
  $scope.players = [
    {
```

```
        number: 17,
        name: 'Alshon',
        position: 'WR'
      },
      {
        number: 15,
        name: 'Brandon',
        position: 'WR'
      },
      {
        number: 22,
        name: 'Matt',
        position: 'RB'
      },
      {
        number: 83,
        name: 'Martellus',
        position: 'TE'
      },
      {
        number: 6,
        name: 'Jay',
        position: 'QB'
      }
    ];

    $scope.team = {
      '3B': {
        number: 9,
        name: 'Brandon'
      },
      '2B': {
        number: 19,
        name: 'Marco'
      },
      '3B': {
        number: 48,
        name: 'Pablo'
      },
      'C': {
        number: 28,
        name: 'Buster'
      },
      'SS': {
```

```
        number: 35,
        name: 'Brandon'
    }
  };
});
```

How to do it...

The ngOptions directive allows you to populate a `<select>` element with both an array and an object's attributes.

Populating with an array

The comprehension expression lets you define how you want to map the data array to a set of `<option>` tags and its string label and corresponding values. The easier implementation is to only define the label string, in which case the application will default to set the `<option>` value to the entire array element, as follows:

```
(index.html)

<div ng-app="myApp">
  <div ng-controller="Ctrl">
    <!-- label for value in array -->
    <select ng-model="player"
            ng-options="p.name for p in players">
    </select>
  </div>
</div>
```

This will compile into the following (with the form CSS classes stripped):

```
<select ng-model="player"
        ng-options="player.name for player in players">
  <option value="?" selected="selected"></option>
  <option value="0">Alshon</option>
  <option value="1">Brandon</option>
  <option value="2">Matt</option>
  <option value="3">Martellus</option>
  <option value="4">Jay</option>
</select>
```

 JSFiddle: http://jsfiddle.net/msfrisbie/vy62c575/

Here, the values of each option are the array indices of the corresponding element. As the model it is attached to is not initialized to any of the present elements, AngularJS inserts a temporary null value into the list until a selection is made, at which point the empty value will be stripped out. When a selection is made, the player model will be assigned to the entire object at that array index.

Explicitly defining the option values

If you don't want to have the `<option>` HTML value assigned the array index, you can override this with a `track by` clause, as follows:

```
(index.html)

<div ng-app="myApp">
  <div ng-controller="Ctrl">
    <!-- label for value in array -->
    <select ng-model="player"
            ng-options="p.name for p in players track by p.number">
    </select>
  </div>
</div>
```

This will compile into the following:

```
<select ng-model="player"
        ng-options="p.name for p in players track by p.number">
  <option value="?" selected="selected"></option>
  <option value="17">Alshon</option>
  <option value="15">Brandon</option>
  <option value="22">Matt</option>
  <option value="83">Martellus</option>
  <option value="6">Jay</option>
</select>
```

 JSFiddle: `http://jsfiddle.net/msfrisbie/umehb407/`

Making a selection will still assign the corresponding object in the array to the `player` model.

Explicitly defining the option model assignment

If instead you wanted to explicitly control the value of each `<option>` element and force it to be the number attribute of each array element, you can do the following:

```
(index.html)

<div ng-app="myApp">
  <div ng-controller="Ctrl">
    <!-- label for value in array -->
    <select ng-model="player"
            ng-options="p.number as p.name for p in players">
    </select>
  </div>
</div>
```

This will compile into the following (with the form CSS classes stripped):

```
<select ng-model="player"
        ng-options="p.number as p.name for p in players">
  <option value="?" selected="selected"></option>
  <option value="17">Alshon</option>
  <option value="15">Brandon</option>
  <option value="22">Matt</option>
  <option value="83">Martellus</option>
  <option value="6">Jay</option>
</select>
```

 JSFiddle: `http://jsfiddle.net/msfrisbie/jtsz46cp/`

However, now when an `<option>` element is selected, the `player` model will only be assigned the number attribute of the corresponding object.

Implementing option groups

If you want to take advantage of the grouping abilities for the `<select>` elements, you can add a `group by` clause, as follows:

```
(index.html)

<div ng-app="myApp">
  <div ng-controller="Ctrl">
    <!-- label for value in array -->
    <select ng-model="player"
```

```
          ng-options="p.name group by p.position for p in
             players">
    </select>
  </div>
</div>
```

This will compile to the following:

```
<select ng-model="player"
        ng-options="p.name group by p.position for p in players">
  <option value="?" selected="selected"></option>
  <optgroup label="WR">
    <option value="0">Alshon</option>
    <option value="1">Brandon</option>
  </optgroup>
  <optgroup label="RB">
    <option value="2">Matt</option>
  </optgroup>
  <optgroup label="TE">
    <option value="3">Martellus</option>
  </optgroup>
  <optgroup label="QB">
    <option value="4">Jay</option>
  </optgroup>
</select>
```

[JSFiddle: http://jsfiddle.net/msfrisbie/2d6mdt9m/]

Null options

If you want to allow a `null` option, you can explicitly define one inside your `<select>` tag, as follows:

```
(index.html)

<select ng-model="player" ng-options="comprehension_expression">
  <option value="">Choose a player</option>
</select>
```

Populating with an object

The `<select>` elements that use `ngOptions` can also be populated from an object's attributes. It functions similarly to how you would process a data array; the only difference being that you must define how the key-value pairs in the object will be used to generate the list of `<option>` elements. For a simple utilization to map the value object's number property to the entire value object, you can do the following:

```
(index.html)

<div ng-app="myApp">
  <div ng-controller="Ctrl">
    <!-- label for value in array -->
    <select ng-model="player"
            ng-options="p.number for (pos, p) in team">
    </select>
  </div>
</div>
```

This will compile into the following:

```
<select ng-model="player"
        ng-options="p.number for (pos, p) in team">
  <option value="?" selected="selected"></option>
  <option value="1B">9</option>
  <option value="2B">19</option>
  <option value="3B">48</option>
  <option value="C">28</option>
  <option value="SS">35</option>
</select>
```

 JSFiddle: `http://jsfiddle.net/msfrisbie/zofojs7n/`

The `<option>` values default to the key string, but the `player` model assignment will still be assigned the entire object that the key refers to.

Explicitly defining option values

If you don't want to have the `<option>` HTML value assigned the property key, you can override this with a `select as` clause:

```
(index.html)

<div ng-app="myApp">
  <div ng-controller="Ctrl">
    <!-- label for value in array -->
```

```
    <select ng-model="player"
            ng-options="p.number as p.name for (pos, p) in team">
    </select>
  </div>
</div>
```

This will compile into the following:

```
<select ng-model="player"
        ng-options="p.number as p.name for (pos, p) in team">
  <option value="?" selected="selected"></option>
  <option value="1B">Brandon</option>
  <option value="2B">Marco</option>
  <option value="3B">Pablo</option>
  <option value="C">Buster</option>
  <option value="SS">Brandon</option>
</select>
```

 JSFiddle: `http://jsfiddle.net/msfrisbie/ssLzvtaf/`

Now, when an `<option>` element is selected, the `player` model will only be assigned the number property of the corresponding object.

How it works...

The `ngOptions` directive simply breaks apart the enumerable entity it is passed, into digestible pieces that can be converted into `<option>` tags.

There's more...

Inside a `<select>` tag, `ngOptions` is heavily preferred to `ngRepeat` for performance reasons. Data binding isn't as necessary in the case of dropdown values, so an `ngRepeat` implementation for a dropdown that must watch many values in the collection adds unnecessary data binding overhead to the application.

Building an event bus

Depending on the purpose of your application, you might find yourself with the need to utilize a **publish-subscribe** (**pub-sub**) architecture to accomplish certain features. AngularJS provides the proper toolkit to accomplish this, but there are considerations that need to be made to prevent performance degradation and keep the application organized.

Formerly, using the `$broadcast` service from a scope with a large number of descendant scopes incurred a significant performance hit due to the large number of potential listeners that needed to be handled. In the AngularJS 1.2.7 release, an optimization was introduced to `$broadcast` that limits the reach of the event to only the scopes that are listening for it. With this, `$broadcast` can be used more freely throughout your application, but there is still a void to be filled to service applications that demand a pub-sub architecture. Simply put, your application should be able to broadcast an event to subscribers throughout the entire application without utilizing `$rootScope.$broadcast()`.

Getting ready

Suppose you have an application that has multiple disparate scopes existing throughout it that need to react to a singular event, as shown here:

```
(app.js)
```

```
angular.module('pubSubApp', [])
.controller('Ctrl', function($scope) {})
.directive('myDir', function() {
  return {
    scope: {},
    link: function(scope, el, attrs) {}
  };
});
```

 Only a single controller and directive are shown here, but an unlimited number of application components that have access to a scope object can tap into the event bus.

How to do it...

In order to avoid using `$rootScope.$broadcast()`, the `$rootScope` will instead be used as a unification point for application-wide messaging. Utilizing `$rootScope.$on()` and `$rootScope.$emit()` allows you to compartmentalize the actual message broadcasting to a single scope and have child scopes inject `$rootScope` and tap into the event bus within it.

Basic implementation

The most basic and naive implementation is to inject `$rootScope` into every location where you need to access the event bus and configure the events locally, as shown here:

```
(index.html)
```

```
<div ng-app="myApp">
```

```
  <div ng-controller="Ctrl">
    <button ng-click="generateEvent()">Generate event</button>
  </div>
  <div my-dir></div>
</div>

(app.js)

angular.module('myApp',[])
.controller('Ctrl', function($scope, $rootScope, $log) {
  $scope.generateEvent = function() {
    $rootScope.$emit('busEvent');
  };
  $rootScope.$on('busEvent', function() {
    $log.log('Handler called!');
  });
})
.directive('myDir', function($rootScope, $log) {
  return {
    scope: {},
    link: function(scope, el, attrs) {
      $rootScope.$on('busEvent', function() {
        $log.log('Handler called!');
      });
    }
  };
});
```

 JSFiddle: `http://jsfiddle.net/msfrisbie/5ot5scja/`

With this setup, even a directive with an isolate scope can utilize the event bus to communicate with a controller that it otherwise would not be able to.

Cleanup

If you're paying close attention, you might have noticed that using this pattern introduces a small problem. Controllers in AngularJS are not singletons, and therefore they require more careful memory management when using this type of cross-application architecture.

Specifically, when a controller in your application is destroyed, the event listener attached to a foreign scope that was declared inside it will not be garbage collected, which will lead to memory leaks. To prevent this, registering an event listener with $on() will return a deregistration function that must be called on the $destroy event. This can be done as follows:

```
(app.js)

angular.module('myApp',[])
.controller('Ctrl', function($scope, $rootScope, $log) {
  $scope.generateEvent = function() {
    $rootScope.$emit('busEvent');
  };

  var unbind = $rootScope.$on('busEvent', function() {
    $log.log('Handler called!');
  });

  $scope.$on('$destroy', unbind);

})
.directive('myDir', function($rootScope, $log) {
  return {
    scope: {},
    link: function(scope, el, attrs) {
      var unbind = $rootScope.$on('busEvent', function() {
        $log.log('Handler called!');
      });

      scope.$on('$destroy', unbind);
    }
  };
});
```

 JSFiddle: http://jsfiddle.net/msfrisbie/xq05p9dt/

Event bus as a service

The event bus logic can be delegated to a service factory. This service can then be dependency-injected anywhere to communicate application-wide events to wherever else listeners exist. This can be done as follows:

```
(app.js)

angular.module('myApp',[])
.controller('Ctrl',function($scope, EventBus, $log) {
  $scope.generateEvent = function() {
    EventBus.emitMsg('busEvent');
  };

  EventBus.onMsg(
    'busEvent',
    function() {
      $log.log('Handler called!');
    },
    $scope
  );
})
.directive('myDir',function($log, EventBus) {
  return {
    scope: {},
    link: function(scope, el, attrs) {
      EventBus.onMsg(
        'busEvent',
        function() {
          $log.log('Handler called!');
        },
        scope
      );
    }
  };
})
.factory('EventBus', function($rootScope) {
  var eventBus = {};
  eventBus.emitMsg = function(msg, data) {
    data = data || {};
    $rootScope.$emit(msg, data);
  };
  eventBus.onMsg = function(msg, func, scope) {
    var unbind = $rootScope.$on(msg, func);
    if (scope) {
```

```
      scope.$on('$destroy', unbind);
    }
    return unbind;
  };
  return eventBus;
});
```

 JSFiddle: http://jsfiddle.net/msfrisbie/m88ruycx/

Event bus as a decorator

The best and cleanest implementation of an event bus is to implicitly add the publish and subscribe utility methods to all scopes by decorating the $rootScope object during the application's initialization, specifically, the config phase:

(app.js)

```
angular.module('myApp',[])
.config(function($provide){
  $provide.decorator('$rootScope', function($delegate){
    // adds to the constructor prototype to allow
    // use in isolate scopes
    var proto = $delegate.constructor.prototype;

    proto.subscribe = function(event, listener) {
      var unsubscribe = $delegate.$on(event, listener);
      this.$on('$destroy', unsubscribe);
    };

    proto.publish = function(event, data) {
      $delegate.$emit(event, data);
    };

    return $delegate;
  });
})
.controller('Ctrl',function($scope, $log) {
  $scope.generateEvent = function() {
    $scope.publish('busEvent');
  };

  $scope.subscribe('busEvent', function() {
    $log.log('Handler called!');
```

```
      });
    })
    .directive('myDir', function($log) {
      return {
        scope: {},
        link: function(scope, el, attrs) {
          scope.subscribe('busEvent', function() {
            $log.log('Handler called!');
          });
        }
      };
    });
```

 JSFiddle: `http://jsfiddle.net/msfrisbie/5madmyzt/`

How it works...

The event bus acts as a single target of indirection between the disparate entities in the application. As the events do not escape the $rootScope object, and $rootScope can be dependency-injected, you are creating an application-wide messaging network.

There's more...

Performance is always a consideration when it comes to events. It is cleaner and more efficient to delegate as much of your application as possible to the data binding/model layer, but when there are global events that require you to propagate events (such as a login/logout), events can be an extremely useful tool.

6

Testing in AngularJS

In this chapter, we will cover the following recipes:

- ▸ Configuring and running your test environment in Yeoman and Grunt
- ▸ Understanding Protractor
- ▸ Incorporating E2E tests and Protractor in Grunt
- ▸ Writing basic unit tests
- ▸ Writing basic E2E tests
- ▸ Setting up a simple mock backend server
- ▸ Writing DAMP tests
- ▸ Using the Page Object test pattern

Introduction

Since its inception, AngularJS has always been a framework built with maximum testability in mind. Developers are often averse to devoting substantial time towards creating a test suite for their application, yet we all know only too well how wrong things can go when untested or partially tested code is shipped to production.

One could fill an entire book with the various tools and methodologies available for testing AngularJS applications, but a pragmatic developer likely desires a solution that is uncomplicated and gets out of the way of the application's development. This chapter will focus on the most commonly used components and practices that are at the core of the majority of test suites, as well as the best practices that yield the most useful and maintainable tests.

Furthermore, preferred testing utilities have evolved substantially over the AngularJS releases spanning the past year. This chapter will only cover the most up-to-date strategies used for AngularJS testing.

 The AngularJS testing ecosystem is incredibly dynamic in nature. It would be futile to attempt to describe the exact methods by which you can set up an entire testing infrastructure as their components and relationships constantly evolve, and will certainly differ as the core team continues to churn out new releases. Instead, this chapter will describe the supporting test software setup from a high level and the test syntax at the code level of detail. I will add errata and updates to this chapter at `https://gist.github.com/msfrisbie/b0c6eceb11adfbcbf482`.

Configuring and running your test environment in Yeoman and Grunt

The Yeoman project is an extremely popular scaffolding tool that allows the quick startup and growth of an AngularJS codebase. Bundled in it is Grunt, which is the JavaScript task runner that you will use in order to automate your application's environment, including running and managing your test utilities. Yeoman will provide much of your project structure for you out of the box, including but not limited to the npm and Bower dependencies and also the Gruntfile, which is the file used for the definition of the Grunt automation.

How to do it...

There is some disagreement over the taxonomy of test types, but with AngularJS, the tests will fall into two types: unit tests and end-to-end tests. Unit tests are the black-box-style tests where a piece of the application is isolated, has external components mocked out for simulation, is fed controlled input, and has its functionality/output verified. End-to-end tests simulate proper application-level behavior by simulating a user interacting with components of the application and making sure that they operate properly by creating an actual browser instance that loads and executes your application code.

Using the right tools for the job

AngularJS unit tests utilize the Karma test runner to run unit tests. Karma has long been the gold standard for AngularJS tests, and it integrates well with Yeoman and Grunt for automatic test file generation and test running. Much of the setup for Karma unit testing is already done for you with Yeoman.

Formerly, AngularJS provided a tool called the Angular Scenario Runner to run end-to-end tests. This is no longer the case; a modern test suite will now utilize Protractor, which is a new end-to-end testing framework built specifically for AngularJS. Protractor currently does not come configured by default when bootstrapping AngularJS project files, so a manual integration of it into your Gruntfile will be necessary.

Conveniently, both Karma unit tests and Protractor end-to-end tests utilize the Jasmine test syntax.

Both Karma and Protractor will require `*.conf.js` files, which will act as the test suite directors when invoked by Grunt. Protractor installation requires manual work, which is provided in detail in the *Incorporating E2E tests and Protractor in Grunt* recipe.

How it works...

Once the testing is set up, running and evaluating your test suite is simple. Karma and Protractor will run separately, one after the other (depending on which comes first in the `grunt test` task). Each of them will spawn some form of browser in which they will perform the tests. Karma will generally utilize PhantomJS to run the unit tests in a headless browser, and Protractor will utilize Selenium WebDriver to spawn an actual browser instance (or instances, depending on how it is configured) and run the end-to-end tests on your actual application that is running in the browser, which you will be able to see happening if it is running on your local environment.

Downloading the example code

You can download the example code files for all Packt books you have purchased from your account at `http://www.packtpub.com`. If you purchased this book elsewhere, you can visit `http://www.packtpub.com/support` and register to have the files e-mailed directly to you.

There's more...

After running the test suite, the console output of Grunt will inform you of any test failures and other metadata about the test run. The output of a successfully run test suite, both unit tests and end-to-end tests with no errors, will include something similar to the following:

```
Running "karma:unit" (karma) task
INFO [karma]: Karma v0.12.23 server started at http://localhost:8080/
INFO [launcher]: Starting browser PhantomJS
INFO [PhantomJS 1.9.7 (Mac OS X)]: Connected on socket
sYgu4c8ZxNFs73zBe_xq with id 75044421
```

```
PhantomJS 1.9.7 (Mac OS X): Executed 3 of 3 SUCCESS (0.017 secs /
0.015 secs)

Running "protractor:run" (protractor) task
Starting selenium standalone server...
Selenium standalone server started at http://192.168.1.120:59539/wd/
hub
. . . . .

Finished in 7.965 seconds
5 tests, 19 assertions, 0 failures

Shutting down selenium standalone server.

Done, without errors.
Total 19.3s
```

Error messages in AngularJS are always getting better, and the AngularJS team is actively working to make failures easier to diagnose by providing detailed error messages and better stack traces. When a test fails, the string identifiers that Jasmine allows you to provide while writing the tests will quickly allow the developer who is running the tests to identify the problem. This is shown in the following error output:

```
Running "karma:unit" (karma) task
INFO [karma]: Karma v0.12.23 server started at http://localhost:8080/
INFO [launcher]: Starting browser PhantomJS
INFO [PhantomJS 1.9.7 (Mac OS X)]: Connected on socket
HVy4JBfIMACzUGR8gPFY with id 29687037
PhantomJS 1.9.7 (Mac OS X) Controller: HandleCtrl Should mark handles
which are too short as invalid FAILED
    Expected false to be true.
PhantomJS 1.9.7 (Mac OS X): Executed 3 of 3 (1 FAILED) (0.018 secs /
0.014 secs)
Warning: Task "karma:unit" failed. Use --force to continue.

Aborted due to warnings.
```

See also

> The *Understanding Protractor* recipe provides greater insight into what the Protractor test runner really is

> The *Incorporating E2E tests and Protractor in Grunt* recipe gives a thorough explanation of how to set up your test suite in order to use Protractor as its end-to-end test runner

Understanding Protractor

Protractor is new to the scene in AngularJS and is intended to fully supplant the now deprecated Angular Scenario Runner.

How it works...

Selenium WebDriver (also referred to as just "WebDriver") is a browser automation tool that provides faculties to script the control of web browsers and the applications that run within them. For the purposes of end-to-end testing, the test runner manifests as three interacting components, as follows:

▶ The formal Selenium WebDriver process, which takes the form of a standalone server with the ability to spawn a browser instance and pipe native events into the page

▶ The test process, which is a Node.js script that runs and checks all the test files

▶ The actual browser instance, which runs the application

Protractor is built on top of WebDriver. It acts as both an extension of WebDriver and also provides supporting software utilities to make end-to-end testing easier. Protractor includes the `webdriver-manager` binary, which exists to make the management of WebDriver easier.

There's more...

Within the tests themselves, Protractor exports a couple of global variables for you to use, which are as follows:

▶ `browser`: This exists to enable you to interact with the URL of the page and the page source. It acts as a WebDriver wrapper, so anything that WebDriver does, Protractor can do too.

▶ `element`: This enables you to interact with specific elements in the DOM using selectors. Besides standard CSS selectors, this also allows you to select the elements with a specific `ng-model` directive or binding.

See also

▶ The *Incorporating E2E tests and Protractor in Grunt* recipe gives a thorough explanation of how to set up your test suite in order to use Protractor as its end-to-end test runner

▶ The *Writing basic E2E tests* recipe demonstrates how to build an end-to-end test foundation for a simple application

Incorporating E2E tests and Protractor in Grunt

Out of the box, Yeoman does not integrate Protractor into its test suite; doing so requires manual work. The Grunt Protractor setup is extremely similar to that of Karma, as they both use the Jasmine syntax and `*.conf.js` files.

 This recipe demonstrates the process of installing and configuring Protractor, but much of this can be generalized to incorporate any new package into Grunt.

Getting ready

The following is a checklist of things to do in order to ensure that your test suite will run correctly:

- Ensure that the `grunt-karma` extension is installed using the `npm install grunt-karma --save-dev` command
- Save yourself the trouble of having to list out all the needed Grunt tasks in your Gruntfile by automatically loading them, as follows:
    - Install the `load-grunt-tasks` module using the `npm install load-grunt-tasks --save-dev` command
    - Add `require('load-grunt-tasks')(grunt);` inside the `module.exports` function in your Gruntfile

How to do it...

Adding Protractor to your application's test configuration requires you to follow a number of steps in order to get it installed, configured, and automated.

Installation

Incorporating Protractor into Grunt requires the following two npm packages to be installed:

- `protractor`
- `grunt-protractor-runner`

They can be installed by being added to the `package.json` file and by running `npm install`. Alternately, they can be installed from the command line as follows:

```
npm install protractor grunt-protractor-runner --save-dev
```

The `--save-dev` flag will automatically add the packages to the `devDependencies` object in `package.json` if it is present.

Selenium's WebDriver manager

Protractor requires Selenium, a web browser automation tool, to operate. The previous commands will have already incorporated the needed dependencies into your `package.json` file. As a convenience, you should bind the Selenium WebDriver update command to run when you invoke `npm install`. This can be accomplished by adding the highlighted line of the following code snippet (the path to the `webdriver-manager` binary might differ in your local environment):

```
(package.json)

{
  "devDependencies": {
    // long list of node package dependencies
  },
  "scripts": {
    // additional existing script additions may be listed here
    "install": "node node_modules/protractor/bin/webdriver-manager
update"
  }
}
```

The order in which the dependencies are listed is not important.

 JSON does not support comments; they are shown in the preceding code only to provide you context within the file. Attempting to provide a JSON file with JavaScript-style comments in it to the npm installer will cause the installer to fail.

Modifying your Gruntfile

Grunt needs to be informed of where to look for the Protractor configuration file as well as how to use it now that the `npm` module has been installed. Modify your `Gruntfile.js` file as follows:

```
(Gruntfile.js)

module.exports = function (grunt) {

  ...

  // Define the configuration for all the tasks
  grunt.initConfig({

    // long list of configuration options for
```

```
    // grunt tasks like minification, JS linting, etc.

  protractor: {
    options: {
      keepAlive: true,
      configFile: "protractor.conf.js"
    },
    run: {}
  }
}
```

If this is done correctly, it should enable you to call `protractor:run` within a Grunt task.

In order to run Protractor and the E2E test suite when you invoke the `grunt test` command, you must extend the relevant Grunt task, as follows:

```
(Gruntfile.js)

grunt.registerTask('test', [
  // list of subtasks to run during `grunt test`
  'karma',
  'protractor:run'
]);
```

The order of these tasks is not set in stone, but `karma` and `protractor:run` must be ordered to follow any tasks that are involved with the setup of the test servers; so it is prudent to list them last.

Setting your Protractor configuration

Obviously, the Protractor configuration you just set in the Gruntfile refers to a file that doesn't exist yet. Create the `protractor.conf.js` file and add the following:

```
(protractor.conf.js)

exports.config = {
  specs: ['test/e2e/*_test.js'],
  baseUrl: 'http://localhost:9001',
  // your filenames, versions, and paths may differ
  seleniumServerJar: 'node_modules/protractor/selenium/selenium-
server-standalone-2.42.2.jar',
  chromeDriver: 'node_modules/protractor/selenium/chromedriver'
}
```

This points Protractor to your test directory(ies), the Yeoman `baseUrl` that acts as the default test port (9001), and the Selenium server and browser setup files. This Protractor configuration will boot a new instance of a Selenium server every time you run tests, run the E2E tests in the Chrome browser, and strip it down when the tests have finished running.

Running the test suite

If all of these steps were successfully accomplished, running `grunt test` should pound out your entire test suite.

How it works...

Much of the power and utility that Grunt has to offer stems from its modular automation topology. The setup you just configured works roughly as follows:

1. The `grunt test` command is run from the command line.
2. Grunt matches the test to its corresponding task definition in the `Gruntfile.js` file.
3. The tasks defined within the test are run sequentially, eventually coming to the `protractor:run` entry.
4. Grunt runs `protractor:run` and matches this to the Protractor configuration definition, which resides in the `protractor.conf.js` file.
5. Protractor locates `protractor.conf.js`, which at a minimum tells Grunt how to boot a Selenium server, where to find the test files, and the location of the test server.
6. All found tests are run.

See also

▸ The *Understanding Protractor* recipe provides greater insight into what the Protractor test runner really is

▸ The *Writing basic E2E tests* recipe demonstrates how to build an end-to-end test foundation for a simple application

Writing basic unit tests

Unit tests should be the foundation of your test suite. Compared to end-to-end tests, they are generally faster, easier to write, easier to maintain, require less overhead while setting up, more readily scale with the application, and provide a more obvious path to the problem area of the application when you debug a failed test run.

There is a surplus of extremely simplistic testing examples available online and rarely do they present a component or test case that is applicable in a real-world application. Instead, this recipe will jump directly to an understandable application component and show you how to write a full set of tests for it.

Getting ready

For this recipe, it is assumed that you have correctly configured your local setup so that Grunt will be able to find your test file(s) and run them on the Karma test runner.

Suppose that you have the following controller within your application:

```
(app.js)

angular.module('myApp')
.controller('HandleCtrl', function($scope, $http) {
    $scope.handle = '';
    $scope.$watch('handle', function(value) {
        if (value.length < 6) {
            $scope.valid = false;
        } else {
            $http({
                method: 'GET',
                url: '/api/handle/' + value
            }).success(function(data, status) {
                if (status == 200 &&
                    data.handle == $scope.handle &&
                    data.id === null) {
                    $scope.valid = true;
                } else {
                    $scope.valid = false;
                }
            });
        }
    });
});
```

In this example application, a user named Jake Hsu will go through a signup flow and attempt to select a unique handle. In order to guarantee the selection of a unique handle while still in the signup flow, a scope watcher is set up against the server to check whether that handle already exists. Through a mechanism outside the controller (and presumably in the view), the value of $scope.handle will be manipulated, and each time its value changes, the application will send a request to the backend server and set $scope.valid based on what the server returns.

How to do it...

An exhaustive set of unit tests for something like the situation mentioned in the previous section can become quite lengthy. When writing tests for a production application, rarely is it prudent to spend time to create an exhaustive set of unit tests for a component, unless it is critical to the application (payments and authentication come to mind).

Here, it is probably sufficient to create a set of tests that attempts to cover scenarios that mark a handle as invalid on the client side, invalid on the server side, and valid on the server side.

Initializing the unit tests

Before writing the actual tests, it is necessary to create and mock the external components that the test component will interact with. This can be done as follows:

```
(handle_controller_test.js)

// monolithic test suite for HandleCtrl
describe('Controller: HandleCtrl', function() {
  // the components to be tested reside in the myApp module
  // therefore it must be injected
  beforeEach(module('myApp'));

  // values which will be used in multiple closures
  var HandleCtrl, scope, httpBackend, createEndpointExpectation;

  // this will be run before each it(function() {}) clause
  // to create or refresh the involved components
  beforeEach(inject(function($controller, $rootScope, $httpBackend) {

    // creates the mock backend server
    httpBackend = $httpBackend;

    // creates a fresh scope
    scope = $rootScope.$new();

    // creates a new controller instance and inserts
    // the created scope into it
    HandleCtrl = $controller('HandleCtrl', {
      $scope: scope
    });

    // configures the httpBackend to match outgoing requests
    // that are expected to be generated by the controller
```

```
      // and return payloads based on what the request contained;
      // this will only be invoked when needed
      createEndpointExpectation = function() {
        // URL matching utilizes a simple regex here
        // expectGET requires that a request be created
        httpBackend.expectGET(/\/api\/handle\/\w+/i).respond(
          function(method, url, data, headers){
            var urlComponents = url.split("/")
              , handle = urlComponents[urlComponents.length - 1]
              , payload = {handle: handle};

            if (handle == 'jakehsu') {
              // handle exists in database, return ID
              payload.id = 1;
            } else {
              // handle does not exist in database
              payload.id = null;
            };

            // AngularJS allows for this return format;
            // [status code, data, configuration]
            return [200, payload, {}];
          }
        );
      };
  }));

  // configures the httpBackend to check that the mock
  // server did not receive extra requests or did not
  // see a request when it should have expected one
  afterEach(function() {
    // verify that all expect<HTTPverb>() expectations were filled
    httpBackend.verifyNoOutstandingExpectation();
    // verify that the mock server did not receive requests it
    // was not expecting
    httpBackend.verifyNoOutstandingRequest();
  });

  // unit tests go here

});
```

Creating the unit tests

With the unit test initialization complete, you will now be able to formally create the unit tests. Each `it(function() {})` clause will count as one unit test towards the counted total, which can be found in the `grunt test` readout. The unit test is as follows:

```
(handle_controller_test.js)

// describe() serves to annotate what the module will test
describe('Controller: HandleCtrl', function() {

  // unit test initialization
  beforeEach( ... );
  afterEach( ... );

  // client invalidation unit test
  it('Should mark handles which are too short as invalid',
    function() {
      // attempt test handle beneath the character count floor
      scope.handle = 'jake';
      // $watch will not be run until you force a digest loop
      scope.$apply();
      // this clause must be fulfilled for the test to pass
      expect(scope.valid).toBe(false);
    }
  );

  // client validation, server invalidation unit test
  it('Should mark handles which exist on the server as invalid',
    function() {
      // server is set up to expect a specific request
      createEndpointExpectation();
      // attempt test handle above character count floor,
      // but which is defined in the mock server to have already
      // been taken
      scope.handle = 'jakehsu';
      // force a digest loop
      scope.$apply();
      // the mock server will not return a response until
      // flush() is invoked
      httpBackend.flush();
      // this clause must be fulfilled for the test to pass
      expect(scope.valid).toBe(false);
    }
```

```
    );

    // client validation, server invalidation unit test
    it('Should mark handles available on the server as valid',
      function() {
        // server is set up to expect a specific request
        createEndpointExpectation();
        // attempt handle above character floor and
        // which is defined to be available on the mock server
        scope.handle = 'jakehsu123';
        // force a digest loop
        scope.$apply();
        // return a response
        httpBackend.flush();
        // this clause must be fulfilled for the test to pass
        expect(scope.valid).toBe(true);
      }
    );
```

How it works...

Each unit test describes the sequential components that describe a scenario that the application is supposed to handle. Though the JavaScript that is natively executed in the browser is heavily asynchronous, the unit test faculties provide a great deal of control over these operations such that you can control the completion of asynchronous operations, and therefore test your application's handling of it in different ways. The $http and $digest cycles are both components of AngularJS that are expected to take indeterminate amounts of time to complete. Here though, you are given fine-grained control over their execution, and it is to your advantage to incorporate that ability into the test suite for more extensive test coverage.

Initializing the controller

To test the controller, it and the components it uses must be created or mocked. Creating the controller instance can be easily accomplished with $controller(), but in order to test how it handles scope transformations, it must be provided with a scope instance. Since all scopes prototypically inherit from $rootScope, it is sufficient here to create an instance of $rootScope and provide that as the created controller's scope.

Initializing the HTTP backend

Mocking a backend server can at times seem to be tedious and verbose, but it allows you to very precisely define how your single-page application is expected to interact with remote components.

Here, you invoke `expectGET()` with a URL regex in order to match an outgoing request generated by the controller. You are able to define exactly what happens when that URL sees a request come through, much in the same way that you would when you build a server API.

Here, it is prudent to encapsulate all the backend endpoint initialization within a function because its definition specifies how the application controller must behave for the test to pass. The `$httpBackend` service offers `expect<HTTPverb>()` and `when<HTTPverb>()` for use, and together they allow powerful unit test definition. The `expect()` methods require that they see a matching request to the endpoint during the unit test, whereas the `when()` methods merely enable the mock backend to appropriately handle that request. At the conclusion of each unit test, the `afterEach()` clause verifies that the mock backend has seen all the requests that it was expected to, using the `verifyNoOutstandingExpectation()` method, and that it didn't see any requests it wasn't expected to, using the `verifyNoOutstandingRequest()` method.

Formally running the unit tests

When running the unit tests, AngularJS makes no assumptions about how your application should or might behave with regard to interfacing with components that involve variable latent periods and asynchronous callbacks. The `$watch` expressions and `$httpBackend` will behave exactly as instructed and exactly when instructed.

By their nature, the `$watch` expressions can take a variable amount of time depending on how long it takes the model changes to propagate throughout the scope, and how many digest loops are required for the model to reach equilibrium. When you run a unit test, a scope change (as demonstrated here) will not trigger a `$watch` expression callback until `$apply()` is explicitly invoked. This allows you to use the intermediate logic and other modifications to be made in different ways to fully exercise the conditions under which a `$watch` expression might occur.

Furthermore, it should be obvious that a remote server cannot be relied upon to respond in a timely fashion, or even at all. When you run a unit test, requests can be dispatched to the mock server normally, but the server will delay sending a response and triggering the asynchronous callbacks until it is explicitly instructed to with `flush()`. In a similar fashion, the `$watch` expressions allow you to test the handling of requests that return normally or slowly, as malformed or failed, or time out altogether.

There's more...

Unit tests should be the core of your test suite as they provide the best assurance that the components of your application are behaving as expected. The rule of thumb is: if it's possible to effectively test a component with a unit test, then you should use a unit test.

Writing basic E2E tests

End-to-end tests effectively complement unit tests. Unit tests make no assumptions about the state of the encompassing systems (and thereby require manual work to mock or fabricate that state for the sake of simulation). Unit tests are also intended to test extremely small and often irreducible pieces of functionality. End-to-end tests take an orthogonal approach by creating and manipulating the system state via the means that are usually available to the client or end user and make sure that a complete user interface *flow* can be successfully executed. End-to-end test failures often cannot pinpoint the exact coordinate from which the error originated. However, they are absolutely a necessity in a testing suite since they ensure cooperation between the interacting application components and provide a safety net to catch the application's misbehavior that results from the complexities of a software interconnection.

Getting ready

This recipe will use the same application controller setup from the preceding recipe, *Writing basic unit tests*. Please refer to the setup instructions and code explained there.

In order to provide an interface to utilize the controller, the application will also incorporate the following:

```
(app.js)

angular.module('myApp', [
  'ngRoute'
])
  .config([
    '$routeProvider',
    function($routeProvider){
      $routeProvider
        .when('/signup', {
          templateUrl: 'views/main.html'
        })
        .otherwise({
          redirectTo: '/',
          template: '<a href="/#/signup">Go to signup page</a>'
        });
    }
  ]);

(views/main.html)

<div ng-controller="HandleCtrl">
  <input type="text" ng-model="handle" />
```

```
  <h2 id="success-msg" ng-show="valid">
    That handle is available!
  </h2>
  <h2 id="failure-msg" ng-hide="valid">
    Sorry, that handle cannot be used.
  </h2>
</div>

(index.html)
<body ng-app="myApp">
  <div ng-view=""></div>
</body>
```

 Take note that here, these files are only the notable pieces required for a working application that the Protractor test runner will use. You will need to incorporate these into a full AngularJS application for Protractor to be able to use them.

How to do it...

Your end-to-end test suite should cover all user flows as best as you can. Ideally, you will optimize for a balance between modularity, independence, and redundancy avoidance when you write tests. For example, each individual test probably doesn't need you to log out at the end of the test since this would only serve to slow down the completion of the tests. However, if you are writing E2E tests to verify that your application's authentication scheme prevents unwanted navigation after authentication credentials have been revoked. Then, an array of tests that test actions after logout would be very appropriate. The focus of your tests will vary depending on the style and purpose of your application, and also the bulk and complexity of the codebase behind it.

Since the `protractor.conf.js` file has been instructed to look for test files in the `test/e2e/` directory, the following would be an appropriate test suite in that location:

```
(test/e2e/signup_flow_test.js)

describe('signup flow tests', function() {

  it('should link to /signup if not already there', function() {
    // direct browser to relative url,
    // page will load synchronously
    browser.get('/');

    // locate and grab <a> from page
```

```
    var link = element(by.css('a'));

    // check that the correct <a> is selected
    // by matching contained text
    expect(link.getText()).toEqual('Go to signup page');

    // direct browser to nonsense url
    browser.get('/#/hooplah');

    // simulated click
    link.click();

    // protractor waits for the page to render,
    // then checks the url
    expect(browser.getCurrentUrl()).toMatch('/signup');
  });
});

describe('routing tests', function() {

  var handleInput,
      successMessage,
      failureMessage;

  function verifyInvalid() {
    expect(successMessage.isDisplayed()).toBe(false);
    expect(failureMessage.isDisplayed()).toBe(true);
  }

  function verifyValid() {
    expect(successMessage.isDisplayed()).toBe(true);
    expect(failureMessage.isDisplayed()).toBe(false);
  }

  beforeEach(function() {
    browser.get('/#/signup');

    var messages = element.all(by.css('h2'));

    expect(messages.count()).toEqual(2);

    successMessage = messages.get(0);
```

```
      failureMessage = messages.get(1);

      handleInput = element(by.model('handle'));

      expect(handleInput.getText()).toEqual('');

   })

   it('should display invalid handle on pageload', function() {

      verifyInvalid();

      expect(failureMessage.getText()).
        toEqual('Sorry, that handle cannot be used.');
   });

   it('should display invalid handle for insufficient characters',
function() {

      // type to modify model and trigger $watch expression
      handleInput.sendKeys('jake');

      verifyInvalid();
   })

   it('should display invalid handle for a taken handle', function() {

      // type to modify model and trigger $watch expression
      handleInput.sendKeys('jakehsu');

      verifyInvalid();
   })

   it('should display valid handle for an untaken handle', function() {

      // type to modify model and trigger $watch expression
      handleInput.sendKeys('jakehsu123');

      verifyValid();
   })
});
```

How it works...

Protractor utilizes a Selenium server and WebDriver to fully render your application in the browser and to simulate a user interacting with it. The end-to-end test suite provides faculties for you to simulate native browser events in the context of an actual running instance of your application. The end-to-end tests verify correctness not by the JavaScript object state of the application, but rather by inspecting the state of either the browser or the DOM.

Since end-to-end tests are interacting with an actual browser instance, they must be able to manage asynchronicity and uncertainty during execution. To do this, each of the element selectors and assertions in these end-to-end tests return promises. Protractor automatically waits for each promise to get completed before continuing to the next test statement.

There's more...

AngularJS provides the `ngMockE2E` module, which allows you to mock a backend server. Incorporating the module gives you the ability to prevent the application from making actual requests to a server, and instead simulates request handling in a fashion similar to that of the unit tests. However, incorporating this module into your application is actually not recommended in many cases, for the following reasons:

> ▶ Currently, integrating `ngMockE2E` correctly into your end-to-end test runner involves a lot of red tape and can cause problems involving synchronization with Protractor.

> ▶ Mocking out the spectrum of end-to-end backend server responses in the `ngMock` syntax can become very tedious and verbose, as larger applications will demand more complexity in the mock server's response logic.

> ▶ Mocking out the backend endpoints for end-to-end tests defeats much of the purpose of the tests in the first place. The end-to-end tests you write are intended to simulate all components of the application that bind and perform together properly in the context of the user interface. Creating fake responses from the server might ameliorate edge cases that involve backend communication that would otherwise be caught by tests that send requests to a real server.

Therefore, it is encouraged to structure your end-to-end tests in order to send requests to a legitimate backend in order to effectively and more realistically simulate client-server HTTP conversations.

See also

> ▶ The *Setting up a simple mock backend server* recipe demonstrates a clever method that will allow you to iterate quickly with your test suite and application

▶ The *Writing DAMP tests* recipe demonstrates even more best practices for writing AngularJS tests effectively

▶ The *Using the Page Object test pattern* recipe demonstrates even more best practices for writing AngularJS tests effectively

Setting up a simple mock backend server

It isn't hard to realize why having end-to-end tests that communicate with a real server that returns mock responses can be useful. Outside of the testing complexity that involves the business logic your application uses to handle the data returned from the server, the spectrum of possible outcomes when relying upon HTTP communication (timeouts, server errors, and more) should be included in a robust end-to-end test suite. It's no stretch of the imagination then that a superb way of testing these corner cases is to actually create a mock server that your application can hit. You can then configure the mock server to support different endpoints that will have predetermined behavior, such as failing, slow response times, and different response data payloads to name a few.

You are fully able to have your end-to-end tests communicate with the API as they normally would, as the end-to-end test runner does not mock the backend server by default. If this is suitable for your testing purposes, then setting up a mock backend server is probably unnecessary. However, if you wish for your tests to cover operations that are not idempotent or will irreversibly change the state of the backend server, then setting up a mock server makes a good deal of sense.

How to do it...

Selecting a mock server style has essentially no limitations as the only requirement is for it to allow you to manually configure responses upon expected HTTP requests. As you might imagine, this can get as simple or as complex as you want, but the nature of end-to-end testing tends to lead to frequent overhaul and repair of large pieces of the mock HTTP endpoints if they try and replicate large amounts of the production application logic.

If you are able to (and in most cases, you absolutely should be able to) design or refactor your tests in such a way) have your end-to-end tests perform more concise application user flows and mock out the API that it communicates with as simply as possible, you should do it—usually, this mostly means hardcoding the responses. Enter the file-based API server!

```
(httpMockBackend.js)

// Define some initial variables.
var applicationRoot = __dirname.replace(/\\/g,'/')
  , ipaddress = process.env.OPENSHIFT_NODEJS_IP || '127.0.0.1'
  , port = process.env.OPENSHIFT_NODEJS_PORT || 5001
  , mockRoot = applicationRoot + '/test/mocks/api'
```

```
  , mockFilePattern = '.json'
  , mockRootPattern = mockRoot + '/**/*' + mockFilePattern
  , apiRoot = '/api'
  , fs = require("fs")
  , glob = require("glob");

// Create Express application
var express = require('express');
var app = express();

// Read the directory tree according to the pattern specified above.
var files = glob.sync(mockRootPattern);

// Register mappings for each file found in the directory tree.
if(files && files.length > 0) {
  files.forEach(function(filePath) {

    var mapping = apiRoot + filePath.replace(mockRoot, '').
replace(mockFilePattern,'')
      , fileName = filePath.replace(/^.*[\\\/]/, '');

    // set CORS headers so this can be used with local AJAX
    app.all('*', function(req, res, next) {
      res.header("Access-Control-Allow-Origin", "*");
      res.header(
        'Access-Control-Allow-Headers',
        'X-Requested-With'
      );
      next();
    });

    // any HTTP verbs you might need
    [/^GET/, /^POST/, /^PUT/, /^PATCH/, /^DELETE/].forEach(
      function(httpVerbRegex) {

        // perform the initial regex of the HTTP verb
        // against the filename
        var match = fileName.match(httpVerbRegex);

        if (match != null) {
          // remove the HTTP verb prefix from the filename
          mapping = mapping.replace(match[0] + '_', '');

          // create the endpoint
```

```
        app[match[0].toLowerCase()](mapping, function(req,res) {

          // handle the request by responding
          // with the JSON contents of the file
          var data = fs.readFileSync(filePath, 'utf8');
          res.writeHead(200, {
            'Content-Type': 'application/json'
          });
          res.write(data);
          res.end();
        });
      }
    }
  );

  console.log('Registered mapping: %s -> %s', mapping,
    filePath);
});
} else {
  console.log('No mappings found! Please check the
    configuration.');
}

// Start the API mock server.
console.log('Application root directory: [' + applicationRoot
  +']');
console.log('Mock Api Server listening: [http://' + ipaddress +
  ':' + port + ']');
app.listen(port, ipaddress);
```

This is a simple node program that can be run using the following command:

```
$ node httpMockServer.js
```

 This Node.js program is dependent on several npm packages, which can be installed using the `npm install glob fs express` command.

How it works...

This simple `express.js` server conveniently matches the incoming request URLs to the corresponding JSON file in the `test/mocks/api/` child directory, and it matches the HTTP verb of the request to the file prefixed with that verb. So, a GET request to `localhost:5001/api/user` will return the JSON contents of `/test/mocks/api/GET_user.json`, a PATCH request to `localhost:5001/api/user/1` will return the JSON contents of `/test/mocks/api/user/PATCH_1.json`, and so on. Since files are automatically discovered and added to the express routing, this allows you to easily simulate a backend server with very different request types, quickly.

There's more...

This setup is obviously extremely limited in a number of ways, including conditional request handling and authentication, to name a few. This is not intended as a full replacement for a backend by any means, but if you are trying to quickly build a test suite or build a piece of your application that sits atop an HTTP API, you will find this tool very useful.

See also

▶ The *Writing E2E tests* recipe demonstrates the core strategies that should be incorporated into your end-to-end test suite

Writing DAMP tests

Any seasoned developer will almost certainly be familiar with the **Don't Repeat Yourself** (**DRY**) programming principle. When architecting production applications, the DRY principle promotes improved code maintainability by ensuring that there is no logic duplication (or as little as feasibly possible) in order to allow efficient system additions and modifications.

Descriptive And Meaningful Phrases (**DAMP**) on the other hand promotes improved code readability by ensuring that there is not too much abstraction to cause the code to be difficult to understand, even if it is at the expense of introducing redundancy. Jasmine encourages this by providing a **Domain Specific Language** (**DSL**) syntax, which approximates how humans would linguistically declare and reason about how the program should work.

How to do it...

The following tests are a sample of unit tests from the *Writing basic unit tests* recipe, presented here unchanged:

```
it('should display invalid handle for insufficient characters',
function() {

    // type to modify model and trigger $watch expression
    handleInput.sendKeys('jake');

    verifyInvalid();
})

it('should display invalid handle for a taken handle', function() {

    // type to modify model and trigger $watch expression
    handleInput.sendKeys('jakehsu');

    verifyInvalid();
})
```

As is, this would be considered a set of DAMP tests. A developer running these tests would have little trouble quickly piecing together what is supposed to happen, where in the code it's happening, and why the tests might be failing.

However, a DRY-minded developer would examine these tests, identify the redundancy between them, and refactor them into something like the following:

```
it('should reject invalid handles', function() {
    // type to modify model and trigger $watch expression
    ['jake', 'jakehsu'].forEach(function(handle){
        handleInput.clear();
        handleInput.sendKeys(handle);
        verifyInvalid();
    });
});
```

This code is definitely more in line with the DRY principle than the previous one, and the tests will still pass and still test the proper behavior, but there is already a measurable loss of information that hurts the quality of the tests. The initial version of the unit tests presented two test cases that were both supposed to be marked as invalid, but for different reasons—one because of a minimum handle length, one because the request to the mock server reveals that the handle is already taken. If one of those tests were to fail, the developer running them would be directed to the exact test case that was failing, would have good insight into which aspect of the validation was failing, and would be able to quickly act accordingly. In the DRY version of the unit tests, the developer running them would see a failed test, but since the two unit tests were condensed, it isn't immediately obvious which one of them is causing the failure or why it is failing. In this scenario, the DAMP tests are more conducive to rapidly locate and repair bugs that might crop up in the application.

There's more...

The example in this recipe is a relatively simple one, but it demonstrates the fundamental difference between the DAMP and DRY practices. In general, the rule of thumb is for production code to be as DRY as possible, and for test suites to be as DAMP as possible. Production code should be optimized for maintainability, and tests for understandability.

Perhaps counterintuitively, the DAMP principle is not necessarily mutually exclusive with the DRY principle—they are merely suited for different purposes. Unit and end-to-end tests should be DRYed wherever it will make the code more maintainable as long as it doesn't hurt the readability of the tests. Generally, this will fall under the setup and teardown routines for tests—use the DRY principle for these routines as much as possible, since they infrequently contain information or procedures that are relevant to the application component(s) that the test is covering. Authentication and navigation are both good examples of test setup/teardown that respond well to DRY refactoring.

See also

- The *Writing basic E2E tests* recipe demonstrates the core strategies that should be incorporated into your end-to-end test suite
- The *Using the Page Object test pattern* recipe demonstrates even more best practices for writing AngularJS tests effectively

Using the Page Object test pattern

Creating and maintaining a test suite for an application is a considerable amount of overhead, and a prudent developer will mold a test suite such that the normal evolution of a software application will not force developers to spend an unduly long amount of time to maintain the test code.

A surprisingly sensible design pattern called the Page Object pattern encapsulates segments of the page-specific user experience and abstracts it away from the logic of the actual tests.

How to do it...

The `test/e2e/signup_flow_test.js` file presented in the *Writing basic E2E tests* recipe can be refactored into the following files using the Page Object pattern.

The `test/pages/main.js` file can be refactored as follows:

```
(test/pages/main.js)

var MainPage = function () {
  // direct the browser when the page object is initialized
  browser.get('/');
};

MainPage.prototype = Object.create({},
  {
    // getter for element in page
    signupLink: {
      get: function() {
        return element(by.css('a'));
      }
    }
  }
);

module.exports = MainPage;
```

The `test/pages/signup.js` file can be refactored as follows:

```
(test/pages/signup.js)

var SignupPage = function () {
  // direct the browser when the page object is initialized
  browser.get('/#/signup');
};

SignupPage.prototype = Object.create({},
  {
    // getters for elements in the page
    messages: {
      get: function() {
        return element.all(by.css('h2'));
```

```
        }
      },
      successMessage: {
        get: function() {
          return this.messages.get(0);
        }
      },
      failureMessage: {
        get: function() {
          return this.messages.get(1);
        }
      },
      handleInput: {
        get: function() {
          return element(by.model('handle'));
        }
      },
      // getters for page validation
      successMessageVisibility: {
        get: function() {
          return this.successMessage.isDisplayed();
        }
      },
      failureMessageVisibility: {
        get: function() {
          return this.failureMessage.isDisplayed();
        }
      },
      // interface for page element
      typeHandle: {
        value: function(handle) {
          this.handleInput.sendKeys(handle);
        }
      }
    }
  );
```

```
module.exports = SignupPage;
```

The `test/e2e/signup_flow_test.js` file can be refactored as follows:

```
(test/e2e/signup_flow_test.js)
```

```
var SignupPage = require('../pages/signup.js')
```

```
  , MainPage = require('../pages/main.js');

describe('signup flow tests', function() {

  var page;

  beforeEach(function() {
    // initialize the page object
    page = new MainPage();
  });

  it('should link to /signup if not already there', function() {

    // check that the correct <a> is selected
    // by matching contained text
    // expect(link.getText()).toEqual('Go to signup page');
    expect(page.signupLink.getText()).toEqual('Go to signup page');

    // direct browser to nonsense url
    browser.get('/#/hooplah');

    // simulated click
    page.signupLink.click();

    // protractor waits for the page to render,
    // then checks the url
    expect(browser.getCurrentUrl()).toMatch('/signup');
  });
});

describe('routing tests', function() {

  var page;

  function verifyInvalid() {
    expect(page.successMessageVisibility).toBe(false);
    expect(page.failureMessageVisibility).toBe(true);
  }

  function verifyValid() {
    expect(page.successMessageVisibility).toBe(true);
```

```
      expect(page.failureMessageVisibility).toBe(false);
  }

  beforeEach(function() {

    // initialize the page object
    page = new SignupPage();

    // check that there are two messages on the page
    expect(page.messages.count()).toEqual(2);

    // check that the handle input text is empty
    expect(page.handleInput.getText()).toEqual('');

  });

  it('should display invalid handle on pageload', function() {

    // check that initial page state is invalid
    verifyInvalid();

    expect(page.failureMessage.getText()).
      toEqual('Sorry, that handle cannot be used.');
  });

  it('should display invalid handle for insufficient characters',
function() {

    // type to modify model and trigger $watch expression
    page.typeHandle('jake');

    verifyInvalid();
  })

  it('should display invalid handle for a taken handle', function() {

    // type to modify model and trigger $watch expression
    page.typeHandle('jakehsu');

    verifyInvalid();
  })

  it('should display valid handle for an untaken handle', function() {

    // type to modify model and trigger $watch expression
```

```
    page.typeHandle('jakehsu123');

    verifyValid();
  })
})
```

How it works...

It should be immediately obvious as to why this test pattern is desirable. Looking through the actual tests, you now do not need to know any information about the specifics of the page contents to understand how the test is manipulating the application.

The page objects take advantage of the second and optional `objectProperties` argument of `Object.create()` to build a very pleasant interface to the page. By using these page objects, you are able to avoid all of the nastiness of creating a sea of local variables to store references to the pieces of the page. They also offer a great deal of flexibility in terms of where the bulk of your test logic lies. These tests could potentially be refactored even more to move the validation logic into the page objects. Decisions like these are ultimately up to the developer, and it boils down to their preference in terms of how dense the page objects should be.

There's more...

In this example, the page object getter interface is especially useful since the nature of end-to-end tests implies that you will need to evaluate the page state at several checkpoints in the lifetime of the test, and a defined getter that performs this evaluation while appearing as a page object property yields an extremely clean test syntax.

Also note the multiple layers of indirection within the `SignupPage` object. Layering in this fashion is absolutely to your advantage, and the page object is a prime place in your end-to-end tests where it really does pay to be DRY. Repetitious location of elements on the page is not the place for verbosity!

See also

- ▶ The *Writing basic E2E tests* recipe demonstrates the core strategies that should be incorporated into your end-to-end test suite

- ▶ The *Writing DAMP tests* recipe demonstrates even more best practices for writing AngularJS tests effectively

7
Screaming Fast AngularJS

In this chapter, we will cover the following recipes:

- ▸ Recognizing AngularJS landmines
- ▸ Creating a universal watch callback
- ▸ Inspecting your application's watchers
- ▸ Deploying and managing `$watch` types efficiently
- ▸ Optimizing the application using reference `$watch`
- ▸ Optimizing the application using equality `$watch`
- ▸ Optimizing the application using `$watchCollection`
- ▸ Optimizing the application using `$watch` deregistration
- ▸ Optimizing template-binding watch expressions
- ▸ Optimizing the application with the compile phase in `ng-repeat`
- ▸ Optimizing the application using track by in `ng-repeat`
- ▸ Trimming down watched models

Introduction

As with most technologies, in AngularJS, the devil is in the details.

In general, the lion's share of encounters with AngularJS's sluggishness is a result of overloading the application's data-binding bandwidth. Doing so is quite easy, and a normative production application contains a substantial amount of data binding, which makes architecting a snappy application all the more difficult. Thankfully, for all the difficulties and snags that one can encounter involving scaled data binding, the use of regimented best practices and gaining an appreciation of the underlying framework structure will allow you to effectively circumnavigate performance pitfalls.

Recognizing AngularJS landmines

Implementation of configurations and combinations that lead to severe performance degradation is often difficult to pinpoint as the contributing components by themselves often appear to be totally innocuous.

How to do it...

The following scenarios are just a handful of the commonly encountered scenarios that degrade the application's performance and responsiveness.

Expensive filters in ng-repeat

Filters will be executed every single time the enumerable collection detects a change, as shown here:

```
<div ng-repeat="val in values | filter:slowFilter"></div>
```

Building and using filters that require a great deal of processing is not advisable as you must assume that filters will be called a huge number of times throughout the life of the application.

Deep watching a large object

You might find it tempting to create a scope watcher that evaluates the entirety of a model object; this is accomplished by passing in `true` as the final argument, as shown here:

```
$scope.$watch(giganticObject, function() { ... }, true);
```

This is a poor design decision as AngularJS needs to be able to determine whether or not the object has changed between `$digest` cycles, which of course means storing a history of the object's exact value, as well as exhaustively comparing it each time.

Using $watchCollection when the index of change is needed

Although it is extremely convenient in a number of scenarios, $watchCollection can trap you if you try to locate the index of change within it. Consider the following code:

```
$scope.$watchCollection(giganticArray, function(newVal, oldVal, scope)
{
  var count = 0;
  // iterate through newVal array
  angular.forEach(newVal, function(oldVal) {
    // if the array snapshot index doesn't match,
    // this implies a change in model value
    if (newVal[count] !== oldVal[count]) {
      // logic for matched object delta
    }
    count++;
  });
});
```

In every $digest cycle, the watcher will iterate through each watched array in order to find the index/indices that have changed. Since this watcher is expected to be invoked quite often, this approach has the potential to introduce performance-related problems as the watched collection grows.

Keeping template watchers under control

Each bound expression in a template will register its own watch list entry in order to keep the data fully bound to the view. Suppose that you were working with data in a 2D grid, as follows:

```
<div ng-repeat="row in rows">
  <div ng-repeat="val in row">
    {{ val }}
  </div>
</div>
```

Assuming that rows is an array of arrays, this template fragment creates a watcher for every individual element in the 2D array. Since watch lists are processed linearly, this approach obviously has the potential to severely degrade the application's performance.

There's more...

These are only a handful of scenarios that can cause problems for your application. There is a virtually unlimited number of possible configurations that can cause an unexpected slowdown in your application, but being vigilant and watching out for common performance anti-patterns will ameliorate much of the headache that comes along with debugging the slowness of an application.

See also

▸ The *Creating a universal watch callback* recipe provides the details of how to keep track of how often your application's watchers are being invoked

▸ The *Inspecting your application's watchers* recipe shows you how to inspect the internals of your application in order to find where your watchers are concentrated

▸ The *Deploying and managing $watch types efficiently* recipe describes the methods for keeping your application's watch bloat under control

Creating a universal watch callback

Since a multiplicity of AngularJS watchers is so commonly the root cause of performance problems, it is quite valuable to be able to monitor your application's watch list and activity. Few beginner level AngularJS developers realize just how often the framework is doing the dirty checking for them, and having a tool that gives them direct insight into when the framework is spending time to perform model history comparisons can be extremely useful.

How to do it...

The `$scope.$watch()`, `$scope.$watchGroup()`, and `$scope.$watchCollection()` methods are normally keyed with a stringified object path, which becomes the target of the change listener. However, if you wish to register a callback for any watch callback irrespective of the change listener target, you can decline to provide a change listener target, as follows:

```
// invoked once every time $scope.foo is modified
$scope.$watch('foo', function(newVal, oldVal, scope) {
  // newVal is the current value of $scope.foo
  // oldVal is the previous value of $scope.foo
  // scope === $scope
});

// invoked once every time $scope.bar is modified
$scope.$watch('bar', function(newVal, oldVal, scope) {
  // newVal is the current value of $scope.bar
  // oldVal is the previous value of $scope.bar
  // scope === $scope
});

// invoked once every $digest cycle
$scope.$watch(function(scope) {
  // scope === $scope
});
```

JSFiddle: `http://jsfiddle.net/msfrisbie/r36ak6my/`

How it works...

There's no trickery here; the universal watcher is a feature that is explicitly provided by AngularJS. Although it invokes `$watch()` on a scope object, the callback will be executed for every model's modification, independent of the scope upon which it is defined.

There's more...

Although the watch callback will occur for model modifications anywhere, the lone `scope` parameter for the callback will always be the scope upon which the watcher was defined, not the scope in which the modification occurred.

 Since using a universal watcher attaches additional logic to every `$digest` cycle, it will severely degrade the application's performance and should only be used for debugging purposes.

See also

▶ The *Inspecting your application's watchers* recipe shows you how to inspect the internals of your application in order to find where your watchers are concentrated

▶ The *Deploying and managing $watch types efficiently* recipe describes the methods to keep your application's watch bloat under control

Inspecting your application's watchers

The Batarang browser plugin allows you to inspect the application's watch tree, but there are many scenarios where dynamically inspecting the watch list within the console or application code can be more helpful when debugging or making design decisions.

How to do it...

The following function can be used to inspect all or part of the DOM for watchers. It accepts an optional DOM element as an argument.

```
var getWatchers = function (element) {
  // convert to a jqLite/jQuery element
  // angular.element is idempotent
```

```
    var el = angular.element(
        // defaults to the body element
        element || document.getElementsByTagName('body')
      )
      // extract the DOM element data
      , elData = el.data()
      // initalize returned watchers array
      , watchers = [];

    // AngularJS lists watches in 3 categories
    // each contains an independent watch list
    angular.forEach([
        // general inherited scope
        elData.$scope,
        // isolate scope attached to templated directive
        elData.$isolateScope,
        // isolate scope attached to templateless directive
        elData.$isolateScopeNoTemplate
      ],
      function (scope) {
        // each element may not have a scope class attached
        if (scope) {
          // attach the watch list
          watchers = watchers.concat(scope.$$watchers || []);
        }
      }
    );

    // recurse through DOM tree
    angular.forEach(el.children(), function (childEl) {
      watchers = watchers.concat(getWatchers(childEl));
    });

    return watchers;
  };
```

 JSFiddle: http://jsfiddle.net/msfrisbie/d58g77m1/

With this, you are able to call the function with a DOM node and ascertain which watchers exist inside it, as follows:

```
// all watchers in the document
getWatchers(document);

// all watchers in the signup form with a selector
getWatchers(document.getElementById('signup-form'));

// all watchers in <div class="container"></div>
getWatchers($('div.container'));
```

How it works...

It is possible to access a DOM element's `$scope` object (without injecting it) through the jQuery/jqLite element object's `data()` method. The `$scope` object has a `$$watchers` property that lists how many watchers are actively defined upon that `$scope` object.

The preceding function exhaustively recurses through the DOM tree and inspects each node in order to determine whether it has a scope attached to it. If it does, any watchers defined on that scope are read and entered into the master watch list.

There's more...

This is only a single, general implementation of watcher inspection. Since watchers are localized to a single scope, it might behoove you to utilize components of this function in order to inspect single scope instances instead of the child DOM subtree.

See also

- The *Recognizing AngularJS landmines* recipe demonstrates common performance-leeching scenarios

- The *Creating a universal watch callback* recipe provides the details of how to keep track of how often your application's watchers are being invoked

- The *Deploying and managing $watch types efficiently* recipe describes the methods for keeping your application's watch bloat under control

Deploying and managing $watch types efficiently

The beast behind AngularJS's data binding is its dirty checking and the overhead that comes along with it. As you tease apart your application's innards, you will find that even the most elegantly architected applications incur a substantial amount of dirty checking. This, of course, is normal, and the framework is architected as to be able to handle the hugely variable loads of dirty checking that different sorts of applications might throw at it. Nevertheless, the nature of object comparison performance at scale (hint—*it is slow*) requires that dirty checking is minimally deployed, efficiently organized, and appropriately targeted. Even with the rigorous engineering and optimization behind AngularJS's dirty checking, it remains the case that it is still deceptively easy to bog down an application's performance with superfluous data comparison. In the same way that a single uncooperative person backpaddling in a canoe can bring a vessel to a halt, a single careless watch statement can bring an AngularJS application's responsiveness to its knees.

How to do it...

Strategies to deploy watchers efficiently can be summed up as follows.

Watch as little of the model as possible

Watchers check the portion of the model they are bound to extremely frequently. If a change in a piece of the model does not affect what the watch callback does, then the watcher shouldn't need to worry about it.

Keep watch expressions as lightweight as possible

The watch expression `$scope.$watch('myWatchExpression', function() {});` will be evaluated in every digest cycle in order to determine the output. You'll be able to put expressions such as `3 + 6` or `myFunc()` as the expression, but these will be evaluated in every single digest cycle in an effort to obtain a fresh return value in order to compare it against the last recorded return value. Very rarely is this necessary, so stick to binding watchers to model properties.

Use the fewest number of watchers possible

It stands to reason that, as the entire watch list must be evaluated in every `$digest` cycle, fewer watchers in that list will yield a speedier `$digest` cycle.

Keep the watch callbacks small and light

The watch callbacks get called as often as the watch expression changes, which can be quite a lot depending on the application. As a result, it is unwise to keep high-latency calculations or requests in the callback.

Create DRY watchers

Though unrelated to performance, maintaining huge groups of watchers can become extremely tedious. The `$watchCollection` and `$watchGroup` utilities provided by AngularJS greatly assist in watcher consolidation.

See also

▶ The *Recognizing AngularJS landmines* recipe demonstrates common performance-leeching scenarios

▶ The *Optimizing the application using reference $watch* recipe demonstrates how to effectively deploy the basic watch type

▶ The *Optimizing the application using equality $watch* recipe demonstrates how to effectively deploy the deep watch type

▶ The *Optimizing the application using $watchCollection* recipe demonstrates how to utilize the intermediate depth watcher in your application

▶ The *Optimizing the application using $watch deregistration* recipe shows how your application can evict watch list entries when they are no longer required

▶ The *Optimizing template-binding watch expressions* recipe explains how AngularJS manages your implicitly-created watchers for template data binding

Optimizing the application using reference $watch

Reference watches register a listener that uses strict equality (===) as the comparator, which verifies the congruent object identity or primitive equality. The implication of this is that a change will only be registered if the model the watcher is listening to is assigned to a new object.

How to do it...

The reference watcher should be used when the object's properties are unimportant. It is the most efficient of the `$watch` types as it only demands top-level object comparison.

The watcher can be created as follows:

```
$scope.myObj = {
  myPrim: 'Go Bears!',
  myArr: [3,1,4,1,5,9]
};

// watch myObj by reference
```

```
$scope.$watch('myObj', function(newVal, oldVal, scope) {
  // callback logic
});

// watch only the myPrim property of myObj by reference
$scope.$watch('myObj.myPrim', function(newVal, oldVal, scope) {
  // callback logic
});

// watch only the second element of myObj.myArr by reference
$scope.$watch('myObj.myArr[1]', function(newVal, oldVal, scope) {
  // callback logic
});
```

 An observant reader will note that some of these examples are technically redundant in what they demonstrate; this will be explained further in the *How it works...* section.

How it works...

The reference comparator will only invoke the watch callback upon object reassignment.

Suppose that a `$scope` object was initialized as follows:

```
$scope.myObj = {
  myPrim: 'Go Bears!'
};
$scope.myArr = [3,1,4,1,5,9];

// watch myObj by reference
$scope.$watch('myObj', function() {
  // callback logic
});
// watch myArr by reference
$scope.$watch('myArr', function() {
  // callback logic
});
```

Any assignment of the watched object to a different primitive or object will register as dirty. The following examples will cause a callback to execute:

```
$scope.myArr = [];
$scope.myObj = 1;
$scope.myObj = {};
```

Beneath the top-level reference watching, any changes that affect the *inside* of the object will not register as changes. This includes modification, creation, and deletion. The following will *not* cause the callback to execute:

```
// replace existing property
$scope.myObj.myPrim = 'Go Giants!';

// add new property
$scope.myObj.newProp = {};

// push onto array
$scope.myArr.push(2);

// modify element of array
$scope.myArr[0] = 6;

// delete property
delete myObj.myPrim;
```

[JSFiddle: `http://jsfiddle.net/msfrisbie/h7hvbfkg/`]

There's more...

The long and short of it is that reference watchers are the most efficient type of watchers, so when you are looking to set up a watcher, reach for this one first.

See also

▸ The *Optimizing the application using equality $watch* recipe demonstrates how to effectively deploy the deep watch type

▸ The *Optimizing the application using $watchCollection* recipe demonstrates how to utilize the intermediate depth watcher in your application

▸ The *Optimizing the application using $watch deregistration* recipe shows how your application can evict watch list entries when no longer required

Optimizing the application using equality $watch

Equality watches register a listener that uses `angular.equals()` as the comparator, which exhaustively examines the entirety of all objects to ensure that their respective object hierarchies are identical. Both a new object assignment and property modification will register as a change and invoke the watch callback.

This watcher should be used when any modification to an object is considered as a change event, such as a user object having its properties at various depths modified.

How to do it...

The equality comparator is used when the optional Boolean third argument is set to `true`. Other than that, these watchers are syntactically identical to reference comparator watchers, as shown here:

```
$scope.myObj = {
  myPrim: 'Go Bears!',
  myArr: [3,1,4,1,5,9]
};

// watch myObj by equality
$scope.$watch('myObj', function(newVal, oldVal, scope) {
  // callback logic
}, true);
```

How it works...

The equality comparator will invoke the watch callback on every modification anywhere on or inside the watched object.

Suppose that a `$scope` object is initialized as follows:

```
$scope.myObj = {
  myPrim: 'Go Bears!'
};
$scope.myArr = [3,1,4,1,5,9];

// watch myObj by equality
$scope.$watch('myObj', function() {
  // callback logic
}, true);
// watch myArr by equality
```

```
$scope.$watch('myArr', function() {
  // callback logic
}, true);
```

All of the following examples will cause a callback to be executed:

```
$scope.myArr = [];
$scope.myObj = 1;
$scope.myObj = {};
$scope.myObj.myPrim = 'Go Giants!';
$scope.myObj.newProp = {};
$scope.myArr.push(2);
$scope.myArr[0] = 6;
delete myObj.myPrim;
```

 JSFiddle: `http://jsfiddle.net/msfrisbie/w24mrkfm/`

There's more...

Since a watcher must store the past version of the watched object to compare against it and perform the actual comparison, equality watchers utilize both the angular.copy() method to store the object and the angular.equals() method to test the equality. For large objects, it is not difficult to discern that these operations will introduce latency into the application. Equality comparator watchers should not be used unless absolutely necessary.

See also

▶ The *Optimizing the application using reference $watch* recipe demonstrates how to effectively deploy the basic watch type

▶ The *Optimizing the application using $watchCollection* recipe demonstrates how to utilize the intermediate depth watcher in your application

▶ The *Optimizing the application using $watch deregistration* recipe shows how your application can evict watch list entries when they are no longer required

Optimizing the application using $watchCollection

AngularJS offers the `$watchCollection` intermediate watch type to register a listener that utilizes a shallow watch depth for comparison. The `$watchCollection` type will register a change event when any of the object's properties are modified, but it is unconcerned with what those properties refer to.

How to do it...

This watcher is best used with arrays or flat objects that undergo frequent top-level property modifications or reassignments. Currently, it does not provide the modified property(s) responsible for the callback, only the entire objects, so the callback is responsible for determining which properties or indices are incongruent. This can be done as follows:

```
$scope.myObj = {
  myPrimitive: 'Go Bears!',
  myArray: [3,1,4,1,5,9]
};

// watch myObj and all top-level properties by reference
$scope.$watchCollection('myObj', function(newVal, oldVal, scope) {
  // callback logic
});

// watch myObj.myArr and all its elements by reference
$scope.$watchCollection('myObj.myArr', function(newVal, oldVal, scope)
{
  // callback logic
});
```

How it works...

The `$watchCollection` utility will set up reference watchers on the model object and all its existing properties. This will invoke the watch callback upon object reassignment or upon top-level property reassignment.

Suppose that a `$scope` object is initialized as follows:

```
$scope.myObj = {
  myPrim: 'Go Bears!',
  innerObj: {
    innerProp: 'Go Bulls!'
  }
```

```
};
$scope.myArr = [3,1,4,1,5,9];

// watch myObj as a collection
$scope.$watchCollection('myObj', function() {
  // callback logic
});
// watch myArr as a collection
$scope.$watchCollection('myArr', function() {
  // callback logic
});
```

The following examples will cause a callback to be executed:

```
// object reassignment
$scope.myArr = [];
$scope.myObj = 1;
$scope.myObj = {};

// top-level property reassignment
$scope.myObj.myPrim = 'Go Giants!';

// array element reassignment
$scope.myArr[0] = 6;

// deletion of top level property
delete myObj.myPrim;
```

The following will *not* cause the callback to be executed:

```
// add new property
$scope.myObj.newProp = {};

// push new element onto array
$scope.myArr.push(2);

// modify, create, or delete nested property
$scope.myObj.innerObj.innerProp = 'Go Blackhawks!';
$scope.myObj.innerObj.otherProp = 'Go Sox!';
delete $scope.myObj.innerObj.innerProp;
```

 JSFiddle: http://jsfiddle.net/msfrisbie/jnL12sck/

There's more...

The name $watchCollection is a bit deceptive (depending on how you think about enumerable collections in JavaScript) as it might not perform how you would expect—especially since it doesn't watch for elements that are being added to the collection. Since explicitly-defined properties and array indices are effectively identical at the object property level, $watchCollection is really more of a single-depth reference watcher.

See also

- ▸ The *Deploying and managing $watch types efficiently* recipe describes methods to keep your application's watch bloat under control
- ▸ The *Optimizing the application using reference $watch* recipe demonstrates how to effectively deploy the basic watch type
- ▸ The *Optimizing the application using equality $watch* recipe demonstrates how to effectively deploy the deep watch type
- ▸ The *Optimizing the application using $watch deregistration* recipe shows how your application can evict watch list entries when they are no longer required

Optimizing the application using $watch deregistration

Nothing boosts watcher performance quite like destroying the watcher altogether. Should you encounter a scenario where you no longer have a need to watch a model component, invoking watch creation returns a deregistration function that will unbind that watcher when called.

How to do it...

When a watcher is initialized, it will return its deregistration function. You must store this deregistration function until it needs to be invoked. This can be done as follows:

```
$scope.myObj = {}

// watch myObj by reference
var deregister = $scope.$watch('myObj', function(newVal, oldVal,
  scope) {
  // callback logic
});

// prevent additional modifications from invoking the callback
deregister();
```

JSFiddle: `http://jsfiddle.net/msfrisbie/yLhwfvwL/`

How it works...

The `$watch` destruction will normally be needed when a change in application state causes a watch to no longer be useful while the scope that it is defined inside still exists. When a scope is destroyed—either manually or automatically—the watchers defined upon it will be flagged as eligible for garbage collection, and therefore, manual teardown is not required.

However, this is contingent upon the scope on which the watcher is destroyed. If your application has watchers defined on a parent scope or `$rootScope`, they will not be flagged for garbage collection and must be destroyed manually upon scope destruction (usually accomplished with `$scope.$on('$destroy', function() {})`), or else your application is subject to potential memory leaks in the form of orphaned watchers.

See also

▸ The *Deploying and managing $watch types efficiently* recipe describes methods to keep your application's watch bloat under control

▸ The *Optimizing the application using reference $watch* recipe demonstrates how to effectively deploy the basic watch type

▸ The *Optimizing the application using equality $watch* recipe demonstrates how to effectively deploy the deep watch type

▸ The *Optimizing the application using $watchCollection* recipe demonstrates how to utilize the intermediate depth watcher in your application

Optimizing template-binding watch expressions

Any AngularJS template expression inside double braces (`{{ }}`) will register an equality watcher using the enclosed AngularJS expression upon compilation.

How to do it...

Curly braces are easily recognized as the AngularJS syntax for template data binding. The following is an example:

```
<div ng-show="{{myFunc()}}">
  {{ myObj }}
</div>
```

On a high level, even to a beginner level AngularJS developer, this is painfully obvious.

Interpolating the two preceding expressions into the view implicitly creates two watchers for each of these expressions. The corresponding watchers will be approximately equivalent to the following:

```
$scope.$watch('myFunc()', function() { ... }, true);
$scope.$watch('myObj', function() { ... }, true);
```

How it works...

The AngularJS expression contained within {{ }} in the template will be the exact entry registered in the watch list. Any method or logic within that expression will necessarily be evaluated for its return value every time dirty checking is performed. An observant developer will note that any logic contained in `myFunc()` will be evaluated on every single digest cycle, which can degrade the performance extremely rapidly. Therefore, it will benefit your application greatly to have the value of the watch entry calculable as quickly as possible. An easy way to accomplish this is to not provide methods or logic as expressions at all, but to calculate the output of the method and store it in a model property, which can then be passed to the template.

There's more...

Template watch entries have setup and teardown processes automatically taken care of for you. You must be careful though, as using {{ }} in your template will sneakily cause your watch count to balloon. AngularJS 1.3 introduces **bind once** capabilities, which allow you to interpolate model data into the view upon compilation, but not to bring along the overhead of data binding, if it will not be necessary.

See also

- The *Inspecting your application's watchers* recipe shows you how to inspect the internals of your application to find where your watchers are concentrated
- The *Deploying and managing $watch types efficiently* recipe describes methods to keep your application's watch bloat under control
- The *Optimizing the application with the compile phase in ng-repeat* recipe demonstrates how to reduce redundant processing inside repeaters
- The *Optimizing the application using track by in ng-repeat* recipe demonstrates how to configure your application to prevent unnecessary rendering inside a repeater
- The *Trimming down watched models* recipe provides the details of how you can consolidate deep-watched models to reduce comparison and copy latency

Optimizing the application with the compile phase in ng-repeat

An extremely common pattern in an AngularJS application is to have an `ng-repeat` directive instance spit out a list of child directives corresponding to an enumerable collection. This pattern can obviously lead to performance problems at scale, especially as directive complexity increases. One of the best ways to curb directive processing bloat is to eliminate any processing redundancy by migrating it to the compile phase.

Getting ready

Suppose that your application contains the following pseudo-setup. This is what we need for the next section:

```
(index.html)

<div ng-repeat="element in largeCollection">
  <span my-directive></span>
</div>

(app.js)

angular.module('myApp', [])
.directive('myDirective', function() {
  return {
    link: function(scope, el, attrs) {
      // general directive logic and initialization
      // instance-specific logic and initialization
    }
  };
});
```

How to do it...

A clever developer will note that since a directive's `link` function executes once for each instance of the directive in the repeater, the current implementation is wasting time performing the same actions for each instance.

Since the compile phase will only occur once for all directives inside an `ng-repeat` directive, it makes sense to perform all generalized logic and initialization within that phase, and share the results with the returned `link` function. This can be done as follows:

```
(app.js)

angular.module('myApp', [])
.directive('myDirective', function() {
```

```
    return {
      compile: function(el, attrs) {
        // general directive logic and initialization
        return function link(scope, el, attrs) {
          // instance-specific logic and initialization
          // link function closure can access compile vars
        };
      }
    };
  });
```

 JSFiddle: `http://jsfiddle.net/msfrisbie/mopuxn8h/`

How it works...

The `ng-repeat` directive will implicitly reuse the same `compile` function for all the directive instances it creates. Therefore, it's a no-brainer that any redundant processing done inside `link` functions should be moved to the `compile` function as far as possible.

There's more...

This is by no means a fix all for the sluggishness of `ng-repeat`, as high latency can stem from a large number of common problems when iterating through huge amounts of bound data. However, using the compile phase effectively is an often overlooked strategy that has the potential to yield huge performance gains from a relatively simple refactoring.

Furthermore, even though this condenses logic into a single compile phase per `ng-repeat`, the compile logic will still get executed once for every instance of the directive in the template. If you truly want the logic to only get executed once for the entire application, use the fact that service types are singletons to your advantage, and migrate the logic inside one of them.

See also

- The *Recognizing AngularJS landmines* recipe demonstrates common performance-leeching scenarios
- The *Deploying and managing $watch types efficiently* recipe describes methods to keep your application's watch bloat under control
- The *Optimizing the application using track by in ng-repeat* recipe demonstrates how to configure your application to prevent unnecessary rendering inside a repeater
- The *Trimming down watched models* recipe provides the details of how you can consolidate deep-watched models to reduce comparison and copy latency

Optimizing the application using track by in ng-repeat

By default, ng-repeat creates a DOM node for each item in the collection and destroys that DOM node when the item is removed. It is often the case that this is suboptimal for your application's performance, as a constant stream of re-rendering a sizeable collection will rarely be necessary at the repeater level and will tax your application's performance heavily. The solution is to utilize the track by expression, which allows you to define how AngularJS associates DOM nodes with the elements of the collection.

How to do it...

When track by $index is used as an addendum to the repeat expression, AngularJS will reuse any existing DOM nodes instead of re-rendering them.

The original, suboptimal version is as follows:

```
<div ng-repeat="element in largeCollection">
  <!-- element repeater content -->
</div>
```

The optimized version is as follows:

```
<div ng-repeat="element in largeCollection track by $index">
  <!-- element repeater content -->
</div>
```

 JSFiddle: http://jsfiddle.net/msfrisbie/0dbj5rgt/

How it works...

By default, ng-repeat associates each collection element by reference to a DOM node. Using the track by expression allows you to customize what that association is referencing instead of the collection element itself. If the element is an object with a unique ID, that is suitable. Otherwise, each repeated element is provided with $index on its scope, which can be used to uniquely identify that element to the repeater. By doing this, the repeater will not destroy the DOM node unless the index changes.

▸ The *Recognizing AngularJS landmines* recipe demonstrates common performance-leeching scenarios

▸ The *Inspecting your application's watchers* recipe shows you how to inspect the internals of your application to find where your watchers are concentrated

▸ The *Deploying and managing $watch types efficiently* recipe describes methods to keep your application's watch bloat under control

▸ The *Optimizing the application with the compile phase in ng-repeat* recipe demonstrates how to reduce redundant processing inside repeaters

▸ The *Trimming down watched models* recipe provide the details of how you can consolidate deep-watched models to reduce comparison and copy latency

Trimming down watched models

The equality comparator watcher can be a fickle beast when tuning the application for better performance. It's always best to avoid it when possible, but of course, that holds true until you actually need to deep watch a collection of large objects. The overhead of watching a large object is so cumbersome that sometimes distilling objects down to a subset for the purposes of comparison can actually yield performance gains.

How to do it...

The following is the naïve method of an exhaustive equality comparator watch:

```
$scope.$watch('bigObjectArray', function() {
  // watch callback
}, true);
```

Instead of watching the entire object, it is possible to call `map()` on a collection of large objects in order to extract only the components of the objects that actually need to be watched. This can be done as follows:

```
$scope.$watch(
  // function that returns object to be watched
  function($scope) {
    // map the array to distill the relevant properties
    // this return value is what will be compared against
    return $scope.bigObjectArray.map(function(bigObject) {
      // return only the property we want
```

```
      return bigObject.relevantProperty;
    });
  },
  function(newVal, oldVal, scope) {
    // watch callback
  },
  // equality comparator
  true
);
```

JSFiddle: `http://jsfiddle.net/msfrisbie/p45jb4dh/`

How it works...

The `$watch` expression can be passed anything that it can compare to a past value; it does not have to be an AngularJS string expression. The outer function is evaluated for its return value, which is used as the value to compare against. For each cycle, the dirty checking mechanism will map the array, test it against the old value, and record the new value.

There's more...

If the time it takes to copy and compare the entire object array is greater than the time it takes to use `map()` on the array and compare the subsets, then using the watcher in this way will yield a performance boost.

See also

- The *Recognizing AngularJS landmines* recipe demonstrates common performance-leeching scenarios

- The *Deploying and managing $watch types efficiently* recipe describes the methods to keep your application's watch bloat under control

- The *Optimizing the application with the compile phase in ng-repeat* recipe demonstrates how to reduce redundant processing inside repeaters

- The *Optimizing the application using track-by in ng-repeat* recipe demonstrates how to configure your application to prevent unnecessary rendering inside a repeater

8
Promises

In this chapter, we will cover the following recipes:

- ▸ Understanding and implementing a basic promise
- ▸ Chaining promises and promise handlers
- ▸ Implementing promise notifications
- ▸ Implementing promise barriers with `$q.all()`
- ▸ Creating promise wrappers with `$q.when()`
- ▸ Using promises with `$http`
- ▸ Using promises with `$resource`
- ▸ Using promises with Restangular
- ▸ Incorporating promises into native route resolves
- ▸ Implementing nested `ui-router` resolves

Introduction

AngularJS promises are an odd and fascinating component of the framework. They are integral to a large number of core components, and yet many references only mention them in passing. They offer an extremely robust and advanced mechanism of application control, and as application complexity begins to scale up, you as an AngularJS developer will find that promises are nearly impossible to ignore. This, however, is a good thing; promises are extraordinarily powerful, and they will make your life much simpler once they are fully understood.

AngularJS promises will soon be subjected to a good deal of modification with the upcoming ES6 promise implementation. Currently, they are a bit of a hybrid implementation, with the CommonJS promise proposal as the primary influence. As ES6 becomes more widely disseminated, the AngularJS promise implementation will begin to converge with that of native ES6 promises.

Understanding and implementing a basic promise

Promises are absolutely essential to many of the core aspects of AngularJS. When learning about promises for the first time, the formal terms can be an impediment to their complete understanding as their literal definitions convey very little about how the actual promise components act.

How to do it...

A promise implementation in one of its simplest forms is as follows:

```
// create deferred object through $q api
var deferred = $q.defer();

// deferred objects are created with a promise attached
var promise = deferred.promise;

// define handlers to execute once promise state becomes definite
promise.then(function success(data) {
  // deferred.resolve() handler
  // in this implementation, data === 'resolved'
}, function error(data) {
  // deferred.reject() handler
  // in this implementation, data === 'rejected'
});

// this function can be called anywhere to resolve the promise
function asyncResolve() {
  deferred.resolve('resolved');
};

// this function can be called anywhere to reject the promise
function asyncReject() {
  deferred.reject('rejected');
};
```

To a person seeing promises for the first time, what makes them difficult to comprehend is quite plain: much of what is going on here is not intuitive.

How it works...

The promise ecosystem can be more readily decoded by gaining a better understanding of the nomenclature behind it, and what problems it intends to solve.

Promises are by no means a new concept in AngularJS, or even in JavaScript; part of the inspiration for $q was taken from Kris Kowal's Q library, and for a long time, jQuery has had key promise concepts incorporated into many of its features.

Promises in JavaScript confer to the developer the ability to write asynchronous code in parallel with synchronous code more easily. In JavaScript, this was formerly solved with nested callbacks, colloquially referred to as *callback hell*. A single callback-oriented function might be written as follows:

```
// a prototypical asynchronous callback function
function asyncFunction(data, successCallback, errorCallback) {
  // this will perform some operation that may succeed,
  // may fail, or may not return at all, any of which
  // occurs in an unknown amount of time

  // this pseudo-response contains a success boolean,
  // and the returned data if successful
  var response = asyncOperation(data);

  if (response.success === true) {
    successCallback(response.data);
  } else {
    errorCallback();
  }
};
```

If your application does not demand any semblance of in-order or collective completion, then the following will suffice:

```
function successCallback(data) {
  // asyncFunction succeeded, handle data appropriately
};
function errorCallback() {
  // asyncFunction failed, handle appropriately
};

asyncFunction(data1, successCallback, errorCallback);
asyncFunction(data2, successCallback, errorCallback);
asyncFunction(data3, successCallback, errorCallback);
```

This is almost never the case though, since your application will often demand either that the data should be acquired in a sequence or that an operation that requires multiple asynchronously-acquired pieces of data should only be executed once all the pieces have been successfully acquired. In this case, without access to promises, the callback hell emerges, as follows:

```
asyncFunction(data1, function(foo) {
  asyncFunction(data2, function(bar) {
    asyncFunction(data3, function(baz){
      // foo, bar, baz can now all be used together
      combinatoricFunction(foo, bar, baz);
    }, errorCallback);
  }, errorCallback);
}, errorCallback);
```

This so-called callback hell is really just attempting to serialize three asynchronous calls, but the parametric topology of these asynchronous functions forces the developer to subject their application to this ugliness. Promises to the rescue!

 From this point forward in this recipe, promises will be discussed pertaining to how they are implemented within AngularJS, rather than the conceptual definition of a promise API. There is a substantial overlap between the two, but for your benefit, the discussion in this recipe will lean towards the side of implementation rather than theory.

Basic components and behavior of a promise

The AngularJS promise architecture exposed by the $q service decomposes into a dichotomy: deferreds and promises.

Deferreds

A deferred is the interface through which the application will set and alter the state of the promise.

An AngularJS deferred object has exactly one promise attached to it by default, which is accessible through the promise property, as follows:

```
var deferred = $q.defer()
  , promise = deferred.promise;
```

In the same way that a single promise can have multiple handlers bound to a single state, a single deferred can be resolved or rejected in multiple places in the application, as shown here:

```
var deferred = $q.defer()
  , promise = deferred.promise;

// the following are pseudo-methods, each of which can be called
```

```
// independently and asynchronously, or not at all
function canHappenFirst() { deferred.resolve(); }
function mayHappenFirst() { deferred.resolve(); }
function mightHappenFirst() { deferred.reject(); }
```

Once a deferred's state is set to resolved or rejected anywhere in the application, attempts to reject or resolve that deferred further will be silently ignored. A promise state transition occurs only once, and it cannot be altered or reversed. Refer to the following code:

```
var deferred = $q.defer()
  , promise = deferred.promise;

// define handlers on the promise to gain visibility
// into their execution
promise.then(function resolved() {
  $log.log('success');
}, function rejected() {
  $log.log('rejected');
});

// verify initial state
$log.log(promise.$$state.status); // 0

// resolve the promise
deferred.resolve();
// >> "resolved"

$log.log(promise.$$state.status); // 1
// output and state check verify state transition

// attempt to reject the already resolved promise
deferred.reject();

$log.log(promise.$$state.status); // 1
// output and state check verify no state transition
```

 JSFiddle: `http://jsfiddle.net/msfrisbie/e4saopyr/`

Promises

A promise represents an unknown state that could transition into a known state at some point in the future.

A promise can only exist in one of three states. AngularJS represents these states within the promises with an integer status:

- **0**: This is the pending state that represents an unfulfilled promise waiting for evaluation. This is the initial state. An example is as follows:

```
var deferred = $q.defer()
  , promise = deferred.promise;

$log.log(promise.$$state.status); // 0
```

- **1**: This is the resolved state that represents a successful and fulfilled promise. A transition to this state cannot be altered or reversed. An example is as follows:

```
var deferred = $q.defer()
  , promise = deferred.promise;

$log.log(promise.$$state.status); // 0

deferred.resolve('resolved');

$log.log(promise.$$state.status); // 1
$log.log(promise.$$state.value);  // "resolved"
```

- **2**: This is the rejected state that represents an unsuccessful and rejected promise caused by an error. A transition to this state cannot be altered or reversed. An example is as follows:

```
var deferred = $q.defer()
  , promise = deferred.promise;

$log.log(promise.$$state.status); // 0

deferred.reject('rejected');

$log.log(promise.$$state.status); // 2
$log.log(promise.$$state.value);  // "rejected"
```

States do not necessarily have a data value associated with them—they only confer to the promise a defined state of evaluation. Take a look at the following code:

```
var deferred = $q.defer()
  , promise = deferred.promise;

promise.then(successHandler, failureHandler);

// state can be defined with any of the following:
// deferred.resolve();
// deferred.reject();
// deferred.resolve(myData);
// deferred.reject(myData);
```

An evaluated promise (resolved or rejected) is associated with a handler for each of the states. This handler is invoked upon the promise's transition into that respective state. These handlers can access data returned by the resolution or rejection, as shown here:

```
var deferred = $q.defer()
  , promise = deferred.promise;

// $log.info is the resolve handler,
// $log.error is the reject handler
promise.then($log.info, $log.error);

deferred.resolve(123);
// (info) 123

// reset to demonstrate reject()
deferred = $q.defer();
promise = deferred.promise;

promise.then($log.log, $log.error);

deferred.reject(123);
// (error) 123
```

[JSFiddle: http://jsfiddle.net/msfrisbie/rz2s9uaq/]

Unlike callbacks, handlers can be defined at any point in the promise life cycle, including after the promise state has been defined, as shown here:

```
var deferred = $q.defer()
  , promise = deferred.promise;

// immediately resolve the promise
deferred.resolve(123);

// subsequently define a handler, will be immediately
// invoked since promise is already resolved
promise.then($log.log);
// 123
```

In the same way that a single deferred can be resolved or rejected in multiple places in the application, a single promise can have multiple handlers bound to a single state. For example, a single promise with multiple resolved handlers attached to it will invoke all of the handlers if the resolved state is reached; the same is true for rejected handlers as well. This is shown here:

```
var deferred = $q.defer()
  , promise = deferred.promise
  , cb = function() { $log.log('called'); };

promise.then(cb);
promise.then(cb);

deferred.resolve();
// called
// called
```

 Variables, object properties, or methods preceded with $$ denote that they are private, and while they are very handy for inspection and debugging purposes, they shouldn't be touched in production applications without good reason.

See also

▶ The *Chaining promises and promise handlers* recipe provides the details of combinatorial strategies involving promises in order to create an advanced application flow

▶ The *Implementing promise notifications* recipe demonstrates how to use notifications for intermediate communication when a promise takes a long time to get resolved

▶ The *Implementing promise barriers with $q.all()* recipe shows how to combine a group of promises into a single, all-or-nothing promise

▶ The *Creating promise wrappers with $q.when()* recipe shows how to normalize JavaScript objects into promises

Chaining promises and promise handlers

Much of the purpose of promises is to allow the developer to serialize and reason about independent asynchronous actions. This can be accomplished by utilizing promise chaining in AngularJS.

Getting ready

Assume that all the examples in this recipe have been set up in the following manner:

```
var deferred = $q.defer()
    , promise = deferred.promise;
```

Also, assume that $q and other built-in AngularJS services have already been injected into the current lexical scope.

How to do it...

The promise handler definition method `then()` returns another promise, which can further have handlers defined upon it in a *chain* handler, as shown here:

```
var successHandler = function() { $log.log('called'); };

promise
  .then(successHandler)
  .then(successHandler)
  .then(successHandler);

deferred.resolve();
// called
// called
// called
```

Data handoff for chained handlers

Chained handlers can pass data to their subsequent handlers, as follows:

```
var successHandler = function(val) {
  $log.log(val);
  return val+1;
};

promise
  .then(successHandler)
  .then(successHandler)
  .then(successHandler);

deferred.resolve(0);
// 0
// 1
// 2
```

 JSFiddle: `http://jsfiddle.net/msfrisbie/n03ncuby/`

Rejecting a chained handler

Returning normally from a promise handler will, by default, signal child promise states to become resolved. If you want to signal child promises to get rejected, you can do so by returning `$q.reject()`. This can be done as follows:

```
promise
.then(function () {
  // initial promise resolved handler instructs handlers
  // child promise(s) to be rejected
  return $q.reject(123);
})
.then(
  // child promise resolved handler
  function(data) {
    $log.log("resolved", data);
  },
  // child promise rejected handler
  function(data) {
    $log.log("rejected", data);
  }
```

```
);

deferred.resolve();
// "rejected", 123
```

[
JSFiddle: `http://jsfiddle.net/msfrisbie/h5au7j2f/`
]

How it works...

A promise reaching a final state will trigger child promises to follow it in turn. This simple but powerful concept allows you to build broad and fault-tolerant promise structures that elegantly mesh collections of dependent asynchronous actions.

There's more...

The topology of AngularJS promises lends itself to some interesting utilization patterns, as follows.

Promise handler trees

Promise handlers will be executed in the order that the promises are defined. If a promise has multiple handlers attached to a single state, then that state will execute all its handlers before resolving the following chained promise. This is shown here:

```
var incr = function(val) {
  $log.log(val);
  return val+1;
}

// define the top level promise handler
promise.then(incr);
// append another handler for the first promise, and collect
// the returned promise in secondPromise
var secondPromise = promise.then(incr);
// append another handler for the second promise, and collect
// the returned promise in thirdPromise
var thirdPromise = secondPromise.then(incr);

// at this point, deferred.resolve() will:
// resolve promise; promise's handlers executes
// resolve secondPromise; secondPromises's handler executes
```

```
// resolve thirdPromise; no handlers defined yet

// additional promise handler definition order is
// unimportant; they will be resolved as the promises
// sequentially have their states defined
secondPromise.then(incr);
promise.then(incr);
thirdPromise.then(incr);

// the setup currently defined is as follows:
// promise -> secondPromise -> thirdPromise
// incr()      incr()             incr()
// incr()      incr()
// incr()

deferred.resolve(0);
// 0
// 0
// 0
// 1
// 1
// 2
```

JSFiddle: `http://jsfiddle.net/msfrisbie/4msybmc9/`

Since the return value of a handler decides whether or not the promise state is resolved or rejected, any of the handlers associated with a promise are able to set the state—which, as you may recall, can only be set once. The defining of the parent promise state will trigger the child promise handlers to execute.

It should now be apparent how trees of the promise functionality can be derived from the combinations of promise chaining and handler chaining. When used properly, they can yield extremely elegant solutions to difficult and ugly asynchronous action serialization.

The catch() method

The `catch()` method is a shorthand for `promise.then(null, errorCallback)`. Using it can lead to slightly cleaner promise definitions, but it is no more than syntactical sugar. It can be used as follows:

```
promise
.then(function () {
  return $q.reject();
})
.catch(function(data) {
```

```
    $log.log("rejected");
});

deferred.resolve();
// "rejected"
```

 JSFiddle: `http://jsfiddle.net/msfrisbie/rLg79m29/`

The finally() method

The `finally()` method will execute irrespective of whether the promise was rejected or resolved. It is convenient for applications that need to perform some sort of cleanup, independent of what the final state of the promise becomes. It can be used as follows:

```
var deferred1 = $q.defer();
  , promise1 = deferred1.promise
  , deferred2 = $q.defer()
  , promise2 = deferred2.promise
  , cb = $log.log("called");

promise1.finally(cb);
promise2.finally(cb);

deferred1.resolve();
// "called"
deferred2.reject();
// "called"
```

 JSFiddle: `http://jsfiddle.net/msfrisbie/owucqmea/`

See also

- The *Understanding and implementing a basic promise* recipe goes into more detail about how AngularJS promises work

- The *Implementing promise notifications* recipe demonstrates how to use notifications for intermediate communication when a promise takes a long time to get resolved

- The *Implementing promise barriers with $q.all()* recipe shows how to combine a group of promises into a single, all-or-nothing promise

- The *Creating promise wrappers with $q.when()* recipe shows how to normalize JavaScript objects into promises

Implementing promise notifications

AngularJS also offers the ability to provide notifications about promises before a final state has been reached. This is especially useful when promises have long latencies and updates on their progress is desirable, such as progress bars.

How to do it...

The `promise.then()` method accepts a third argument, a notification handler, which can be accessed through the deferred an unlimited number of times until the promise state has been resolved. This is shown here:

```
promise
.then(
  // resolved handler
  function() {
    $log.log('success');
  },
  // empty rejected handler
  null,
  // notification handler
  $log.log
);

function resolveWithProgressNotifications() {
  for (var i=0; i<=100; i+=20) {
    // pass the data to the notification handler
    deferred.notify(i);
    if (i>=100) { deferred.resolve() };
  };
}

resolveWithProgressNotifications();
// 0
// 20
// 40
// 60
// 80
// 100
// "success"
```

 JSFiddle: `http://jsfiddle.net/msfrisbie/5798q0ru/`

How it works...

The notification handler allows the notifications to be enqueued upon the promise, and they are sequentially executed at the conclusion of the `$digest` cycle. Another example is as follows:

```
promise
.then(
  function() {
    $log.log('success');
  },
  null,
  $log.log
);

function asyncNotification() {
  deferred.notify('Hello, ');
  $log.log('world!');
  deferred.resolve();
};

// this function is invoked by some non-AngularJS entity
asyncNotification();
// world!
// Hello,
// success
```

 JSFiddle: `http://jsfiddle.net/msfrisbie/cn4pLbcw/`

The order of the console log statements might surprise you. Since the notifications often arrive from an event that is not bound to the AngularJS `$digest` cycle, a call to `$scope.$apply()` will push through the execution of the notification handler(s) immediately. This is shown here:

```
promise
.then(
  function() {
    $log.log('success');
  },
  null,
  $log.log
);

function newAsyncNotification() {
  deferred.notify('Hello, ');
```

```
  $scope.$apply();
  $log.log('world!');
  deferred.resolve();
};

// this function is invoked by some non-AngularJS entity
newAsyncNotification();
// Hello,
// world!
// success
```

 JSFiddle: `http://jsfiddle.net/msfrisbie/0rpbu07z/`

There's more...

The notification handler cannot transit the promise into a final state with its return value, although it can use the deferred object to cause a state transition, as demonstrated earlier in this recipe.

Notifications will not be executed after the promise has transitioned to a final state, as shown here:

```
// resolve or reject handlers not needed in this example
promise.then(null, null, $log.log);

deferred.notify('Hello, ');
deferred.resolve();
deferred.notify('world!');

// Hello,
```

Implementing promise barriers with $q.all()

You might find that your application requires the use of promises in an all-or-nothing type of situation. That is, it will need to collectively evaluate a group of promises, and that collection will be resolved as a single promise if and only if all of the contained promises are resolved; if any one of them is rejected, the aggregate promise will be rejected.

How to do it...

The `$q.all()` method accepts an enumerable collection of promises, either an array of promise objects or an object with a number of promise properties, and will attempt to resolve all of them as a single aggregate promise. The parameter of the aggregate resolved handler will be an array or object that matches the resolved values of the contained promises. This is shown here:

```
var deferred1 = $q.defer()
  , promise1 = deferred1.promise
  , deferred2 = $q.defer()
  , promise2 = deferred2.promise;

$q.all([promise1, promise2]).then($log.log);

deferred1.resolve(456);
deferred2.resolve(123);
// [456, 123]
```

 JSFiddle: `http://jsfiddle.net/msfrisbie/L8Lxf1ho/`

If any of the promises in the collection are rejected, the aggregate promise will be rejected. The parameter of the aggregate rejected handler will be the returned value of the rejected promise. This is shown here:

```
var deferred1 = $q.defer()
  , promise1 = deferred1.promise
  , deferred2 = $q.defer()
  , promise2 = deferred2.promise;

$q.all([promise1, promise2]).then($log.log, $log.error);

// resolve a collection promise, no handler execution
deferred1.resolve(456);

// reject a collection promise, rejection handler executes
deferred2.reject(123);
// (error) 123
```

 JSFiddle: `http://jsfiddle.net/msfrisbie/0mjbn62L/`

How it works...

As demonstrated, the aggregate promise will reach a final state only when all of the enclosed promises are resolved, or when a single enclosed promise is rejected. Using this type of promise is useful when the promises in a collection do not need to reason about one another, but their collective completion is the only metric of success for the group.

In the case of a contained rejection, the aggregate promise will not wait for the remaining promises to get completed, but those promises will not be prevented from reaching their final state. Only the first promise to be rejected will be able to pass the rejection data to the aggregate promise rejection handler.

There's more...

The $q.all() method is in many ways extremely similar to an operating-system-level process synchronization barrier. A process barrier is a common point in a thread instruction execution, which a collection of processes will reach independently and at different times, and none can proceed until all have reached this point. In the same way, $q.all() will not proceed unless either all of the contained promises have been resolved (reached the barrier) or a single contained rejection has prevented that state from ever being achieved, in which case the failover handler logic will take over.

Since $q.all() allows the *recombination* of promises, this also allows your application's promise chains to become a **directed acyclic graph** (**DAG**). The following diagram is an example of a promise progression graph that has diverged and later converged:

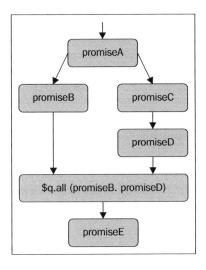

This level of complexity is uncommon, but it is available for use should your application require it.

See also

▶ The *Understanding and implementing a basic promise* recipe goes into more detail about how AngularJS promises work

▶ The *Chaining promises and promise handlers* recipe provides the details of combinatorial strategies that involve promises to create an advanced application flow

▶ The *Implementing promise barriers with $q.all()* recipe shows how to combine a group of promises into a single, all-or-nothing promise

▶ The *Creating promise wrappers with $q.when()* recipe shows how to normalize JavaScript objects into promises

Creating promise wrappers with $q.when()

AngularJS includes the `$q.when()` method that allows you to normalize JavaScript objects into promise objects.

How to do it...

The `$q.when()` method accepts promise and non-promise objects, as follows:

```
var deferred = $q.defer()
  , promise = deferred.promise;

$q.when(123);
$q.when(promise);
// both create new promise objects
```

If `$q.when()` is passed a non-promise object, it is effectively the same as creating an immediately resolved promise object, as shown here:

```
var newPromise = $q.when(123);

// promise will wait for a $digest cycle to update $$state.status,
// this forces it to update for inspection
$scope.$apply();

// inspecting the status reveals it has already resolved
$log.log(newPromise.$$state.status);
// 1

// since it is resolved, the handler will execute immediately
newPromise.then($log.log);
// 123
```

JSFiddle: `http://jsfiddle.net/msfrisbie/ftgydnqn/`

How it works...

The `$q.when()` method wraps whatever is passed to it with a new promise. If it is passed a promise, the new promise will retain the state of that promise. Otherwise, if it is passed a non-promise value, the new promise created will get resolved and pass that value to the resolved handler.

 Keep in mind that the `$q.reject()` method returns a rejected promise, so `$q.when($q.reject())` is simply wrapping an already rejected promise.

There's more...

Since `$q.when()` will return an identical promise when passed a promise, this method is effectively idempotent. However, the `promise` argument and the returned promise are different promise objects, as shown here:

```
$log.log($q.when(promise)===promise);
// false
```

See also

- ▶ The *Understanding and implementing a basic promise* recipe goes into more detail about how AngularJS promises work

- ▶ The *Chaining promises and promise handlers* recipe provides the details of combinatorial strategies that involve promises to create an advanced application flow

- ▶ The *Implementing promise notifications* recipe demonstrates how to use notifications for intermediate communication when a promise takes a long time to get resolved

- ▶ The *Implementing promise barriers with $q.all()* recipe shows how to combine a group of promises into a single, all-or-nothing promise

Using promises with $http

HTTP requests are the quintessential variable latency operations that demand a promise construct. Since it would appear that developers are stuck with the uncertainty stemming from TCP/IP for the foreseeable future, it behooves you to architect your applications to account for this.

How to do it...

The $http service methods return an AngularJS promise with some extra methods, success() and error(). These extra methods will return the same promise returned by the $http service, as opposed to .then(), which returns a new promise. This allows you to chain the methods as $http().success().then() and have the .success() and .then() promises attempt to resolve simultaneously.

The following two implementations are more or less identical, as everything is being chained upon the $http promise:

```
// Implementation #1
// $http.get() returns a promise
$http.get('/myUrl')
// .success() is an alias for the resolved handler
.success(function(data, status, headers, config, statusText) {
  // resolved handler
})
// .error() is an alias for the rejected handler
.error(function(data, status, headers, config, statusText) {
  // rejected handler
});

// Implementation #2
$http.get('/myUrl')
.then(
  // resolved handler
  function(response) {
    // response object has the properties
    // data, status, headers, config, statusText
  },
  // rejected handler
  function(response) {
    // response object has the properties
    // data, status, headers, config, statusText
  }
);
```

However, the following two implementations are *not* identical:

```
// Implementation #3
// $http.get() returns a promise
$http.get('/myUrl')
// .success() is an alias for the resolved handler
.success(function(data, status, headers, config, statusText) {
```

```
  // resolved handler
})
// .error() is an alias for the rejected handler
.error(function(data, status, headers, config, statusText) {
  // rejected handler
})
.then( ... );

// Implementation #4
$http.get('/myUrl')
.then(
  // resolved handler
  function(response) {
    // response object has the properties
    // data, status, headers, config, statusText
  },
  // rejected handler
  function(response) {
    // response object has the properties
      // data, status, headers, config, statusText
  }
)
.then( ... );
```

The differences are explained in the following example:

```
// these are split into variables to be able to inspect
// the returned promises
var a = $http.get('/')
  , b = a.success(function() {})
  , c = b.error(function() {})
  , d = c.then(function() {});

$log.log(a===b, a===c, a===d, b===c, b===d, c===d);
//        true   true   false  true    false  false

var e = $http.get('/')
  , f = e.then(function() {})
  , g = e.then(function() {});

$log.log(e===f, e===g, f===g);
//        false  false  false
```

JSFiddle: `http://jsfiddle.net/msfrisbie/sh60bhc8/`

For the sake of this example, the `$http.get()` requests are only accessing routes from the same domain that served the page. Keep in mind that using a foreign origin URL in the context of this example will bring about **Cross-origin resource sharing (CORS)** errors unless you properly modify the request headers to allow CORS requests.

How it works...

The success/error dichotomy for an HTTP request is decided by the response status code, as follows:

- Any code between 200 and 299 will register as a successful request and the resolved handler will be executed
- Any code between 300 and 399 will indicate a redirect, and `XMLHttpRequest` will follow the redirect to acquire a concrete status code
- Any code between 400 and 599 will register as an error and the rejected handler will be executed

See also

- The *Using promises with $resource* recipe discusses how `ngRoute` can be used as a promise-centric resource manager
- The *Using promises with Restangular* recipe demonstrates how the popular third-party resource manager is extensively integrated with AngularJS promise conventions

Using promises with $resource

As part of the `ngResource` module, `$resource` provides a service to manage connections with RESTful resources. As far as vanilla AngularJS goes, this is in some ways the closest you'll get to a formal data object model infrastructure. The `$resource` tool is highly extensible and is an excellent standalone tool upon which to build applications if third-party libraries like Restangular aren't your cup of tea.

As the API-focused wrapper for `$http`, `$resource` also provides an interface for using promises in conjunction with the HTTP requests that it generates.

How to do it...

Although it wraps $http, $resource actually does not use promises in its default implementation. The $promise property can be used to access the promise object of the HTTP request, as follows:

```
// creates the resource object, which exposes get(), post(), etc.
var Widget = $resource('/widgets/:widgetId', {widgetId: '@id'});

// resource object must be coaxed into returning its promise
// this can be done with the $promise property
Widget.get({id: 8})
.$promise
.then(function(widget) {
  // widget is the returned object with id=8
});
```

 JSFiddle: `http://jsfiddle.net/msfrisbie/upzh1f97/`

How it works...

A $resource object accepts success and error function callbacks as its second and third arguments, which can be utilized if the developer desires a callback-driven request pattern instead of promises. Since it does use $http, promises are still very much integrated and available to the developer.

See also

▶ The *Using promises with $http* recipe demonstrates how AngularJS promises are integrated with AJAX requests

▶ The *Using promises with Restangular* recipe demonstrates how the popular third-party resource manager is extensively integrated with AngularJS promise conventions

Using promises with Restangular

Restangular, the extremely popular REST API extension to AngularJS, takes a much more promise-centric approach compared to $resource.

How to do it...

The Restangular REST API mapping will always return a promise. This is shown here:

```
(app.js)

angular.module('myApp', ['restangular'])
.controller('Ctrl', function($scope, Restangular) {
  Restangular
  .one('widget', 4)
  // get() will return a promise for the GET request
  .get()
  .then(
    function(data) {
      // consume response data in success handler
      $scope.status = 'One widget success!';
    },
    function(response) {
      // consume response message in error handler
      $scope.status = 'One widget failure!';
    }
  );

  // generally, the API mapping is stored in a variable,
  // and the promise-returning method will be invoked as needed
  var widgets = Restangular.all('widgets');

  // create the request promise
  widgets.getList()
  .then(function(widgets) {
    // success handler
    $scope.status = 'Many widgets success!';
  }, function() {
    // error handler
    $scope.status = 'Many widgets failure!';
  });
});
```

[JSFiddle: http://jsfiddle.net/msfrisbie/5ud5210n/]

Since Restangular objects don't create promises until the request method is invoked, it is possible to chain Restangular route methods before creating the request promise, in order to match the nested URL structure. This can be done as follows:

```
// GET request to /widgets/6/features/11
Restangular
.one('widgets', 6)
.one('features', 11)
.get()
.then(function(feature) {
  // success handler
});
```

[JSFiddle: `http://jsfiddle.net/msfrisbie/8qrkkyyv/`]

How it works...

Every Restangular object method can be chained to develop nested URL objects, and every request to a remote API through Restangular returns a promise. In conjunction with its flexible and extensible resource CRUD methods, it creates a powerful toolkit to communicate with REST APIs.

See also

- ▶ The *Using promises with $http* recipe demonstrates how AngularJS promises are integrated with AJAX requests
- ▶ The *Using promises with $resource* recipe discusses how `ngRoute` can be used as a promise-centric resource manager

Incorporating promises into native route resolves

AngularJS routing supports resolves, which allow you to demand that some work should be finished before the actual route change process begins. Routing resolves accept one or more functions, which can either return values or promise objects that it will attempt to resolve.

How to do it...

Resolves are declared in the route definition, as follows:

```
(app.js)

angular.module('myApp', ['ngRoute'])
.config(function($routeProvider){
  $routeProvider
  .when('/myUrl', {
    template: '<h1>Resolved!</h1>',
    // resolved values are injected by property name
    controller: function($log, myPromise, myData) {
      $log.log(myPromise, myData);
    },
    resolve: {
      // $q injected into resolve function
      myPromise: function($q) {
        var deferred = $q.defer()
          , promise = deferred.promise;
        deferred.resolve(123);
        return promise;
      },
      myData: function() {
        return 456;
      }
    }
  });
})
.controller('Ctrl', function($scope, $location) {
  $scope.navigate = function() {
    $location.url('myUrl')
  };
});

(index.html)

<div ng-app="myApp">
  <div ng-controller="Ctrl">
    <button ng-click="navigate()">Navigate!</button>
    <div ng-view></div>
  <div>
</div>
```

With this configuration, navigating to /myUrl will log 123, 456 and render the template.

 JSFiddle: http://jsfiddle.net/msfrisbie/z0fymttz/

How it works...

The premise behind route resolves is that the promises gather data or perform tasks that need to be done before the route changes and the controller is created. A resolved promise signals the router that the page is safe to be rendered.

The object provided to the route resolve evaluates the functions provided to it and consequently makes injectables available in the route controller.

There are several important details to keep in mind involving route resolves, which are as follows:

> Route resolve functions that return raw values are not guaranteed to be executed until they are injected, but functions that return promises are guaranteed to have those promises get resolved or rejected before the route changes and the controller is initialized.

> Route resolves can only be injected into controllers defined in the route definition. Controllers named in the template via ng-controller cannot have the route resolve dependencies injected into them.

> Routes with a specified route controller but without a specified template will never initialize the route controller, but the route resolve functions will still get executed.

> Route resolves will wait for either all the promises to get resolved or one of the promises to get rejected before proceeding to navigate to the URL.

There's more...

By definition, promises are not guaranteed to undergo a final state transition, and the AngularJS router diligently waits for promises to get resolved unless they get rejected. Therefore, if a promise never gets resolved, the route change will never occur and your application will appear to hang.

See also

> The *Implementing nested ui-router resolves* recipe provides the details of basic and advanced strategies used to integrate promises into nested views and their accompanying resources

Implementing nested ui-router resolves

As you gain experience as an AngularJS developer, you will come to realize that the built-in router faculties are quite brittle in a number of ways—mainly that there can only be a single instance of `ng-view` for dynamic route templating. AngularUI provides a superb solution to this in `ui-router`, which allows nested states and views, named views, piecewise routing, and nested resolves.

How to do it...

The `ui-router` framework supports resolves for states in the same way that `ngRoute` does for routes. Suppose your application displayed individual widget pages that list the features each widget has, as well as individual pages for each widget's features.

State promise inheritance

Since nested states can be defined with relative state routing, you might encounter the scenario where the URL parameters are only available within the state in which they are defined. For this application, the child state has a need to use the `widgetId` and the `featureId` value in the child state controller. This can be solved with nested route promises, as shown here:

```
(app.js)

angular.module('myApp', ['ui.router'])
.config(function($stateProvider) {
  $stateProvider
  .state('widget', {
    url: '/widgets/:widgetId',
    template: 'Widget ID: {{ widgetId }} <div ui-view></div>',
    controller: function($scope, $stateParams, widgetId){
      // the widgetId is only available in this state due to
      // the :widgetId variable definition in the state url
      $scope.widgetId = $stateParams.widgetId;
    },
    resolve:{
      // the stateParam widget property is wrapped in a property
      // to enable it to be injected in child states
      widgetId: function($stateParams){
        return $stateParams.widgetId;
      }
    }
  })
  .state('widget.feature', {
```

```
    url: '/features/:featureId',
    template: 'Feature ID: {{ featureId }}',
    // widgetId can now be injected from the parent state
    controller: function($scope, $stateParams, widgetId){
      // both widgetId and featureId are made available
      // in this state controller
      $scope.featureId = $stateParams.featureId;
      $scope.widgetId = widgetId;
    }
  });
});
```

```
(index.html)
```

```html
<div ng-app="myApp">
  <a ui-sref="widget({widgetId:6})">
    See Widget 6
  </a>
  <a ui-sref="widget.feature({widgetId: 6, featureId:11})">
    See Feature 11 of Widget 6
  </a>
  <div ui-view></div>
</div>
```

 JSFiddle: http://jsfiddle.net/msfrisbie/0kpos1xt/

Here, the child state has access to the injected `widgetId` value through the inherited resolution defined in the parent state.

Single-state promise dependencies

A state's resolve promises have the ability to depend on one another, which allows you the convenience of requesting data without explicitly defining the order or dependence. This can be done as follows:

```
(app.js)
```

```javascript
angular.module('myApp', ['ui.router'])
.config(function($stateProvider) {
  $stateProvider
  .state('widget', {
    url: '/widgets',
    template: 'Widget: {{ widget }} Features: {{ features }}',
```

```
    controller: function($scope, widget, features){
      // resolve promises are injectable in the route controller
      $scope.widget = widget;
      $scope.features = features;
    },
    resolve: {
      // standard resolve value promise definition
      widget: function() {
        return {
          name: 'myWidget'
        };
      },
      // resolve promise injects sibling promise
      features: function(widget) {
        return ['featureA', 'featureB'].map(function(feature) {
          return widget.name+':'+feature;
        });
      }
    }
  });
});
```

(index.html)

```
<div ng-app="myApp">
  <a ui-sref="widget({widgetId:6})">See Widget 6</a>
  <div ui-view></div>
</div>
```

With this setup, navigating to /widgets will print the following:

```
Widget: {"name":"myWidget"}
Features: ["myWidget:featureA","myWidget:featureB"]
```

JSFiddle: http://jsfiddle.net/msfrisbie/ugsx6c1w/

How it works...

Route resolves effectively represent an amount of work that needs to be completed before a route change can happen. These units of work, represented in the resolve as promises, are able to be dependency injected anywhere in the route state construct, which allows you a great deal of flexibility. Since the route change will only occur once all promises have resolved, you are able to effectively chain the promises within the route by chaining them using dependency injection.

 Be careful with promise dependencies within routes. It is entirely possible to create circular dependencies with such types of dependent declarations.

See also

> ▸ The *Incorporating promises into native route resolves* recipe demonstrates how vanilla AngularJS routing incorporates promises into the route life cycle

9
What's New in AngularJS 1.3

In this chapter, we will cover the following recipes:

- ▶ Using HTML5 datetime input types
- ▶ Combining watchers with `$watchGroup`
- ▶ Sanity checking with `ng-strict-di`
- ▶ Controlling model input with `ngModelOptions`
- ▶ Incorporating `$touched` and `$submitted` states
- ▶ Cleaning up form errors with `ngMessages`
- ▶ Trimming your watch list with lazy binding
- ▶ Creating and integrating custom form validators

Introduction

The release of AngularJS 1.3 incorporates a sizeable number of additions that focus on form usability and extensibility, maximizing an application's performance and integration with modern browsers. These recipes aren't an exhaustive list of all the changes in AngularJS 1.3, but here you will find all the new components that you will definitely want to start incorporating into your applications right away.

Using HTML5 datetime input types

Formerly, AngularJS was limited to using antiquated input field types in forms. The 1.3 AngularJS release added the AngularJS field and model support for HTML5 date and time types, which will gracefully degrade when used on older browsers.

How to do it...

With AngularJS 1.3, your application is now able to bind to the date and time HTML5 input types while preserving their native data format.

The <input type="date"> type

The `<input type="date">` date input type binds to a JavaScript `Date` object and extracts only the date from the `Date` object, ignoring the time component by letting it go unmodified (it will not be forced to midnight). The string value for the date October 31, 2014 would be `2014-10-31`.

The <input type="datetime-local"> type

The `<input type="datetime-local">` date input type binds to a JavaScript `Date` object and associates it with a time zone (by default, the browser time zone). The string value for 10:30 P.M. on October 31, 2014 would be `2014-10-31T20:30:00`.

The <input type="time"> type

This `<input type="time">` date input type binds to a JavaScript `Date` object and extracts only the time from the `Date` object. The date value of the `Date` object will always be January 1, 1970, the Unix epoch time. The string value for 10:30 P.M. would be `20:30:00`.

The <input type="week"> type

The `<input type="week">` date input type binds to a JavaScript `Date` object and extracts only the week from the `Date` object. This is a year-aware week field, for example, the string value of the sixth week in 2014 would be `2014-W06`.

The <input type="month"> type

The `<input type="month">` date input type binds to a JavaScript `Date` object and extracts only the month from the `Date` object. This is a year-aware month field, for example, the string value of the sixth month in 2014 would be `2014-06`.

 JSFiddle: `http://jsfiddle.net/msfrisbie/52b93whx/`

How it works...

All of these input types offer built-in comprehension of `Date` objects, including their bi-directional ISO 8601 conversion.

There's more...

If the browser does not support the HTML5 input type, the field will degrade to a simple text field. AngularJS will then handle it as a simple ISO date string to the `Date` object conversion mechanism.

All of the fields default to the browser time zone. If you wish to override the time zone, you can specify this in `ngModelOptions`.

See also

▸ The *Controlling model input with ngModelOptions* recipe provides the details of all the ways the `ngModelOptions` option lets you define how and when your input-bound models will change

Combining watchers with $watchGroup

You might find that multiple model components need to be tied to the same `$watch` type callback. As of the 1.3 release, AngularJS provides the `$watchGroup` method that accepts a collection of watch targets in which all the watch targets need to bind to the same callback.

How to do it...

The change event callback parameters can be an ordered array of the current values, followed by an ordered array of the previous values. This is shown here:

```
(app.js)

angular.module('myApp',[])
.controller('Ctrl', function($scope, $log) {
  $scope.ping = 'pong';

  $scope.ding = {
    dong: 'ditch'
  };

  // watch ping and the ding.dong property by reference
```

```
    $scope.$watchGroup(['ping', 'ding.dong'], function(newVals, oldVals,
  scope) {
      // callback logic
      $log.log(newVals, oldVals, scope);
    });
  });

  (index.html)

  <div ng-app="myApp">
    <div ng-controller="Ctrl">
      <input ng-model="ping" />
      <input ng-model="ding.dong" />
    </div>
  </div>
```

 JSFiddle: `http://jsfiddle.net/msfrisbie/80yr36qn/`

How it works...

Invoking $watchGroup will create a set of reference watchers for each model component provided in the first argument. Using $watchGroup does not reduce the number of watchers created, as AngularJS still needs to independently check each element in the set to both determine whether any of the watched values are dirty, and to determine what the new values are that should be provided as arguments to the watch callback.

There's more...

Although $watchGroup() does not provide a direct performance benefit to your application, the primary gain from using $watchGroup() is to use the DRY principle on your controllers.

See also

▶ The *Trimming your watch list with lazy binding* recipe provides the details of how the new *bind once* functionality can help you greatly streamline your application

Sanity checking with ng-strict-di

The `ng-strict-di` directive is new and extremely simple to understand. When declaring the parent DOM node for your application, if `ng-strict-di` is included in that element, functions without the minification-safe dependency injection syntax will fail to execute.

How to do it...

Using the `ng-strict-di` directive is as simple as adding an extra attribute to your `ng-app` node, as follows:

```
(app.js)

angular.module('myApp', [])
.controller('Ctrl', function($scope) {});

(index.html)

<div ng-app="myApp" ng-strict-di>
  <div ng-controller="Ctrl"></div>
</div>
```

If you try to load the page in your browser, you will be greeted with the following error:

```
Error: [$injector:strictdi] function($provide) is not using explicit
annotation and cannot be invoked in strict mode
```

 JSFiddle: `http://jsfiddle.net/msfrisbie/snqvypgL/`

There's more...

The `ng-strict-di` directive recognizing a minification-vulnerable application and consequently throwing on the brakes is for the developer's benefit. Utilities such as `ng-annotate` and `ng-min` are used to avoid the verbosity of minification-safe notations, but having a safeguard like `ng-strict-di` to protect against the nastiness of minification-vulnerable code is extremely useful when checking your application's validity.

Controlling model input with ngModelOptions

This new helper directive introduces a new vector of control over model access and updating to the developer. Formerly, using `ng-model` bound to an input meant that validation or any verification of value change needed to happen in a controller helper method or in a scope watcher, neither of which ever felt very clean. With `ngModelOptions`, you are now able to make decisions about how and when the model will get updated.

Getting ready

The `ngModelOptions` directive will most directly benefit you while developing an AngularJS form, since it implicitly provides namespaces to the inputs within the form that are used by some of this directive's features. Suppose that for all the examples in this recipe, you begin, as follows:

```
<div ng-controller="PlayerCtrl">
  <form name="playerForm">
    Name:
    <input type="text"
           name="playerName"
           ng-model="player.name"
           ng-model-options="" />
  </form>
</div>
```

How to do it...

The `ngModelOptions` directive exposes several options that can be defined within its template expression as object literals.

The updateOn option

When the `updateOn` option is set, the model does not change the value until a trigger event occurs. The `updateOn` option accepts one or more DOM events in order to trigger the update. In addition to normal DOM events, there is a special default event that matches the default events belonging to the control. Using the default option allows you to incorporate extra events on top of the standard ones. This can be done as follows:

```
(app.js)

angular.module('myApp', []);

(index.html)

<div ng-app="myApp">
```

```
<form name="playerForm">
  Name:
  <input type="text"
         name="playerName"
         ng-model="player.name"
         ng-model-options="{updateOn: 'blur click mousemove'}" />
</form>
{{ player.name }}
</div>
```

Of course, these DOM events are silly in the context of a text input, but they demonstrate that there are broad possibilities when using updateOn.

 JSFiddle: http://jsfiddle.net/msfrisbie/tz319dpe/

The debounce option

The debounce option allows you to set a delay between when the value of the input changes and when the model updates itself with that changed value. This can either accept an integer millisecond value for all updateOn events, or it can accept an object with integer delay values for each event. This can be done as follows:

```
<input type="text"
       name="playerName"
       ng-model="player.name"
       ng-model-options="{ updateOn: 'blur click mousemove', debounce:
500 }" />
```

Alternately, this can also be done as follows:

```
<input type="text"
       name="playerName"
       ng-model="player.name"
       ng-model-options="{ updateOn: 'blur click mousemove', debounce:
{'blur': 500, 'click': 300, 'mousemove': 0} }" />
```

 JSFiddle: http://jsfiddle.net/msfrisbie/rjxrgv7h/

The origin of the term *debounce* comes from the world of circuits. Mechanical buttons or switches utilize metal contacts to open and close circuit connections. When the metal contact switches are closed, they will collide with each other and rebound before settling, causing the *bounce*. This bounce is problematic in the circuit as it is often registered as a repeat toggling of the switch or button—obviously buggy behavior. The workaround is to find a way to ignore the expected bounce noise—debouncing! This can be accomplished either by ignoring the bounce noise or introducing a delay before reading the value, both of which can be done with hardware or software.

The allowInvalid option

The `allowInvalid` option is quite uncomplicated. The normal behavior of validated input is to not propagate an invalid value to the model, but to set it to undefined. Setting `allowInvalid` to `true` overrides this behavior and propagates the invalid value through to the model. You will still be able to catch the invalid value while validating the form as normal.

 JSFiddle: `http://jsfiddle.net/msfrisbie/ejzpoo75/`

The getterSetter option

The `getterSetter` option is an interesting option that allows you to inform the application that the `ng-model` value should be used as a combination getter/setter instead of just a value. This can be done as follows:

```
(index.html)

<div ng-app="myApp">
  <div ng-controller="Ctrl">
    <form name="playerForm">
      Name:
      <input type="text"
             name="playerName"
             ng-model="player.name"
             ng-model-options="{ getterSetter: true }" />
    </form>
  </div>
</div>

(app.js)

angular.module('myApp', [])
.controller('Ctrl', function($scope) {
  // private player name
```

```
    var playerName = 'Jordan Wilson';

    // public getter/setter
    $scope.player = {
      name: function (newName) {
        console.log(newName)
        if (angular.isUndefined(newName)) {
          // getter
          return playerName;
        } else {
          // setter
          playerName = newName;
        };
      }
    };
});
```

Behind the scenes, `ngModelOptions` is now transparently assigning the model value with `player.name(val)` and reading the model value with `player.name()`. Since you have defined your method of access within the getter/setter paradigm, this of course means that interpolating and assigning the value manually must be done with the getters and setters as well, as shown here:

```
<!-- interpolation with getter syntax -->
Name: <span>{{ player.name() }}</span>

<!-- assignment with setter syntax -->
<button ng-click="player.name('')">Reset Name</button>
```

 JSFiddle: `http://jsfiddle.net/msfrisbie/uqpd7xft/`

The timezone option

The `timezone` option relates to the newly added support for HTML5 datetime input types. The input defaults to the browser time zone. Setting this value allows you to override that default time zone.

The $rollbackViewValue option

The `updateOn` and `debounce` options in `ngModelOptions` introduce a Schrödinger's cat-esque pattern, where there are technically two simultaneous values for a single model that might be resolved at some point in the future. Fortunately, unlike quantum superposition, we are able to reason about which state should get priority in a scenario of uncertainty—the model of course!

The `$rollbackViewValue` option acts as a reset button for the model. Invoking it will reset the input to the value that exists in the model, and will also cancel any outstanding debounce changes that are yet to occur. This can be done as follows:

```
(index.html)

<div ng-app="myApp">
  <form name="playerForm">
    Name:
    <input type="text"
           name="playerName"
           ng-model="player.name"
           ng-model-options="{ updateOn: 'click', debounce: 2000 }" />
    <button ng-click="playerForm.playerName.$rollbackViewValue()">
      Revert changes
    </button>
  </form>
  {{ player.name }}
</div>

(app.js)

angular.module('myApp', []);
```

 JSFiddle: `http://jsfiddle.net/msfrisbie/tbft57zw/`

How it works...

Conceptually, `ngModelOptions` should make a lot of sense to you in terms of how it fits into AngularJS. The `ngModelController` (which existed in previous releases) acts as the intermediary view/model arbiter by managing the parsing, validation, and transportation of data between the model and the view. The `ngModelOptions` directive is simply acting as a supplementary arbiter by giving the developer additional control over how the model should change.

See also

▶ The *Using HTML5 datetime input types* recipe helps you wrap your head around how AngularJS integrates with HTML5 data types

▶ The *Incorporating $touched and $submitted states* recipe takes you through how the new AngularJS form states give you tighter control of the application flow

▸ The *Cleaning up form errors with ngMessages* recipe demonstrates how to use this new module in order to radically reform how you handle form error messages

▸ The *Creating and integrating custom form validators* recipe demonstrates how you can now integrate forms directly with the validation pipeline

Incorporating $touched and $submitted states

Part of what makes form implementation so difficult to get exactly right is that they are highly stateful. DOM events, page history, user state, and countless other factors can all play a role in deciding what should be displayed to the user.

How to do it...

AngularJS 1.3 incorporates two more state representations into forms: `$touched` and `$submitted`.

The $touched state

Formerly, the closest thing to `$touched` was `$pristine`, which would only be unset if some input was entered into a field, but would not change if the field was merely entered and left as is. Now, `$touched` will be set if the field notices a focus event, even if the model value does not change. This can be done as follows:

```
(app.js)
angular.module('myApp', []);

(index.html)

<div ng-app="myApp">
  <form name="playerForm">
    <input type="text"
           name="playerName"
           ng-model="player.name" />
  </form>
  <div ng-if="playerForm.playerName.$touched">
    You touched the playerName field
  </div>
</div>
```

The message in the preceding code will be displayed once the field notices a pair of focus/blur events.

The $submitted state

It is not hard to imagine a scenario where you would only want to display error messages to the user after the form has seen an unsuccessful submit attempt. The `$submitted` flag will be set on the form controller object once it notices an unsuccessful submit attempt. This can be done as follows:

```
(app.js)
angular.module('myApp', []);

(index.html)

<div ng-app="myApp">
  <form name="playerForm">
    <input type="text"
           name="playerName"
           ng-model="player.name" />
    <button type="submit">Submit</button>
  </form>
  <div ng-if="playerForm.$submitted">
    You clicked submit
  </div>
</div>
```

The message in the preceding code will be displayed after a submit attempt.

 JSFiddle: `http://jsfiddle.net/msfrisbie/cng82hn4/`

See also

- ▶ The *Controlling model input with ngModelOptions* recipe provides the details of all the ways in which the `ngModelOptions` option lets you define how and when your input-bound models will change
- ▶ The *Cleaning up form errors with ngMessages* recipe demonstrates how to use this new module in order to radically reform how you handle form error messages
- ▶ The *Creating and integrating custom form validators* recipe demonstrates how you can now integrate forms directly with the validation pipeline

Cleaning up form errors with ngMessages

The addition of the ngMessages directive aims to solve the problem of erratic and complicated organization of error messages in forms. Traditionally, error messages were handled individually and independently, and they also incorporated some semblance of meta-logic in order to decide which messages should take priority, how many should be seen, and so on. The naïve solution is usually accomplished by sprinkling fistfuls of ng-if directives in the page corresponding to the error message corpus and delegating the display logic to the form controller. As you can imagine, this can get messy very quickly in the wake of complex forms.

Getting ready

The ngMessages directive comes packaged in the ngMessage module. To use it, include it in your application as follows:

```
(app.js)

angular.module('myApp', ['ngMessages']);
```

How to do it...

The ngMessages module exists as two separate directives: ng-messages and ng-message. The ng-messages directive defines the error message block that will process a form $error object. It will contain one or many instances of ng-message, which will refer to a specific property within the $error object. This can be done as follows:

```
(index.html)

<div ng-app="myApp">
  <form name="playerForm">
    <input type="text"
           name="playerName"
           ng-model="player.name"
           minlength="4"
           required />
    <!-- ng-messages block will handle the field $error object -->
    <div ng-messages="playerForm.playerName.$error">
      <!-- each ng-message handles a single error condition -->
      <div ng-message="required">
        Player name is required
      </div>
      <div ng-message="minlength">
        A player name must be at least 4 characters
      </div>
```

```
      </div>
    </form>
  </div>
```

 JSFiddle: http://jsfiddle.net/msfrisbie/cd8ud10q/

How it works...

Only a single error message per `ng-messages` block is displayed at a time, and the error message priority is defined by the order in which the `ng-message` entities are ordered within the block. This lets you afford a high degree of control over how and when error messages are displayed.

There's more...

Message blocks can be reused as templates. The preceding example can be refactored as follows:

```
(index.html)

<div ng-app="myApp">
  <form name="playerForm">
    <input type="text"
           name="playerName"
           ng-model="player.name"
           minlength="4"
           required />
    <div ng-messages="playerForm.playerName.$error"
       ng-messages-include="error-messages.html">
    </div>
  </form>

  <script type="text/ng-template" id="error-messages.html">
    <div ng-message="required">
      Player name is required
    </div>
    <div ng-message="minlength">
      A player name must be at least 4 characters
    </div>
  </script>
</div>
```

JSFiddle: `http://jsfiddle.net/msfrisbie/dz7vfd54/`

This `error-messages` template can be reused by any `ng-messages` instance, and it will match up the `$error` object properties to the corresponding `ng-message` fields within the included template. The included error messages can be overridden if necessary by providing an `ng-message` instance with the same `ng-message` value within the actual `ng-messages` block. This can be done as follows:

```
(index.html)

<div ng-app="myApp">
  <form name="playerForm">
    <input type="text"
           name="playerName"
           ng-model="player.name"
           minlength="8"
           required />
    <div ng-messages="playerForm.playerName.$error"
         ng-messages-include="error-messages.html">
      <div ng-message="minlength">
        A player name must be at least 8 characters
      </div>
    </div>
  </form>

  <script type="text/ng-template" id="error-messages.html">
    <div ng-message="required">
      Player name is required
    </div>
    <div ng-message="minlength">
      A player name must be at least 4 characters
    </div>
  </script>
</div>
```

Any `ng-message` defined in the actual `ng-messages` block will be given priority over a matching `ng-message` defined in an included `ng-messages` collection.

JSFiddle: `http://jsfiddle.net/msfrisbie/5hd8d5hz/`

See also

▸ The *Controlling model input with ngModelOptions* recipe provides the details of all the ways in which the `ngModelOptions` option lets you define how and when your input-bound models will change

▸ The *Incorporating $touched and $submitted states* recipe takes you through how the new AngularJS form states give you tighter control of the application flow

▸ The *Creating and integrating custom form validators* recipe demonstrates how you can now integrate forms directly with the validation pipeline

Trimming your watch list with lazy binding

A continuing gripe with AngularJS as a framework is targeted at the perceived inefficiencies of its data binding facilities. While it is true that it can be easy to fall into bad performance traps, a developer who understands what is going on under the hood and is able to make decisions accordingly can wield AngularJS against any architectural challenge.

Bind once is one of the more heralded introductions in the AngularJS 1.3 release. It offers one-time data binding, allowing the developer to reason about the necessity of real-time data being interpolated in the template and elect to opt out of that data binding in order to improve the overall performance of the application.

How to do it...

One-time data binding can be signaled inside the parsed expression at the time of compilation by prepending the expression with `: :`, as demonstrated here:

```
<span ng-show="user.isAuthenticated">{{ ::user.name }}</span>
```

This will maintain normal data binding for the authenticated display state, but the `user.name` value will only be watched until it is assigned a definite value, in which case, AngularJS will schedule that watcher for deletion. The heuristic in this example would be that the application should always check whether the user is still authenticated, but the user's name isn't anticipated to ever change over the lifetime of the application, so it is senseless to watch a value that you know won't change.

 JSFiddle: `http://jsfiddle.net/msfrisbie/Lxxmcveq/`

How it works...

This *bind once* logic, also referred to as *lazy binding*, occurs at the scope watcher level. Recall that each expression in the template is registered with its own watcher. Prepending that expression with : : signals the digest loop to store the value of the expression upon its first evaluation. If that value is defined, AngularJS will mark that value as stabilized, and it will schedule deregistration of that watch entry at the end of the digest loop. At the end of the digest loop, AngularJS will check each scheduled watch removal for its value again; if the value is still defined, the watch entry will deregister, otherwise the scheduled deregistration is thrown out.

In short, AngularJS will watch the expression until it becomes defined. This being the case, in some ways, the term "bind once" doesn't seem to exactly match what is going on, which is really that AngularJS will "bind until" a defined value is assigned.

 In this explanation, the quality of being *defined* refers to any value that is not a JavaScript undefined value.

There's more...

Bind once will only take effect when the parsed expression (which returns a function) is passed to a watch expression. This can be demonstrated directly using the $parse service, as follows:

```
// uses lazy binding
var playerGetter = $parse('::player');
scope.$watch(playerGetter);
```

The preceding code is effectively what happens when an expression is bound in the view. The parse function will communicate to the watcher that it needs to use lazy binding. Consider the following code:

```
// does not use lazy binding
var playerGetter = $parse('::player');
playerGetter($scope);
```

The preceding code will not use lazy binding; the return value from invoking the parse function will provide you with the up-to-date value each time.

Bind once expression universality

AngularJS does not discriminate on the basis of where the expression is coming from while registering the watcher, so the bind once feature is available anywhere you use expressions.

The ng-repeat directive

The `ng-repeat` directive's attribute string is parsed as piecewise expressions, so it is entirely possible to target one-time binding in the enumerable collection, as follows:

```
<div ng-repeat="player in ::roster.players">
  {{ ::player.name }}
</div>
```

Also notice here that the encapsulated repeat expression has one-time binding. Even though the collection is bound once, the repeated elements are still bound to the existing instances and create separate watch entries unless instructed not to, as done here.

 JSFiddle: `http://jsfiddle.net/msfrisbie/dg45qdpu/`

Isolate scope bindings

Sometimes, directives that have isolate scope attribute expressions do not expect the binding references or content to change. This is an excellent opportunity to cut down on watchers, as shown here:

```
(app.js)

angular.module('myApp', [])
.directive('playerProfile', function() {
  return {
    scope: {
      draft: '@'
    },
    template: '<div>{{player.name}}: {{draft}}</div>'
  };
});


(index.html)

<div ng-app="myApp">
  <input ng-model="draft.year" />
  <player-profile draft="Drafted in {{::draft.year}}">
  </player-profile>
  <hr />
  <pre>{{ draft | json }} </pre>
</div>
```

Since the bindings in the directive declaration are evaluated upon compilation, it makes sense to push the single bind prefix to the directive definition expressions, rather than in the directive template itself.

 JSFiddle: `http://jsfiddle.net/msfrisbie/ft3z53de/`

Methods and expressions requiring execution

AngularJS does not discriminate between types of expressions. Declaring a one-time binding on a method in an expression is an excellent way of preventing that method from being invoked for an insane amount of time. This can be done as follows:

```
<span ng-show="::verySlowMethod()">Show me maybe</span>
```

It is always desirable to make expressions as lightweight as possible, and this usually means that using methods in the view is undesirable. However, if it cannot be avoided, using bind once to cut the method execution count makes the application more efficient.

 JSFiddle: `http://jsfiddle.net/msfrisbie/y3qhdhhp/`

See also

> ▸ The *Combining watchers with $watchGroup* recipe demonstrates how to use the nifty new watch type to funnel multiple watchers to the same callback

Creating and integrating custom form validators

With the addition of the validator pipeline, AngularJS's form validation is now highly extensible and straightforward to expand.

How to do it...

Formerly, custom form validation required messiness involving parsers and formatters; this is no longer the case. Custom validation can now be encapsulated cleanly within a directive.

Synchronous validation

The ngModel directive now exposes the $validators property, which allows you to directly tap into its form validation.

The following directive definition is an example of a custom validator that ensures that a model value is not Packers:

```
(app.js)

angular.module('myApp', [])
.directive('validateFavoriteTeam', function() {
  return {
    require : 'ngModel',
    link : function(scope, element, attrs, ngModel) {
      // define custom validator "favoriteTeam"
      ngModel.$validators.favoriteTeam = function(team) {
        // check string inequivalency
        // a false return value indicates an error
        return team !== "Packers";
      };
    }
  };
});
```

You will then be able to use it as follows:

```
(index.html)

<div ng-app="myApp">
  <form name="fanForm">
    <input name="myTeam"
           type="text"
           ng-model="user.team"
           validate-favorite-team />
    <div ng-if="fanForm.myTeam.$error.favoriteTeam">
      Your favorite team cannot be the Packers
    </div>
  </form>
</div>
```

With this, the error message will only be shown if the input value is Packers.

 JSFiddle: http://jsfiddle.net/msfrisbie/d2t833ag/

Asynchronous validation

Form values are expected to change frequently, so it makes sense that any high-latency validation process should be treated differently from lightweight operations such as regex matches. The most obvious validation class that would fall into this category is a validation that requires an AJAX request to a remote entity, something that ostensibly will take a substantially long time to get completed and should not be done ad nauseam.

The following directive definition is an example of a custom asynchronous validator that ensures that a jersey number is not already taken on a certain team:

```
(app.js)

angular.module('myApp', [])
.directive('validateJerseyAvailable', function($http, $q, $timeout) {
  return {
    require : 'ngModel',
    link : function(scope, element, attrs, ngModel) {
      ngModel.$asyncValidators.jerseyAvailable = function(num) {
        if (!Number.isInteger(num)) {
          // input value is not an int, invalid
          // return rejected promise
          return $q.reject();
        } else {
          // send request to server, return promise
          return $http.get('/player/' + num)
          // assume success() means a 200 response
          .success(function() {
            // jersey number exists
            // is not available, invalid
            return $q.reject();
          })
          // assume error() means a 404 response
          .error(function() {
            // jersey number does not exist
            // is available, valid
            return true;
          });
        }
      };
    }
  };
});
```

You will then be able to use it as follows:

```
(index.html)

<div ng-app="myApp">
  <form name="playerForm">
    <input name="myNumber"
           type="number"
           ng-model="player.number"
           validate-jersey-available />
    <div ng-if="playerForm.myNumber.$pending">
      Checking for jersey number availability...
    </div>
    <div ng-if="playerForm.myNumber.$error.jerseyAvailable">
      That jersey number is taken.
    </div>
  </form>
</div>
```

If the promise is resolved, the model will validate; if the promise is rejected, the validator error will be registered on the $error object. For the sake of efficiency, validators defined on $asyncValidators will not be evaluated until all the validators defined on $validators (including the default ones) pass.

Asynchronous validators, as an unevaluated promise cannot be defined as $valid or $invalid, introduce an intermediate state, $pending. This state follows all the conventions of valid/invalid and can be used as follows:

```
<div ng-if="playerForm.myNumber.$pending">
  Checking for jersey number availability...
</div>
```

 JSFiddle: http://jsfiddle.net/msfrisbie/odL6yLn6/

How it works...

The $validators and $asyncValidators are vectors that allow you to directly integrate with the validation flow of AngularJS forms by defining custom directives that interact with ngModel.

There's more...

Since the AngularJS form ecosystem is quite broad and robust—covering error handling, validation, CSS styling, model transformation, and propagation—it behooves you to utilize custom validators within your own application in order to take advantage of this synergy.

See also

- The *Controlling model input with ngModelOptions* recipe provides the details of all the ways in which this option lets you define how and when your input-bound models will change

- The *Incorporating $touched and $submitted states* recipe takes you through how the new AngularJS form states give you tighter control of the application flow

- The *Cleaning up form errors with ngMessages* recipe demonstrates how to use this new module in order to radically reform how you handle form error messages

10
AngularJS Hacks

In this chapter, we will cover the following recipes:

- ▶ Manipulating your application from the console
- ▶ DRYing up your controllers
- ▶ Using `ng-bind` instead of `ng-cloak`
- ▶ Commenting JSON files
- ▶ Creating custom AngularJS comments
- ▶ Referencing deep properties safely using `$parse`
- ▶ Preventing redundant parsing

Introduction

Mastering a programming language or framework demands more than merely reading through the documentation or cruising through one tutorial; it requires that you read a ton of code written by other developers. For the same reason, art museums don't have works from only one painter, or Beethoven's symphonies aren't written for one instrument, or the best technology companies don't rely on the ideas of one engineer. Complex, analytical, and creative thoughts are best stimulated by multitudinous, diverse, and often orthogonal channels of input. Gleaning the inner machinations of someone else's mind by dissecting their work is an intensely intimate and educational process, and reading their code will provide you with an escape from the echo chamber of your own mind.

As you consume more and more code, you will be inundated with an understanding of the idiomatic methodologies that can make a great technology just a little bit better. Often, within that code, you will discover *hacks*, either of your own or someone else's, that you will become quite fond of, for their sheer utility or clever nature. This chapter consists of a fistful of these hacks that I have derived or encountered and enjoy using, and sincerely hope you will as well.

Manipulating your application from the console

Being able to directly manipulate components of your application manually while testing is an extremely useful tool when debugging. It is often the case that framework abstractions that provide you with improved application organization will, at the same time, make it more difficult to inspect and manipulate application components at the console level. Breakpoint debugging is more than suitable for these purposes most of the time, but being able to easily inspect and manipulate services, scopes, and other AngularJS components at the console level can be extremely useful.

How to do it...

The angular object is exposed in the global browser namespace, and access to the application internals will need to be routed through there. Scopes and services can be manipulated as shown in the following sections:

Scopes

Inspecting and manipulating scopes throughout your application will likely be one of the most common use cases when interacting with an AngularJS application in the console. The Batarang plugin for Google Chrome is an excellent tool available to AngularJS developers, and it offers among other things the ability to inspect your application's scopes.

If you want a floating scope object (that is not associated with any part of your application), using $injector will help you create a new scope instance as follows:

```
(browser console)

// this creates a new scope object that is not yet associated with
// any part of your application
var scope = angular.injector(['ng']).get('$rootScope')
```

Often, you will only need access to $rootScope, or a nonspecific application scope to change data or emit/broadcast events. If this is the case, $rootScope is the quickest to access, and can be done as follows:

```
(browser console)

// if you know which DOM node is the root, you can use a query
// selector and extract with <node>.scope()
// $rootScope typically is associated with <body>
var rs = angular.element(document.querySelector('body')).scope()

// if you don't know the DOM node, use the furthest ancestral DOM
```

```
// node with the ng-scope class
var rs = angular.element(
  document.querySelector('.ng-scope')).scope()

// or if you're not manually bootstrapping,
// use the only node with the ng-app attribute
var rs = angular.element(
  document.querySelector('[ng-app]')).scope()
```

If you're looking for a specific child scope inside the application, you can use the preceding selector techniques to find the exact node associated with the scope.

If you're using Google Chrome, there is a built-in feature in the console that makes DOM node selection easy. Inside the DOM inspector (the **Elements** tab in the inspection panel), if you click on a DOM node to select it, it becomes available as $0 in the console. This can then be used as normal to extract the associated scope:

```
(browser console)

// (user clicks <body> node to select it)

$0
// <body ng-app="playerApp" class="ng-scope">...</body>

angular.element($0).scope()
// Scope {$id: 1, $$childTail: ChildScope, ...}
```

Chrome keeps an in-order history of DOM nodes selected in the inspector, so the last node you clicked is available as $1, two nodes ago is $2, and so on.

Services

Even if your application might not take full advantage of the many benefits of service type abstraction (which it should!), manipulating service types from the console can be an extremely useful debugging tool for testing model manipulation, remote API access, authentication, and more. This can be done as follows:

```
(browser console)

// injector allows you access to dependency injected components
// 'ng' is the umbrella module dependency for built-in services
var $injector = angular.injector(['ng'])
// $http can be now accessed with its string name via
// regular AngularJS dependency injection
  , $http = $injector.get('$http');

// combined into a single line:
var $http = angular.injector(['ng']).get('$http');
```

Of course, you might also access your application's non-AngularJS services as well:

```
(browser console)

var Player = angular.injector(
  // access module in which the Player service is defined
  ['footballApp.players.services.player']
// grab Player service through dependency injection
).get('Player');
```

There's more...

Modification of the model, changing the page location through $location, or any other actions that modify the application state and are performed within the console will likely force a $digest cycle to occur due to the fact that AngularJS does not pay attention to the console. An easy way to do it is as follows:

```
(browser console)

angular.element(
  document.querySelector('.ng-scope')).scope().$apply()
```

Alternately, if you want to avoid a potential $apply() conflict that arises due to the $digest cycle possibly already being executed, an instantaneous $timeout callback will safely begin a new $digest cycle if one is not already in progress. This can be done as follows:

```
(browser console)

angular.injector(['newApp']).get('$timeout')(function() {}, 0)
```

DRYing up your controllers

When defining the model data and methods in controllers, you will quickly become tired of typing $scope repeatedly. Some developers simply take this on the chin and accept it as a necessity of the framework, but there is a superb method that avoids this verbosity and simultaneously makes your controllers more DRY.

Getting ready

Suppose that you have a controller in a fantasy football application, appearing as follows:

```
app.module('myApp', [])
.controller('Ctrl' function($scope) {
  $scope.team = {
    name: 'Bears',
```

```
      city: 'Chicago'
    };
    $scope.player = {
      name: 'Jake Hsu',
      team: 'Bears',
      number: 29,
      position:'RB'
    };
    $scope.trade = function(player1, player2) {
      // $scope.trade() logic
    };
    $scope.drop = function(player) {
      // $scope.drop() logic
    };
  });
```

How to do it...

Even with two scope objects and two methods, the number of times $scope needs to be typed here is extremely annoying. The central reason that demands this verbose syntax is that $scope is an existing object being injected, and you are merely extending it. Therefore, in this scenario, it makes sense to put the built-in angular.extend() method to use.

The controller can be refactored in the following way:

```
(app.js)

angular.module('myApp', [])
.controller('Ctrl', function($scope) {
  angular.extend($scope, {
    team: {
      name: 'Bears',
      city: 'Chicago'
    },
    player: {
      name: 'Jake Hsu',
      team: 'Bears',
      number: 29,
      position:'RB'
    },
    trade: function(player1, player2) {
      // $scope.trade() logic
    },
    drop: function(player) {
      // $scope.drop() logic
```

```
      }
    });
  });
```

 JSFiddle: `http://jsfiddle.net/msfrisbie/3Laxmcn9/`

How it works...

Instead of a cumbersome sequence of value and method property definitions, all of them can be defined upon a single object and that object can be merged into the `$scope` object. Since this only occurs when the controller is initialized, unless this controller is being created a huge number of times, any performance hits taken from this are outweighed by the significantly cleaner code.

There's more...

An observant developer will note that extending `$scope` with a monolithic object in this way takes away a critical component that might be needed: the ability to individually manage the events occurring during each `$scope` property assignment. Since the object that will extend `$scope` must be instantiated before it can be merged, a property in the merged object that throws an exception or takes a long time to complete (for example, a HTTP request), will cause problems.

If one-off exception handling is needed during initialization, an IIFE can be used in a pinch, although an excessive number of these will quickly become cumbersome and the benefit of the `angular.extend()` method's brevity will be lost.

If the initialization data takes a long time to calculate, then that is probably something that you should rethink before putting it in the controller initialization anyway.

Using ng-bind instead of ng-cloak

The `ng-cloak` directive is a workable solution to the rendering latency problem, but to the seasoned developer, blanking out the entire page or sprinkling `ng-cloak` throughout the application's templates seems like a suboptimal solution. In many scenarios, a more elegant fix would be to display as much of the page as possible and interpolate data as it is calculated to make the page load seem snappier to the end user.

How to do it...

The {{ }} interpolation syntax in AngularJS causes problems when the template loads, and is displayed before compilation can occur. The following is an example:

```
<div ng-controller="PlayerCtrl">
  Player: <span>{{ player.name }}</span>
</div>
```

If this template is displayed before compilation, it will suffer from the uncompiled template flash problem and display `Player: {{ player.name }}` momentarily.

The `ng-cloak` fix is as follows:

```
<div ng-cloak ng-controller="PlayerCtrl">
  Player: <span>{{ player.name }}</span>
</div>
```

Of course, this hides the entire `<div>` element until AngularJS can compile it and strip away the `ng-cloak` attribute. This works, but you can do better.

Instead of interpolating using {{ }}, the `ng-bind` directive will replace the contents of that element with the evaluated expression passed to it. This can be done as follows:

```
<div ng-controller="PlayerCtrl">
  Player: <span ng-bind="player.name"></span>
</div>
```

With this, the uncompiled template will simply flash `Player:`, which allows the page to be displayed faster without hiding everything, and the bound data will be interpolated as AngularJS transparently compiles the template.

 JSFiddle: `http://jsfiddle.net/msfrisbie/807L7Lbh/`

How it works...

Since HTML element's attributes in the DOM aren't visible, the page will appear normal, but unfilled until compilation. The bound data is then interpolated as it becomes available, and the user simply sees the data pop into the page after a brief delay.

Commenting JSON files

This isn't quite an AngularJS hack per se, but when you are writing JSON configuration files (for example, in your Grunt configuration, Bower package definition, or npm package definition), you might find that you forgot the purpose of a line. Inconveniently, JSON does not support formal comments, but there are some clever (but highly controversial) workarounds that can be used with a pinch.

How to do it...

If the JSON file is parsed in a certain way, you can take advantage of that by allowing the data format to bleed outside the boundaries of the JSON specification.

Ignored properties

If you know that a section of JSON won't be exhaustively parsed, that is, there is a defined set of keys that it will examine, then the easiest route is to just incorporate a property that the program will ignore. This can be done as follows:

```
(package.json)

{
  "name": "playerApp",
  "version": "1.0.0",
  "_comment_devDependencies": "External test, build, or documentation
framework components that the application does not directly depend
upon",
  "devDependencies": {
    "grunt": "^0.4.1",
    ...
  }
  ...
}
```

Duplicate properties

An ignored property will suffice in many cases, but having to dodge whatever entity is consuming the JSON is a bit like boxing with it, and it will often be the case that you won't be able to sprinkle _comment properties everywhere you want to. If you determine that the JSON parser will use only the last value encountered for a property, then you can incorporate duplicate values for properties that the parser will *theoretically* ignore, as long as the last encountered value is valid. This can be done as follows:

```
(package.json)

{
```

```json
  "name": "playerApp",
  "version": "1.0.0",
  "devDependencies": "External test, build, or documentation framework
components that the application does not directly depend upon",
  "devDependencies": {
    "grunt": "JavaScript task runner",
    "grunt": "^0.4.1",
    "grunt-autoprefixer": "Parse CSS and add vendor-prefixed CSS
properties",
    "grunt-autoprefixer": "^0.7.3",
    ...
  }
  ...
}
```

Don't run with scissors

If you're unwilling to take the risk of a nonstandard JSON file, the proper way of commenting on a JSON file is to strip out the comments with a preprocessor before handing it off to the parser using something such as JSMin.

How it works...

I suspect that Douglas Crockford might like to take a swing at me for recommending the first two solutions, but the fact of the matter is that there are certain scenarios, especially with smaller projects, where they work just fine.

There's more...

As mentioned earlier, this strategy is highly controversial and has the potential to cause trouble if you're not careful.

Since doing this sort of thing goes against the JSON specification, you are at the mercy of whatever is using this JSON file. Various JSON interpreters will handle this in different ways. If the JSON file is fed into a stream parser, or parsed into a dictionary where there is no guarantee of key ordering, this will encounter problems. But hey, it's called a *hack* for a reason.

Creating custom AngularJS comments

An overlooked ability of AngularJS is its ability to wield directives with the intention of streamlining the development process. One awesome way to do this is by using directives to comment in your application.

How to do it...

Normally, nesting HTML comments requires variable syntax as shown here:

```
<!--
<div>
  <p>I am the outer comment</p>
  <!- -
    <p>I am the inner comment</p>
  - ->
</div>
-->
```

This is completely obnoxious. It would be much better to be able to add comments anywhere without having to worry about which comments are already in place. Since the HTML comment convention doesn't suit your needs, you are able to just make your own comment directive, as follows:

```
(app.js)

angular.module('myApp', [])
.directive('x', function() {
  return {
    restrict: 'AE',
    compile: function(el) {
      el.remove();
    }
  };
});
```

Now, you are able to do the following, using attribute comments:

```
(index.html)

<div x>
  <p>I am the outer comment</p>
  <p x>I am the inner comment</p>
</div>
```

Alternately, you can do the following with element comments:

```
(index.html)

<x>
<div>
  <p>I am the outer comment</p>
```

```
<x>
<p>I am the inner comment</p>
</x>
</div>
</x>
```

 JSFiddle: `http://jsfiddle.net/msfrisbie/95nc7j7z/`

How it works...

This commenting style allows you to instruct the client to strip out chunks of the DOM upon template compilation. Every time AngularJS encounters the directive, it will just destroy that entire DOM node during the compile phase and move on.

There's more...

HTML comments aren't quite what you'd expect. The customary `<!--  -->` pairing actually comprises SGML delimiters `<!  >`, and within the delimiters is a single SGML comment that is bookended by `--  --`. This is what prevents you from nesting comments without variable syntax, or using `--` within comments.

You also have quite a bit of freedom to make the HTML-compliant comment directive string or SGML-compliant comment directive string appear how you want it to. Choosing a string of alphabetic characters, such as `x` or `cmnt`, will always be a valid directive name, and you can use this as both an element or attribute directive. However, since AngularJS will be handling the compilation, you are able to choose special characters such as `,` or `|` to act as a directive comment. You usually cannot use these as an element tag by themselves (`<|></|>`—you'll need to use something as `<a |></a>`), but as long as it follows the HTML5 attribute specification and the browser doesn't barf all over the place when it parses the HTML, the comment directive world is your plaything—go crazy.

Keep in mind that this probably isn't something you would include in a production application; this is more of a tool to be used in the development process. Since it's best to not serve the client data you know they won't use or need, a production application's asset preparation is usually smart enough to remove HTML comments during minification, so giving preference to using them is recommended.

Extensibility

It is also completely possible to extend these comment directives in ways that might suit your development process. For example, if you wanted the directive to be cut out only when a flag is set, you could do the following:

```
(app.js)

angular.module('myApp', [])
.directive('x', function() {
  return {
    restrict: 'AE',
    link: function(scope, el) {
      scope.$watch('flags.purgeComments', function(newVal) {
        if (newVal) {
          el.remove();
        }
      });
    }
  };
});
```

 JSFiddle: `http://jsfiddle.net/msfrisbie/5vej1z39/`

Obviously, this example cannot be reversed since the DOM node is being destroyed.

Referencing deep properties safely using $parse

When dealing with object access, a seasoned JavaScript developer will be quite familiar with this error message:

```
TypeError: Cannot read property '...' of undefined
```

This, of course, is the result of attempting to access a property on an object that does not exist in the current lexical scope. It is often the case that the developer is aware of the possibility that the referenced object can be undefined, but it would be preferred that a failed property access returns undefined instead of throwing an error.

How to do it...

The typical use case is an asynchronous method that references a piece of data that isn't necessarily initialized before use.

Suppose that the user object in this example is populated with a user object served from the backend, filled upon login authentication, and cleared upon logging out, as shown here:

```
(app.js)

angular.module('myApp', [])
.controller('Ctrl', function($log, $scope) {
  $scope.$watch('user', function(newUserVal) {
    $log.log(newUserVal.address.city);
  });
});

// console on pageload:
// TypeError: Cannot read property 'address' of undefined
```

This might appear safe, but if the user has not authenticated, this will throw an error when attempts are made to access the `address` property.

To protect your application from this, you can inject the `$parse` service to protect against `TypeError` when referencing a deep property:

```
(app.js)

angular.module('myApp', [])
.controller('Ctrl', function($parse, $log, $scope) {
  $scope.$watch('user', function(newUserVal) {
    $log.log($parse('address.city')(newUserVal));
  });
});

// console on pageload:
// undefined
```

This parses the expression argument and returns a function to check the expression against. The returned value will now be undefined for a reference, as shown here, that caused `TypeError` in the previous example.

 JSFiddle: `http://jsfiddle.net/msfrisbie/oao5rav5/`

The following would be the functional—though less idiomatic—equivalent to the preceding example:

```
(app.js)

angular.module('myApp', [])
.controller('Ctrl', function($parse, $log, $scope) {
  $scope.$watch('user', function() {
    $log.log($parse('user.address.city')($scope));
  });
});

// console on pageload:
// undefined
```

How it works...

Using $parse in this way takes advantage of AngularJS's template interpolation conventions. The $parse service is used implicitly when interpolating expressions in the view, allowing you to use {{ user.name }} in the templates without having to worry about handling an incomplete object hierarchy. If the property can be accessed, it will be returned and interpolated; otherwise, it will be returned as undefined.

There's more...

The $parse service can handle multipart expressions, as follows:

```
(app.js)

angular.module('myApp', [])
.controller('Ctrl', function($log, $scope, $parse) {
  $scope.$watch('user', function(newUserVal) {
    $log.log($parse('"City: " + address.city')(newUserVal));
  });
});

// console on pageload:
// "City: "
```

 Note that this will not log "City: undefined", which is what would happen if you perform "City: " + undefined in a vanilla JavaScript.

It can also handle attempts to invoke of methods that might not exist:

```
(app.js)

angular.module('myApp', [])
.controller('Ctrl', function($log, $scope, $parse) {
  $scope.$watch('user', function(newUserVal) {
    $log.log($parse(
      '"Address: " + address.fullStr()')(newUserVal)
    );
  });
});

// console on pageload:
// "Address: "
```

We can add the scope data as follows:

```
(app.js)

angular.module('myApp', [])
.controller('Ctrl', function($log, $scope, $parse) {
  $scope.user = {
    address: {
      number: 1060,
      street: 'W Addison St',
      city: 'Chicago',
      state: 'IL',
      zipCode: 60613,
      fullStr: function() {
        return this.number + ' ' +
          this.street + ', ' +
          this.city + ', ' +
          this.state + ' ' +
          this.zipCode;
      }
    }
  };

  $scope.$watch('user', function(newUserVal) {
    $log.log($parse('"City: " + address.city')(newUserVal));
  });

  $scope.$watch('user', function(newUserVal) {
    $log.log($parse(
```

```
      '"Address: " + address.fullStr()'
    )(newUserVal));
  });
});

// console on pageload:
// Address: 1060 W Addison St, Chicago, IL 60613
```

JSFiddle: http://jsfiddle.net/msfrisbie/t12ym3as/

See also

▸ The *Preventing redundant parsing* recipe demonstrates how to refactor your application in order to trim down identical expression parsing

Preventing redundant parsing

The $parse operation can often be unnecessarily repetitive in certain situations. If your application scales to the point where this redundancy is starting to become a performance factor, then the parsing can be refactored in order to prevent reparsing the same expression over and over.

Getting ready

Suppose that your application resembles the following code:

```
(index.html)

<div ng-app="myApp">
  <div ng-controller="OuterCtrl">
  <div ng-repeat="player in data.playerIds"
       ng-controller="InnerCtrl">
  </div>
  </div>
</div>

(app.js)

angular.module('myApp', [])
.controller('OuterCtrl', function($scope, $log) {
  $scope.data = {
```

```
        playerIds: [1,2,3]
    };
})
.controller('InnerCtrl', function($scope, $log, $parse) {
    $scope.myExp = function() {
        $log.log('Expression evaluated');
        return 'watchedValue';
    };
    $scope.$watch(
        $parse(
            // this IIFE is structured so you can see when
            // $parse() is being invoked
            (function() {
                $log.log('Parse compilation called');
                return 'myExp()';
            })()
        ),
        function(newVal) {
            $log.log('Watch handler called: ', newVal);
        }
    );
});
```

This will log the following when the page is loaded:

```
(browser console)

Parse compilation called
Parse compilation called
Parse compilation called
Expression evaluated
Watch handler called: watchedValue
Expression evaluated
Watch handler called: watchedValue
Expression evaluated
Watch handler called: watchedValue
Expression evaluated
Expression evaluated
Expression evaluated
```

Here, your application is parsing an identical expression for every `ng-repeat` iteration. This can be prevented!

How to do it...

The `$parse()` method returns a function that takes the object to which the evaluated expression needs to be applied. This function can be saved and reused in order to prevent redundant parsing, as follows:

```
(app.js)
```

```javascript
angular.module('myApp', [])
.controller('OuterCtrl', function($scope, $log, $parse) {
  $scope.data = {
    playerIds: [1,2,3],
    // perform the $parse once and expose the returned
    // function on $scope
    repeatParsed: $parse(
      (function() {
        $log.log("Parse compilation called");
        return 'myExp()';
      })()
    )
  };
})
.controller('InnerCtrl', function($scope, $log) {
  $scope.myExp = function() {
    $log.log("Expression evaluated");
    return 'watchedValue';
  };
  // each watcher will implicitly invoke the $parse() return
  // function with $scope as the parameter
  $scope.$watch($scope.data.repeatParsed, function(newVal) {
    $log.log("Watch handler called: ", newVal);
  });
});
```

[JSFiddle: `http://jsfiddle.net/msfrisbie/hzevdLd7/`]

Now, the parsing occurs when the parent controller is initialized and will occur only once, as shown here:

```
(browser console)
```

```
Parse compilation called
Expression evaluated
```

```
Watch handler called: watchedValue
Expression evaluated
Watch handler called: watchedValue
Expression evaluated
Watch handler called: watchedValue
Expression evaluated
Expression evaluated
Expression evaluated
```

How it works...

The `$parse()` method doesn't evaluate the expression; it only figures out how to extract the expression from the string and prepares it for evaluation. Moving this preparatory computation to earlier in the application setup allows you to reuse it.

See also

▶ The *Referencing deep properties safely using $parse* recipe shows how you can utilize expression parsing to avoid boilerplate object inspection when interacting with deep objects

Index

N

native route resolves
promises, incorporating into 270-272
nested directives
interaction between 24-26
nested ui-router resolves
implementing 273, 276
single-state promise dependencies 274, 275
state promise inheritance 273, 274
ng-bind
ng-cloak, avoiding with 306, 307
ngClass directive
about 115, 120
removeClass animations,
creating with 120-122
ng-cloak
about 306
avoiding, with ng-bind 306, 307
ngController directive 161
ngForm directive 115, 120
ngHide directive 115, 120
ngIf directive
about 92, 98, 165, 166
enter animations, creating with 92, 93
ngInclude directive 92, 98, 161
ngMessage directive 92, 98
ngMessages directive
about 115, 120
used, for cleaning up form errors 289-292
ngMockE2E module 208
ngModel directive 115, 120
ngModelOptions
$rollbackViewValue option 285
allowInvalid option 284
debounce option 283, 284
getterSetter option 284, 285
time zone option 285
updateOn option 282, 283
URL 283
used, for controlling model inputs 282
working 286, 287
ngOptions directive
about 175-177
array, populating within 177, 178
null options 180
object, populating within 181

option groups, implementing 179
option model assignment,
defining explicitly 179
option values, defining 178
option values, defining explicitly 181
ng-repeat directive 240, 294
ngRepeat directive
about 92, 98, 162-165
used, for creating move animations 105-107
ngShow directive
about 115, 120
addClass animations, creating with 115, 116
ng-strict-di directive
sanity checking with 281
ngSwitch directive 92, 98, 167
ngView directive
about 92, 98, 162
leave and concurrent animations,
creating with 98-100
null option 180
number filters
using 48-51

O

object
populating 181
optional nested directive controllers 26-28
option groups
defining, explicitly 179
option model assignment
defining, explicitly 179
option values
defining, explicitly 178-182
orderBy filters 59

P

Page Object test pattern
using 214-219
promise barriers
implementing, $q.all() used 260-263
promise handlers
about 255, 256
and promises, chaining 253
promise notifications
implementing 258-260

Thank you for buying
AngularJS Web Application
Development Cookbook

About Packt Publishing

Packt, pronounced 'packed', published its first book, *Mastering phpMyAdmin for Effective MySQL Management*, in April 2004, and subsequently continued to specialize in publishing highly focused books on specific technologies and solutions.

Our books and publications share the experiences of your fellow IT professionals in adapting and customizing today's systems, applications, and frameworks. Our solution-based books give you the knowledge and power to customize the software and technologies you're using to get the job done. Packt books are more specific and less general than the IT books you have seen in the past. Our unique business model allows us to bring you more focused information, giving you more of what you need to know, and less of what you don't.

Packt is a modern yet unique publishing company that focuses on producing quality, cutting-edge books for communities of developers, administrators, and newbies alike. For more information, please visit our website at www.packtpub.com.

About Packt Open Source

In 2010, Packt launched two new brands, Packt Open Source and Packt Enterprise, in order to continue its focus on specialization. This book is part of the Packt open source brand, home to books published on software built around open source licenses, and offering information to anybody from advanced developers to budding web designers. The Open Source brand also runs Packt's open source Royalty Scheme, by which Packt gives a royalty to each open source project about whose software a book is sold.

Writing for Packt

We welcome all inquiries from people who are interested in authoring. Book proposals should be sent to author@packtpub.com. If your book idea is still at an early stage and you would like to discuss it first before writing a formal book proposal, then please contact us; one of our commissioning editors will get in touch with you.

We're not just looking for published authors; if you have strong technical skills but no writing experience, our experienced editors can help you develop a writing career, or simply get some additional reward for your expertise.

Mastering AngularJS Directives

ISBN: 978-1-78398-158-8   Paperback: 210 pages

Develop, maintain, and test production-ready directives for any AngularJS-based application

1. Explore the options available for creating directives, by reviewing detailed explanations and real-world examples.

2. Dissect the life cycle of a directive and understand why they are the base of the AngularJS framework.

3. Discover how to create structured, maintainable, and testable directives through a step-by-step, hands-on approach to AngularJS.

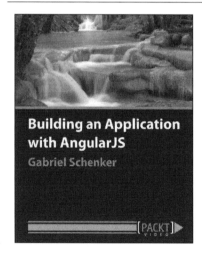

Building an Application with AngularJS [Video]

ISBN: 978-1-78328-369-9   Duration: 02:22 hours

Get creative with AngularJS to develop exciting applications

1. Use views and controllers to build an application from the ground up quickly.

2. Construct Angular services and implement dependency injection with the help of illustrative examples.

3. Master asynchronous programming through the effective use of JavaScript coupled with Angular.

Please check **www.PacktPub.com** for information on our titles

Mastering Web Application Development with AngularJS

ISBN: 978-1-78216-182-0   Paperback: 372 pages

Build single-page web applications using the power of AngularJS

1. Make the most out of AngularJS by understanding the AngularJS philosophy and applying it to real-life development tasks.

2. Effectively structure, write, test, and finally deploy your application.

3. Add security and optimization features to your AngularJS applications.

4. Harness the full power of AngularJS by creating your own directives.

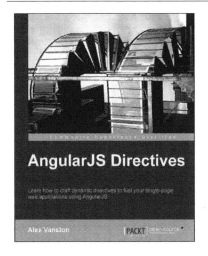

AngularJS Directives

ISBN: 978-1-78328-033-9   Paperback: 110 pages

Learn how to craft dynamic directives to fuel your single-page web applications using AngularJS

1. Learn how to build an AngularJS directive.

2. Create extendable modules for plug-and-play usability.

3. Build apps that react in real time to changes in your data model.

Please check **www.PacktPub.com** for information on our titles

Made in the USA
Lexington, KY
30 April 2015